STUDIES IN AMERICAN POPULAR HISTORY AND CULTURE

Edited by
Jerome Nadelhaft
University of Maine

A ROUTLEDGE SERIES

STUDIES IN AMERICAN POPULAR HISTORY AND CULTURE

JEROME NADELHAFT, *General Editor*

CLEANING UP

The Transformation of Domestic Service in Twentieth Century New York City

Alana Erickson Coble

Routledge
New York & London

Published in 2006 by
Routledge
Taylor & Francis Group
711 Third Avenue
New York, NY 10017

Published in Great Britain by
Routledge
Taylor & Francis Group
2 Park Square
Milton Park, Abingdon
Oxon OX14 4RN

First issued in paperback 2013

© 2006 by Taylor & Francis Group, LLC
Routledge is an imprint of the Taylor & Francis Group, an informa business

International Standard Book Number-10: 0-415-97809-2 (Hardcover)
International Standard Book Number-13: 978-0-415-97809-5 (Hardcover)
International Standard Book Number-13: 978-0-415-64670-3 (Paperback)
Library of Congress Card Number 2005035747

Library of Congress Cataloging-in-Publication Data

Coble, Alana Erickson.
    Cleaning up : the transformation of domestic service in twentieth century New York City/ Alana Erickson Coble.
        p. cm. -- (Studies in American popular history and culture)
    Includes bibliographical references and index.
    ISBN 0-415-97809-2
    1. Domestics--New York (State)--New York--History--20th century. 2. Women domestics--New York (State)--New York--History--20th century. 3. Housekeeping--New York (State)--New York--History--20th century. I. Title. II. Series: American popular history and culture (Routledge (Firm)

HD8039.D52U575 2006
331.7'616480974710904--dc22
    2005035747

informa
Taylor & Francis Group
is the Academic Division of Informa plc.

Visit the Taylor & Francis Web site at
http://www.taylorandfrancis.com

and the Routledge Web site at
http://www.routledge-ny.com

To my beloved son David Leland Coble, the best boy in the world.
I love you, honey, and I miss you.
May 16, 1999–June 29, 2005
And to my darling Julia, who keeps me going.

Contents

List of Tables

List of Charts

List of Figures

List of Exhibits

Acknowledgments

I would like to acknowledge the following people:

My husband, Rick Coble.

My daughter, Julia Amy Coble.

My late son, David Leland Coble.

My parents, John and Nancy Erickson.

My sister, Julia Erickson.

My brother and his family, John, Susi and Helen Erickson.

My brother and his family, Ron, Laura and Ana Erickson.

My great-grandmother, Mum, Anna Hildegard Karolina (Nilsdotter) Andersson Graham, whose experience as a domestic servant helped inspire this dissertation.

My advisor, Kenneth T. Jackson.

Elizabeth Blackmar; Rosalind Rosenberg; Eric Foner; Eric McKitrick; the Columbia University History Department staff, especially Barbara Locurto and Kirsten Olsen; Jeffrey Kroessler; Owen Gutfreund; Michael Green; Elizabeth Hovey; the late Pastor Robert F. Scholz, Ph.D.; the late Matthew (Richardson) Richmond; Tim McCarthy; Herbert Aptheker; Cindy Cegelski Arn; Jenni Watson; Sarah Holt; Ron Newman; Jill Norman Fouad; Liz Bradley Buffa; Grai Rice; Karen Zweig Aronson; Ana Valverde Moore; Cheryl Davis; Tekla Torell; Cynthia Soderholm Hansen; Kent Hansen; Tim DeWerff; all the folks at Menaker & Herrmann; Walter Bourne and the EDS family; the Encyclopedia of New York City crowd, especially Deborah Gardner; my marchFIRST colleagues, especially Bill Kane; the late Virginia Johnson; the late Marvel Cooke; Debbie Cox; Gleason Frye.

Introduction

Over the course of the 20th century, domestic service in the United States was transformed from a strictly hierarchical to a more balanced institution. From a relationship in which mistresses had almost all the control in the relationship, it evolved into one where employer and employee shared control. Workers gained more leverage and were more able to negotiate the terms of the relationship. Domestic service also became more like other occupations, in that it was more standardized and regulated.

Americans came to value domestic service differently between 1920 and 1970 as employers, employees, the media, government and non-governmental organizations all changed the way they looked at paid household labor. The occupation was "industrialized," or standardized; it changed from an invisible occupation with only the individualized standards of employers to one that became the subject of national debate and was regulated. This was a sign of domestic service's increasing perceived value; it and its practitioners were treated with more respect.

The pattern of the 20th century was a reversal of the nineteenth century, when, as Faye Dudden points out, the occupation shifted from one involving "hired help" of more or less the same social standing as their employers to one in which domestic servants and those who hired them were in different social classes. As the work became more menial in the 19th century, mistresses exercised more power. Native-born white women withdrew from the occupation, leaving it to immigrants and African-Americans.[1]

This book picks up in the first years of the 20th century, when maids could readily change employers but not the basic conditions of their job. Most lived in, their workweeks were 72 to 84 hours long, they had almost no real free time (Thursdays and every other Sunday afternoon was normal), and they were at the beck and call of the family for whom they worked. As there were so few other occupations open to women, many were stuck in domestic service.

By contrast, at the beginning of the twenty-first century, most household employees lived in their own homes and worked on a part-time basis for a number of families. They controlled the rhythm of their work and declined to do various unpleasant tasks.

There were limits to the changes, of course. Wages remained low, although they were usually at or above the minimum wage. Vacation and sick pay became more common, but health insurance remained rare. No amount of legal rights could remove the vagaries of personality from the occupation, as the employer-employee ratio was usually one to one. The workplace was still a private home, and as such difficult to police. For undocumented aliens, too, legal rights meant almost nothing, since fear of deportation usually stopped them from availing themselves of those rights.

The essential character of the domestic service relationship, however, had changed. No longer were maids taken for granted and considered subordinate to the needs of those they served. Legally, they had rights the equal of those for whom they worked, and they could leave the occupation for other jobs. Workers had more leverage in their relationship with employers, thus evening the scales of power.

* * *

This book focuses not on a single point of view—employer or employee—but on the relationship between the two parties. I have tried to be even-handed, as I have a foot in both camps.

My great-grandmother emigrated from Sweden and worked as a maid in Brooklyn in the 1890s to earn the money to go to western Pennsylvania. When her family farm needed financial help, she returned briefly to domestic service. In high school, I cleaned houses one summer. It was a memorable experience, both for the good and the bad. As an adult, I have employed a nanny, individual house cleaners and a cleaning service.

* * *

Domestic service's improving relationships were the result of alterations in racial, ethnic and gender relations in a modern industrial society; in the nature of work in public and private spheres; and in the relationship between government and the people.

These caused both the number of private household workers and their proportion to the total U.S. population to decrease, while demand for their labor remained relatively constant.[2]

Servants gained bargaining power, and they used it to get increased wages and a restructuring of the market from full-time to part-time, live-out employment. Workers gained more control over their own lives when they no longer lived in with the families for whom they worked. This resulted in an increase in workers' self-respect. Being in demand and living out made it possible for workers to stand their ground and insist upon being treated better.

There were fewer servants for two main reasons. First, other job opportunities for women opened up. Beginning before World War I and especially in the 1920s, women took clerical jobs. Despite the Depression, the clerical field continued to grow in the 1930s. During World War II, women entered dozens of new fields as their husbands, fathers, and sons fought overseas. In the postwar economic boom, opportunities for clerical positions grew astronomically, along with other areas of employment, even manufacturing.

Second, roughly between 1915 and 1970, immigration to the United States dropped. Young immigrant women had been the primary source of servants in the North, particularly in New York City. The constriction caused by war and legislation limited the number of new arrivals, which consequently cut the supply of immigrant servants. The shortage caused African-American women to become more prominent in the occupation in Northern cities like New York. These women took an active role in changing their working conditions, and their efforts helped to even the relationship scales.

In the last third of the twentieth century, the African-American "servant class" was finally able to move into other occupations as a result of the civil rights movement, the 1964 Civil Rights Act, and the tight labor markets in central cities. New immigrants took African Americans' place; their arrival was spurred by the passage of a liberalized immigration law in 1965.[3]

The twentieth century also saw altered attitudes toward housework. As appliances made cleaning and washing easier to do—and because there was a "servant shortage"—middle- and even upper-class women did their own housework after the Second World War. Housework and the maintenance of family life were associated with white American womanhood, and so housework gained new prestige in the postwar era. The use of appliances lent it technological cachet. Respect for housework rubbed off on paid domestic labor in the form of greater respect for their work and for them.

Attitudes changed also because the sheer number of American women in the labor force rose dramatically. In 1920, 23 percent were employed outside the home; by 1950 that figure had risen to 33 percent, and in 1986,

55 percent. Working women needed help with their housework, and this led to a greater appreciation for domestic help.[4]

Finally, domestics gained leverage in their work relationships because they slowly won legal protections already held by other workers. Initially excluded from Social Security, from unemployment insurance, and from wage and hour regulation, they were covered one piece at a time, beginning with Old Age Social Insurance (OASI) coverage in 1950. In 1974, the federal government covered domestic workers under the Fair Labor Standards Act, which ensured them a minimum wage and, in some cases, overtime pay. Unemployment insurance for some domestics followed in 1978.[5]

As a result of these changes, both the work itself and attitudes about it altered. These attitudes showed up in contemporary newspapers and magazines, in advertisements (classified and mass market), in oral histories, in sociological studies, in government files, and in reform organization files. They reflected the issues with which people were struggling as well as what they took for granted.

The power relationship was transformed. No longer an employer-dominated hierarchy, domestic service now had a more level playing field.

THE NATURE OF DOMESTIC SERVICE

In this book, domestic work is defined solely as those tasks necessary to keep a household running: cooking, cleaning, and laundry. Cooking includes all food gathering and preparation. Cleaning means dusting, vacuuming, sweeping, polishing, and scrubbing surfaces in the house, as well as washing, drying and putting away dishes, pots, pans and kitchen utensils. Laundry consists of washing, drying, pressing and putting away clothing, linens, and shoes and/or arranging for laundry to be done outside the home.[6]

Hard work notwithstanding, two aspects of paid domestic service made it undesirable: 1) wages, schedule, living arrangements, clothing, and other conditions were often abysmal, and 2) there was a social stigma associated with being a maid.

Domestic work was routinely characterized as without dignity, as a "stepping stone to nowhere." This low social status resulted from the lack of value accorded housework in American society and the workers' identity.

Housework, paid or unpaid, has rarely been esteemed. Karl Marx pointed out that a thing could have a price, or a wage, but not a value. Because housekeeping does not produce a marketable product, it theoretically does not produce value. Moreover, if a family cannot afford household help, its members perform the work themselves. This implies that domestic help is a luxury, not a necessity.

Yet over the course of the twentieth century in America, such help became more of a priority as more families had two working spouses and less time to do their own housework—and thus Americans saw such work as having value. As Jeanne Boydston has noted, "What Marx did not consider is that . . . a labor form can also have a value without having a wage."[7]

It would take until almost the end of the twentieth century to reach this perception of value. As production moved out of the household in the nineteenth century, what remained (cooking, cleaning and laundry) was menial and therefore less esteemed. The low value placed upon it accrued to houseworkers. Because domestic servants were not valued, the occupation was prone to abuse, as housewives sought to squeeze as much as they could out of their workers. Those who could leave the occupation did so as soon as possible. George Stigler, a future Nobel Prize-winning economist, noted in 1946:

> The low social status of domestic service, the absence of vocational or educational requirements, and the discrimination practiced in other lines of employment seem adequate to explain the fact that immigrants and negroes have constituted more than half of female servants since 1900."[8]

In addition, housework could not be standardized, since housekeeping needs varied from household to household. Therefore, the occupation operated on a personalized basis, in which the mistress-maid relationship took on a hierarchical structure. The presence of marginalized groups (newly arrived immigrants, African Americans) in the occupation only increased the employer's power.[9]

Ambivalence about the existence of a "servant class" played into this stigmatization. After 1920, African-American women in fact constituted such a group in the North (as they had for centuries in the South). Their prominence as servants in the North belied the myth of a classless republic. In New York City, for example, they comprised between 40 and 60 percent of the servant population for over 50 years. This lack of mobility emphasized the employer's power. The Bronx Slave Market—in which Depression-era domestic workers gathered on New York street corners to wait for extremely low-paid day work—exemplified some of the worst aspects of the employer-employee relationship and reflected the true state of affairs not only on the street but in every home with a servant. Only in gradually taking control of their schedules and obligations were workers able to claim some dignity for their jobs.

Employers resisted workers' efforts. Some did try to attract workers through mild improvements in working conditions. But until well into the 1950s, they blamed the occupation's problems on employees. A carefully constructed and maintained boundary of *difference* between mistress and maid—based on ethnicity, race, language—allowed this. Just as Americans in general believed in the melting pot, in which newcomers would shed their customs to become "American," so employers believed domestics aspired to be like them. Hence, they felt it was necessary to train workers to perform according to employers' standards; in enforcing those standards, they felt they were helping workers establish themselves in American society.

The central period of this study—roughly 1920 to 1970—was one in which there was little immigration. While it may have been true that immigrants wanted to emulate their employers in terms of Americanization, African Americans did not need to. They were already American, and until the 1960s, emulating their employers had no impact on their occupational progress. African-American workers therefore pursued their own agenda, which involved gaining control of their workplaces so they could earn more money, have better hours and command more respect from employers. Until they were able to do so, the occupation remained feudal in nature.

THE LIMITS OF CHANGE

There are several continuing pressures that keep some stigma still attached to the occupation. The movement of women into jobs outside the home has helped to keep domestic work underpaid, since it is still something that must be accounted for out of a household budget. As most women work because their families need the money, budgets do not extend to high pay for household help.

There are castes within the ranks of domestics. Independent, legal housecleaners belong to the upper caste of domestic workers. Normally, they earn over $10 an hour; some can earn $20 to $30 an hour. In the next level are those who work for cleaning services; they are taxed and receive Social Security, but their wages typically hover around $6.50 to $7.50 an hour, which is not, in most cities, enough to live on. The lowest rung of the ladder belongs to illegal aliens, who in some cases are lucky to earn $2.00 an hour for 90-hour weeks. These suffer the most from stigma.[10]

Adding to the occupational stigma is the fact that housework remains tedious, repetitive and necessary. Once done, it is undone almost immediately. Food is eaten, clothing is worn, and floors are dirtied. Cooking and cleaning are not chores most people like doing.

Since domestic workers work in such atomized conditions, it has also been difficult to organize them. However, in recent years, housecleaning companies have sometimes offered their workers benefits like paid vacation, sick days and even health insurance, which private employers have typically not offered. As noted above, however, wages can be very low. Yet even when women are working together on cleaning teams, they know they are expendable, so they do not organize themselves to demand better wages.[11]

If wage/hour/social legislation applied equally to all domestics, it might remove the stigma. However, those laws apply only to those who earn the most and have regular jobs—or at least those who report such things to the government. Because domestic work occurs in private homes, it is practically impossible to enforce any laws. Many workers do not report their employment. Indeed, employers and employees often collude to evade taxes and social security withholding. While this collusion can equalize the relationship, it can also make it difficult for workers to use the leverage the law allows them.[12]

The crux of the matter regarding status remains the low value Americans place on housework and the dislike people have for doing their own "dirty work." Owning a cleaning service, or working for one, is not as low status as being a cleaning person.[13]

Because Americans assume that domestic service is an undesirable job, the corollary is that anyone in the job is a victim to some extent, because who in their right mind would choose this job? But the source of the abuses in the field is also the source of the positives—the personal nature of the job. It may take a while to find a good fit of employer-employee, but when it does happen, it is to both parties' satisfaction.

The key is that the relationship is based upon both parties' view that the job is important. For both, it is simply a job and not a familial commitment. For the worker, the home is merely a workplace. Both acknowledge the inherent difficulties and contradictions in the situation. In these circumstances, the relationship is fairly balanced, and domestic service works as an occupation.[14]

STATISTICS (AND THEIR SHORTCOMINGS)

Two major characteristics of private household workers remained true throughout the twentieth century.

First, females comprised over 90 percent of the occupation.[15]

Second, there has been a steady decrease in the number of private household workers over the course of the century. In 1900, over half of

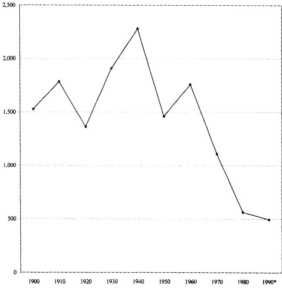

* Categories for occupations other than domestic service differ slightly in 1990 from prior years.

Chart 1. Women Working in Domestic Service in the United States, 1920–1990 (by Number)

Sources: U.S. Bureau of the Census, *Decennial Census of the Population*, 1900, 1920, 1970, 1980; David Katzman, *Seven Days a Week: Domestic Service in Industrializing America* (Urbana, IL: University of Illinois Press, 1981): 56, 60, 290, 291, 292; "Facts About Working Women," *Bulletin of the Women's Bureau* 46 (Washington, G.P.O., 1925): 2, 23; Allyson Sherman Grossman, "Women in Domestic Work, Yesterday and Today," *Monthly Labor Review* 103 (August 1980): 17–21; Janet M. Hooks, "Women's Occupations Through Seven Decades," *Bulletin of the Women's Bureau* 218, U.S. Department of Labor (Washington, D.C.: G.P.O., 1951).

all employed American women were servants. Even as late as 1940, private household workers were the largest group of female laborers (clerical occupations were broken out into several categories—see Table 1). By 1990, however, fewer than 2 percent of American women—495,000—who reported their occupation were in the household help category. New York City experienced a similar pattern; the proportion of women working as domestics dropped from 12 percent in 1920 to 1 percent in 1990.[16]

The decline in the number of household workers meant that employers had to compete for help in the second half of the century. The change in absolute numbers after World War II—from a national high of 2.3 million in 1940 to less than 1.5 million in 1950—is startling enough. But the

* Categories for occupations other than domestic service differ slightly in 1990 from prior years.

Chart 2. Female Domestic Workers as Percentage of Working Women, United States, 1920–1990

Sources: *Decennial Census of the Population*, 1900, 1920, 1970, 1980; Katzman, *Seven Days a Week*: 56, 60, 290, 291, 292; *Facts About Working Women*: 2, 23; Grossman, "Women in Domestic Work, Yesterday and Today"; Hooks, "Women's Occupations Through Seven Decades."

proportion of employed American women who reported domestic service occupations plummeted dramatically as well. And although the number of American servants increased slightly in 1960, the occupation's importance continued to fade. New York City experienced its all-time high in the number of servants in 1930; decline was constant in subsequent years. While the supply of workers decreased, demand remained at least constant. This led to a further restructuring of the market.

Caution must be used when interpreting statistics. One problem with using statistics in the case of domestic service is that many domestic workers did not report their occupation to census takers. I believe that while the absolute number of domestic workers is likely to be higher than reported, the relative size of the occupation according to the available statistics probably reflects reality.

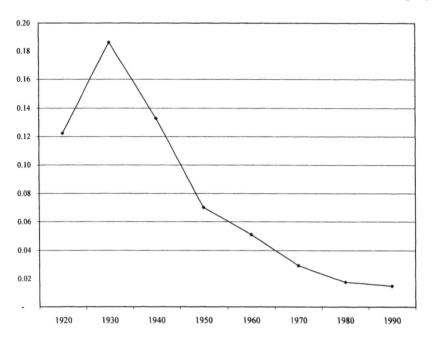

Chart 3. Private Household Workers as Proportion of Working Women, New York City, 1920–1990

Source: *Decennial Census of the Population*, 1920–1990.

Regarding undercounting, stigma is not likely to have been much of a factor. It is true that the stigma of remaining in domestic service may have been higher after World War II, given the great many other job opportunities for women.

Nonetheless, the stigma was great throughout the twentieth century, so it is not necessarily true that underreporting of occupation increased after the Second World War. Moreover, the fact that those other vocations drew women away from private household work did not inevitably increase the latter's stigma. Indeed, many women who did domestic work enjoyed it. The rise in the number of women who reported the occupation in 1960 appears to refute the stigma argument.

Since the inclusion of domestics under Social Security in 1950, the wage deductions involved have probably also had a dampening effect on the reporting of both income and occupation on the part of domestic workers, although that probably was not the case until after the 1960

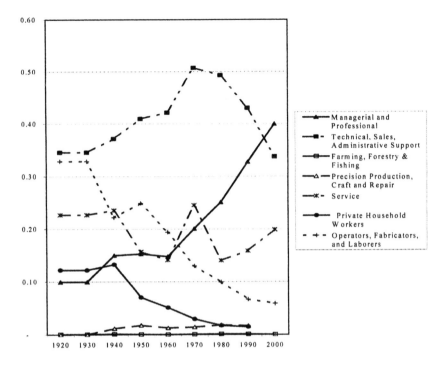

Chart 4. Percent of Women Employed in Occupations, New York City, 1920–2000

Source: *Decennial Census of the Population*, 1920–2000.

Note that private household workers and precision production workers were not broken out in 2000.

census, given that domestics had just been covered at the time of the 1950 census.

The most compelling reasons for undercounting household workers involve schedule and immigration status. People who only occasionally do housework for pay are not likely to view it as an occupation or report it as such. They are an important component of the market, although not nearly so great as undocumented workers.

Illegal immigrants account for a huge number of domestic workers, and they are unlikely to be counted in censuses. There is general agreement among demographers that there are probably between 3 and 5 million undocumented workers in the United States, and New York City probably has about 11 or 12 percent of those.

Table 1. The Leading Ten Occupations of Women Workers, 1900–1940 (in order of size, and as reported in each census regardless of changes in definition)

1900	1910	1920	1930	1940
Servants	Other Servants	Other Servants	Other Servants, Other Domestic and Personal Service	Servants (private family)
Farm Laborers (members of family)	Farm Laborers (home farm)	Teachers (school)	Teachers (school)	Stenographers, Typists and Secretaries
Dressmakers	Laundresses (not in laundry)	Farm Laborers (home farm)	Stenographers and typists	Teachers (not elsewhere classified)
Teachers	Teachers (school)	Stenographers and Typists	Other Clerks (except clerks in stores)	Clerical and Kindred Workers (not elsewhere classified)
Laundry work (hand)	Dressmakers and Seamstresses (not in factory)	Other Clerks (except clerks in stores)	Saleswomen	Saleswomen (not elsewhere classified)

Farmers and planters	Farm Laborers (working out)	Laundresses (not in laundry)	Farm Laborers (unpaid family members)	Operatives and Kindred Workers, Apparel and Accessories
Farm and Plantation Workers	Cooks	Saleswomen	Bookkeepers and Cashiers	Bookkeepers, Accountants and Cashiers
Saleswomen	Stenographers and Typists	Bookkeepers and Cashiers	Laundresses (not in laundry)	Waitresses (except private family)
Housekeepers and Stewards	Farmers	Cooks	Trained Nurses	Housekeepers (private family)
Seamstresses	Saleswomen (stores)	Farmers (general farms)	Other Cooks	Trained Nurses and Student Nurses

Sources: Donna L. Van Raaphorst, *Union Maids Not Wanted: Organizing Domestic Workers 1870–1940* (New York: Praeger, 1988): 4–7; Janet M. Hooks, "Women's Occupations Through Seven Decades," *Bulletin of the Women's Bureau* 218, (Washington, D.C.: Government Printing Office, 1951); Rosalyn Baxandall, Linda Gordon, and Susan Reverby, eds., *America's Working Women: A Documentary History—1600 to the Present* (New York: Vintage 1976): 406–407.

However, because they come from many of the same countries as documented entrants, their occupational distribution tends to mimic that of
officially sanctioned workers. Granted, undocumented workers are more
likely to take lower-paying and lower status jobs, which means they are
over-represented in domestic service compared to their legal compatriots.
Yet some illegal immigrants come from nationalities that typically eschew
domestic work. This means that although the *number* of domestic servants
is likely to actually be higher than reported, illegal aliens probably do not
skew things overmuch. The *proportion* of women working in the occupation is probably similar to the official count.[17]

With regard to those part-time workers who do not declare their
occupation, there were most likely always domestics who did not identify
themselves as such. It is unlikely that their numbers increased sharply over
the century. With regard to immigrants, the number who did not identify themselves as domestics probably increased most sharply after 1970.
Many legal post-1968 immigrants declared their intention of working as
servants. At the end of the twentieth century, there were perhaps 50,000
to 100,000 undocumented domestic workers who were not counted in the
census (demographers believe about half of the country's illegal aliens are
counted). This number was significant compared to the roughly 500,000
workers accounted for in the census. But because of the general rise in the
American population, this does not necessarily mean that domestic service
is a more significant field of work. It does, however, support the argument
that housework is once again an immigrant's occupation.[18]

SCOPE

Although the nature of household help is of course national, it is necessary
to focus on a particular locale. New York City is a very different place than
other American cities, especially those in the South. Yet its statistics closely
mirror national averages, making it a useful place to study. Almost all the
U.S. trends in home economics and management, appliance use, labor force
composition, job structure, compensation, and protective legislation for
private household workers began or were prominent in New York State.
New York is also important since it was (and continues to be) the entry
point for the vast majority of immigrants.

Moreover, New York City and its suburbs constituted the nation's
largest metropolitan area both before and after the half-century under discussion. It was a magnet for immigrants and unskilled labor, and it underwent every economic expansion and contraction that affected the domestic
labor market. The size of that market made New York significant, too. And

the city shared circumstances with other northern urban areas—Chicago, for example, had numerous slave markets during the Depression, and like New York received large numbers of black migrants.[19]

Too, just as federal legislation affected conditions in New York, conditions in the city influenced state and federal legislation. For example, there were scandals in the late 1950s involving New York City employment agencies that lured young women there from the South or Europe with empty promises of good jobs. These led to a federal ban on all domestic servant importation. Only the hue and cry of potential employers caused Congress to reverse that decision.[20]

* * *

Americans tend to want to be egalitarian. The story of domestic service in the twentieth century shows how individuals struggle with realizing that aspiration.

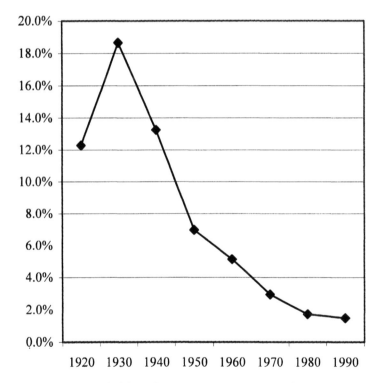

Chart 5. Private Household Workers, 1920–1990, New York City

Table 2. U.S. Women Working in Occupations, 1900–1990

	1900	1910	1920	1930	1940	1950	1960	1970	1980	1990*
Total (000)	5,319	7,445	8,637	10,752	12,574	16,507	22,304	28,930	41,634	52,977
Professional Workers	434	726	1,008	1,482	1,608	1,976	2,793	3,827	5,884	14,753
Clerical	212	688	1,614	2,246	2,700	4,408	6,497	9,351	12,997	14,570
Sales	228	379	541	736	925	1,418	1,746	3,154	4,671	8,551
Operatives	1,264	1,702	1,748	1,870	2,452	3,287	3,612	3,237	3,646	5,724
Domestic Service	1,526	1,784	1,360	1,909	2,277	1,459	1,760	1,110	563	495
Service	359	629	703	1,045	1,422	2,073	3,020	4,649	6,720	8,435
Farm	697	895	892	645	351	481	270	160	**	450

* Occupational categories in 1990 vary slightly from prior years. Clerical is now "administrative support"; Sales is now "Technical, Sales, Administrative Support"; and "Operatives" is now "Precision Production, Craft, Repair" and "Operators, Fabricators, and Laborers."

** Information unavailable.

Sources: David Katzman, *Seven Days a Week: Domestic Service in Industrializing America* (New York, 1978): 56, 60, 290, 291, 292; "Facts About Working Women," *Bulletin of the Women's Bureau* 46 (Washington, G.P.O., 1925): 2, 23; Allyson Sherman Grossman, "Women in Domestic Work, Yesterday and Today," *Monthly Labor Review* (August 1980), 17–21; Janet M. Hooks, "Women's Occupations Through Seven Decades," *Bulletin of the Women's Bureau* 218, (Washington, D.C.: G.P.O., 1951); U.S. Bureau of the Census, *Decennial Census of the Population*, 1900, 1920, 1930, 1940, 1950, 1960, 1970, 1980, 1990.

Table 3. Percent of U.S. Women Working in Occupations, 1900–1990

	1900	1910	1920	1930	1940	1950	1960	1970	1980	1990*
Professional Workers	8.16	9.75	11.67	13.78	12.79	11.97	12.52	13.23	14.13	27.85
Clerical and kindred	3.99	9.24	18.69	20.89	21.47	26.70	29.13	32.32	31.22	27.50
Sales and kindred	4.29	5.09	6.26	6.85	7.36	8.59	7.83	10.90	11.22	16.14
Operatives and kindred	23.76	22.86	20.24	17.39	19.50	19.91	16.19	11.19	8.76	10.80
Domestic Service	28.69	23.96	15.75	17.75	18.11	8.84	7.89	3.84	1.35	0.93
Service (Non-Household)	6.75	8.45	8.14	9.72	11.31	12.56	13.54	16.07	16.14	15.92
Farm Laborers	13.10	12.02	10.33	6.00	2.79	2.91	1.21	0.55	**	0.85

* Note: The categories for the 1990 census are slightly different than the previous decades. Clerical is now "administrative support"; Sales is now "Technical, Sales, Administrative Support"; and "Operatives" is now "Precision Production, Craft, Repair" and "Operators, Fabricators, and Laborers."

** Information unavailable.

Sources: Katzman, *Seven Days a Week*, 56, 60, 290, 291, 292; "Facts About Working Women," 2, 23; Grossman, "Women in Domestic Work," 17–21; Hooks, "Women's Occupations Through Seven Decades"; *Decennial Census of the Population*, 1900, 1920, 1930, 1940, 1950, 1960, 1970, 1980, 1990.

Table 4. Private Household Workers, 1920–1990 (by Number), New York City

	All	Private Household Workers	
Year	Employed Women	Total	As percent of all employed women
1920	692	85	12
1930	863	161	19
1940	875	116	13
1950	1,074	75	7
1960	1,206	62	5
1970	1,293	38	3
1980	1,385	24	2
1990	1,546	23	1.5

Source: *Decennial Census of the Population*, 1920, 1930, 1940, 1950, 1960, 1970, 1980, 1990; Kenneth T. Jackson, ed., *The Encyclopedia of New York City* (New Haven: Yale University Press, 1995).

Table 5. Ethnic Distribution of Private Household Workers, New York City, 1920–1990

		Percentage of Total			
Year	Total	White	Non-White*	Asian	Hispanic
1920	85,000	60	40		
1930	161,000	60	40		
1940	116,000	57	43		
1950	75,000	44	56		
1960	62,000	42	58		
1970	38,000	35	65		1
1980	24,000	20	61	2.5	16
1990	23,000	**	**	**	**

Sources: *Historical Statistics of the U.S., Colonial Times to 1970, Part 1* (U.S. Dept. of Commerce, Bureau of The Census, 1975), Series D182–232: 132; *Decennial Census of the Population*, 1980, 1990.

** 1990 is similar to 1980, but with a higher Hispanic percentage.

Table 6. Women's Occupations, New York City 1920–1990 (by Number)

Total Numbers	1920 ****	1930 ****	1940	1950 **	1960 **	1970 **	1980 ***	1990
Employed Females*	692	863	875	1,074	1,206	1,293	1,385	1,546
Managerial and Professional	69	103	131	164	179	259	348	506
Technical, Sales, Administrative Support	262	363	325	440	508	656	683	665
Farming, Forestry & Fishing	.3	.2	1	.5	.2	.7	1.5	1.4
Precision Production, Craft and Repair	—	—	10	19	16	19	26	26
Service	157	220	206	169	171	317	195	246
Private Household Workers	85	161	116	75	62	38	24	23
Operators, Fabricators, and Laborers	204	177	194	268	234	168	137	103

* For employed women ages 16+ 1960, 1970, 1980, 1990 and 2000; for employed women 14+ in 1940, 1950, and 10+ in 1920.

** Managerial includes technical.

*** From 1980 NY-NJ Standard Metropolitan Statistical Area (SMSA); reduced to 79 percent of that number. The 1970 ratio of NYC to SMSA numbers was 72 percent, and the 1990 ratio was 64 percent, but both of those ratios resulted in a drop in the total number of employed women in 1980, which seemed unreasonable. I therefore used the 1960 ratio, which was 79 percent.

**** Public and professional service make up Managerial and Professional numbers; there was no real "precision production category": manufacturing & mechanical and extraction of minerals were combined into "operators, fabricators and laborers." Trade and Clerical Occupations were combined into Technical, sales and administrative support, as was Transportation & Communication, since it was mostly telephone and telegraph operators. Finally, the only service category was "domestic and personal service," of which "servants" was a sub-category.

Source: *Decennial Census of the United States* 1920, 1930, 1940, 1950, 1960, 1970, 1980, 1990.

Table 7. Women's Occupations, New York City 1920–1990 (by Percentage)

Occupational Distribution (%)	1920 ****	1930 ****	1940	1950 **	1960 **	1970 **	1980 ***	1990
Employed Females*	100	100	100	100	100	100	100	100
Managerial and Professional	0.10	0.12	0.15	0.15	0.15	0.20	0.25	0.33
Technical, Sales, Administrative Support	0.38	0.42	0.37	0.41	0.42	0.51	0.49	0.43
Farming, Forestry & Fishing	0.00	0.00	0.00	0.00	0.00	0.00	0.00	0.00
Precision Production, Craft and Repair	—	—	0.01	0.02	0.01	0.01	0.02	0.02
Service	0.23	0.25	0.24	0.16	0.14	0.25	0.14	0.16
Private Household Workers	0.12	0.19	0.13	0.07	0.05	0.03	0.02	0.015
Operators, Fabricators, and Laborers	0.30	0.20	0.22	0.25	0.19	0.13	0.10	0.07

* For employed women ages 16+ 1960, 1970, 1980, 1990 and 2000; for employed women 14+ in 1940, 1950, and 10+ in 1920.

** Managerial includes technical.

*** From 1980 NY-NJ Standard Metropolitan Statistical Area (SMSA); reduced to 79 percent of that number. The 1970 ratio of NYC to SMSA numbers was 72 percent, and the 1990 ratio was 64 percent, but both of those ratios resulted in a drop in the total number of employed women in 1980, which seemed unreasonable. I therefore used the 1960 ratio, which was 79 percent.

**** Public and professional service make up Managerial and Professional numbers; there was no real "precision production category": manufacturing & mechanical and extraction of minerals were combined into "operators, fabricators, and laborers." Trade and Clerical Occupations were combined into Technical, sales and administrative support, as was Transportation & Communication, since it was mostly telephone and telegraph operators. Finally, the only service category was "domestic and personal service," of which "servants" was a sub-category.

Source: Decennial Census of the United States 1920, 1930, 1940, 1950, 1960, 1970, 1980, 1990.

Table 8. Women's Occupations, New York City and U.S., 1920–1990

	New York Women as a Percentage of U.S. Women (Employed)							
	1920	1930	1940	1950	1960	1970	1980	1990
Managerial and Professional	6.8	7.0	8.2	8.3	6.4	6.8	5.9	3.4
Technical, Sales, Administrative Support	11.1	12.2	9.0	7.5	6.2	5.2	3.9	2.9
Farming, Forestry & Fishing	0.1	0.0	0.3	0.1	0.1	0.5		0.3
Service	7.6	7.4	14.5	4.8	3.2	5.5	2.7	2.8
Private Household Workers	6.2	8.4	5.1	5.2	3.5	3.4	4.3	4.6
Operators, Fabricators, and Laborers	13.0	9.4	8.3	8.7	6.9	5.8	4.5	2.3

Source: *Decennial Census of the United States*, 1920, 1930, 1940, 1950, 1960, 1970, 1980, 1990.

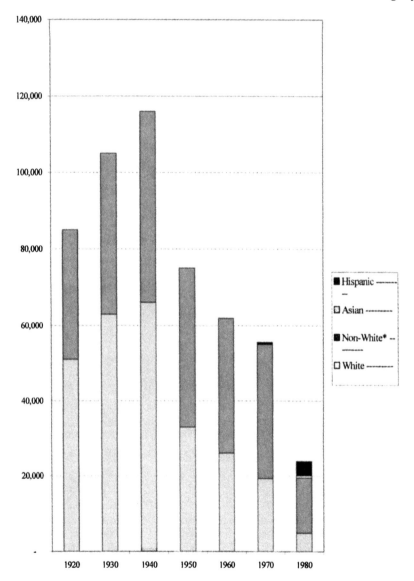

Chart 6. Ethnic Distribution of Private Household Workers, 1920–1980, New York City

Sources: *Historical Statistics of the U.S., Colonial Times to 1970, Part 1; Decennial Census of the Population,* 1980, 1990.

* Nonwhite includes Asian and Hispanic until 1970.It includes Afro-Caribbeans in all years.

Note: 1990 is similar to 1980, but with a higher Hispanic percentage.

Chapter One

Breaking the Mold: Changing Work Structures between the Wars

Gustafsa Gustafson arrived in New York from Sweden in late 1921. Through the Mrs. A.E. Johnson Agency, she immediately found a job as a live-in kitchen maid. Paid $45 a month, Gustafsa worked from early in the morning till after the dinner dishes were done at night. She probably slept in a room at the top of the house, and she may have had to go to the basement to bathe in a copper tub. She had no say in her duties or hours.[1]

Had she come at the end of the 1920s, Gustafsa's experiences were likely to have been very different. There were fewer servants' quarters as well as fewer servants. Wages were higher, and more workers lived in their own homes. Most importantly, the relationship between maid and mistress was beginning to change.

Before World War I, domestic service relations were unequal. There was an employer-dominated hierarchy, largely because there were relatively few employment options for women. Domestic service was the major employer of women in the United States. In the South, things could even be described as feudal, as one author has done, because workers were essentially bound to their jobs. In New York, the market did play a role— i.e., workers were paid wages and were free to change jobs to maximize earnings and better their working conditions. But although servants could and did change jobs, while they were employed, their employers were absolute masters. They dictated hours, tasks, working conditions, and for live-ins, food and living quarters. Of course, there was some give and take in the relationship, but the supremacy of the employer in the hierarchy was unquestioned.[2]

Beginning with the First World War and the resulting servant shortage, this pattern began to shift. First with wage levels, then working hours, and finally with the notion that a servant had to live in, the status quo began to crumble. Servants began to be able to dictate some of their own requirements, shifting the balance of power and disrupting the hierarchical structure. Because wages and hours became more important during the 1920s, the maid-mistress relationship became more market-based and impersonal, one in which both maid and mistress had a say in how things worked between them.

*   *   *

In the early twentieth century, domestic service was woven into the ideal of the American dream. Although the vast majority of families did not have servants, household help was prevalent enough to be taken for granted. If one had enough money, one could have a full-time maid or a cook, or both.[3]

This ideal underwent significant alterations during the 1920s. Perhaps most significantly, housewives of all classes expected less human help with their housework. Even the recessionary cycle begun in 1928, which presaged the Depression and sent laid-off workers into jobs of last resort like household service, could not undo the changes. Household workers now wanted to live in their own homes and to work fewer hours. In short, they wanted to make domestic work more like factory work.

Employers resisted change as long as they could, and only grudgingly began to pay some attention to workers' complaints about job conditions. In two areas, they bowed to reality: Servants' quarters became a thing of the past except for the wealthy. And housewives began to handle their domestic chores with electrical appliances, commercial laundries and prepared foods. The middle-class family became more isolated and engaged in the impersonal purchase of services and tools from outside the home. And when they did hire help, it was in a similar market-oriented way.

WORKING CONDITIONS

Prior to World War I, servants tended to live with the families for whom they worked. As Elizabeth Clark-Lewis put it, "Until World War I, to the employer, the word *servant* meant a live-in servant."[4]

Resident workers worked long hours. A normal day began at 7:00 a.m. or earlier and ended at 9:00 p.m. or later. Fires (in fireplaces and stoves) had to be lit at the beginning of the day, before the family awoke, and the house tidied after the family retired. Live-in domestics usually had a day and a half off each week, most often Thursdays and Sunday afternoons. This made their regular workweek at least 72 hours. Even after their official duties ended, a maid was still on call.[5]

What one irate domestic wrote in 1927 held true for many live-in workers throughout the decades:

The domestic is still working longer hours than a longshoreman works. Her 'day out,' which is once a week, is from 3 o'clock in the afternoon until 10 at night, and when she gets in she is supposed to do all the work that has been left over for her. She has never an hour to call her very own. . . . [6]

Housework was hard to schedule, because the need for it continued throughout the day. A 1924 study found that the most popular time for help was between 5 and 8 p.m., followed by 7 to 11 a.m., when the worker not only prepared breakfast and cleaned up after it, but also made beds and did another daily task, like laundry or the thorough cleaning of one room.[7]

All service jobs were of course not the same. In the 1920s, one New York City agency offered regular cooks, second cooks, dinner cooks, luncheon cooks, kitchen maids, chambermaids, parlormaids, waitresses, chambermaid/waitresses, nurses, ladies maids, day workers, laundresses, general houseworkers, caretakers, housekeepers, couples, hotel help, butlers, second men, and footmen.[8]

Domestic work itself could be divided into five main groups:

1. Those centering around meals: cooking, serving, washing dishes.

2. Those centering around the care of the home: daily care, weekly care.

3. Those having to do with the care of household textiles and clothing: washing, ironing, mending.

4. Those having to do with the care of children: daily care, occasional care during afternoon or evening.

5. Miscellaneous: answering the telephone and doorbell, receiving packages, and so on.[9]

Cooks cooked and ordered food and planned menus, usually in consultation with their mistresses. In larger establishments, they had an additional kitchen maid to chop, clean, scrub the kitchen floor, wash dishes, dispose of garbage and perhaps tend the wood-burning stove.

Chambermaids were responsible for cleaning the bedrooms and bathrooms, parlormaids for the public areas. The latter also answered the door and the telephone. Waitresses and/or footmen served and cleared meals, cleaned silver, and set the table.

Before automatic washing machines, laundresses had to boil vat after vat of water and wash and rinse clothing by hand. As time went on, there were hand-operated and then electric washers, but until the late 1940s there were no automatic dryers, and there was always lots of ironing to do manually. Sometimes laundresses lived in the household, but more often, they came in once or twice a week and worked for several families.[10]

In smaller households, duties were conflated. The chambermaid/waitress combination was very common; she cleaned the private areas of the house, served meals, washed dishes and helped the cook. These classifications were fairly rigid, and served as a kind of protection for workers. In the 1935 movie *Alice Adams,* the black woman hired to cook and serve a meal refused to answer the door. It was not part of her job and would lessen her dignity.[11]

As the number of servants decreased, the general houseworker became predominant. She cleaned the house or apartment, scrubbed floors, washed windows, did "plain cooking," and often did laundry and ironing. Childcare was often mixed in with housework in homes with only one or two servants.

THE NATURE OF HOUSEHOLD WORK

Housework has traditionally been viewed as unskilled, but it requires knowledge and ability. The New York State Employment Service listed the following needs in 1948:

> manual dexterity . . . physical endurance, emotional stability . . . free[dom from] communicable disease or occupationally hazardous disease . . . good muscular coordination . . . [ability] to stand, bend, stretch, stoop, and to lift light objects such as vacuum cleaner, or to move small pieces of furniture such as arm chairs.

Though literacy was "preferred," it was "not necessary," although the worker "[s]hould be sufficiently alert to be able to act in emergencies [and] to give attention to many items simultaneously [and] sufficiently accurate to follow recipes and take telephone messages."[12]

These were not inconsiderable capabilities, particularly when put into the context of the specific knowledge workers were expected to have. A mid-twentieth century training course test covered a variety of normal household tasks, including cooking, cleaning, sewing, laundry and childcare. Some questions were very basic:

19. Dishes should be rinsed in
    a. hot soapy water
    b. hot water
    c. cold soapy water

while others were trickier:

9. In cleaning a bed room one should
    a. first wash the windows, clean the floor, wipe down the walls and then clean the wood work.
    b. first clean the floors, then wash the windows and lastly wipe down the walls and clean the wood work.
    c. first wipe down the walls, clean the wood work, wash the windows, and lastly wipe up the floors.

and others quite sophisticated (as well as beyond the ken of a typical person today):

5. To thicken one cup of medium white sauce use
    a. one tablespoon of flour
    b. two tablespoons of flour
    c. four tablespoons of flour

25. After a dress is fitted the next step is
    a. to sew in the sleeves
    b. to sew on the collar
    c. to finish the seams

43. Vegetables for babies should be cooked
    a. three minutes
    b. five minutes
    c. until they are well done[13]

These questions assumed detailed knowledge. The average house-worker knew how to make rolls, biscuits, waffles, every kind of egg (fried, poached, scrambled, coddled, custard), soups, salads, vegetables, meats, and many desserts; could set and decorate a table and serve a meal, organize cooking and serving while keeping dishes hot, and wash dishes when the meal was done.[14]

Work was psychologically taxing, too. Minnie Barnes, a Washington, D.C. domestic, described her work as "running back and forth to hand them this and that," to reassure the housewife that her staff was busy and focused on her. Supervision was close and personal, which could become irksome, and standards were particular to each household.[15]

Compared to factory and other personal service occupations, paid housework was relatively safe. It nonetheless held very real dangers. Household employees lost more than a week's work due to injury more often than other types of workers.[16]

Amey Watson, who conducted a study of household employment in Philadelphia, wrote:

> The frequency and severity of home accidents . . . indicates the risk in household employment, with its hazards of wet or polished floors; loose rugs; stairs and cellar and attic steps; climbing, reaching, lifting, carrying; fires, gas, electricity, fuel oils, cleaning chemicals; scalding fluids; hot irons; sharp utensils; fragile glass and china; and a multitude of others.[17]

Sexual harassment was common. The notion of a husband having intimate contact with household help was so ingrained that postcards made a joke of it. In one, a portly man kissed a uniformed maid while his wife sat in another room and confided to a friend, "I have so much trouble with the maids. Charles is never satisfied." Such situations may have resulted from the common perception that paid household help was an extension of the unpaid houseworker: the wife, or "the more menial part of herself."[18]

IMMIGRANTS AND DOMESTIC WORK

In the early years of the twentieth century, most of New York City's servants were white, with Irish, Scandinavians, and Germans predominant. By 1920, African-American women who had migrated north helped swell their share of domestic laborers to about 40 percent, even though blacks accounted for less than three percent of the city's population.[19]

Before the 1920s, immigrants had occupied the majority of household positions because domestic service was a useful entrance job. A single woman arriving alone from Europe could get a wage and a place to live at the same time. Immigration was high before World War I: between 1900 and 1910, almost 9 million people arrived in the United States.

Figure 1. Sexual abuse was common enough to engender jokes. General Comics postcard, 1941.

Martin Harris, an investment banker who grew up on New York's Upper East Side, remembered, "We had a cook and a maid. Then, you could get people in. The maid would go down to the boats at Ellis Island. If someone would be congenial to her, she would bring them back." The new arrivals were "very glad to get a place to live." As the occupation was both easy to enter and convenient, it became popular; in 1905, 84 percent of new female arrivals (of all nationalities) in New York went into domestic service.[20]

Newcomers, particularly those without marketable skills, knew where opportunity lay. Evelyn Crookhorn's father, who came from Sweden in 1918, served in the U.S. Army and then went into service, "because that's all the jobs there were for people who were uneducated." Like Gustafsa Gustafson, the "just landed" Marta Byrne rapidly found employment as a general houseworker.[21]

Despite the long hours, hard work and dangers, many European immigrants preferred domestic service to other lines of work. Swedish housemaids, for example, tended to have worked in that occupation at home. And despite the low social status accorded domestics in the United States, it was a step up to do it in America. "[Th]ey were better treated, had lighter duties and regular time off. One was 'treated like a human being'" in comparison with treatment in Sweden.[22]

Evelyn Crookhorn said of her Swedish immigrant parents: "You know, they were all young. They didn't look upon being servants as being demeaning. They considered it an honor. To be in service, as they called it, was wonderful."[23]

Like Swedes, Irish maids chose their occupation. As Hasia Diner has pointed out, "the nature of the work did not jar their cultural patterns or the values they cherished." Irish women were not necessarily interested in getting married and giving up their independence. Live-in work was thus an economical way to live.[24]

For both Swedes and Irish, and presumably the Germans who also made up large numbers of New York's servants in the early part of the twentieth century, domestic work afforded the chance to immerse themselves in their new culture. Swedish women tended to marry other Scandinavian immigrants "whose assimilation to American society the former housemaids, thanks to their familiarity with American customs, doubtless facilitated."[25]

Indeed, domestic work was a "bridging occupation" for immigrants, "a transitional occupation into the formal sector," i.e., non-household jobs. Still, there was a stigma attached to the occupation, partially caused by its unequal power relationship. This was reflected in the fact that very few native-born white Americans chose it.[26]

MATERIAL CONDITIONS

Employers liked to think of their help as "part of the family," but in fact servants were both distinct and invisible. Uniforms, for example, rendered workers anonymous and emphasized their subservience.[27]

The configuration and use of household space also emphasized the distance between employer and employee. Workers were relegated to small areas in service wings or to a tiny maid's room. Around the turn of the century, this description was apt for most urban dwellings: "One apartment-house recently erected in New York . . . has every kitchen and servant's room so arranged as to require gas-light all day long on even bright days, below the sixth story. . . . Comparatively few of the houses in America are arranged to give bathing facilities to servants."[28]

The wealthiest households had small sitting rooms for the help, but most live-in servants had only a 7' x 11' space and the kitchen in which to spend time. The famous Dakota apartment building on Central Park West had separate floors of tiny rooms for servants. Sometimes live-ins were expected to share a room with an infant or child, or if they were in a house, they were stuck in basements, attics, or garages.[29]

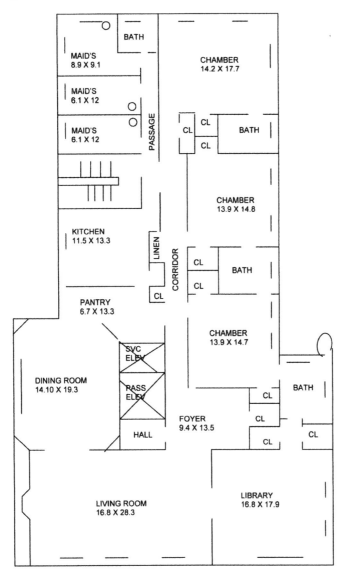

Figure 2. 1922 floorplan for 3 East 84th Street, New York, NY. *Pease & Elliman's Catalogue of East Side of New York Typical Apartment Plans* (New York: Edited and Published by A.G. Blaisdell, 1922?).

Even the kitchen could not belong to the servant alone, since it was part of her employer's property. It was a workplace, not a place to relax. But the worker had to stay there, since she was not allowed to take her ease elsewhere in the home. For live-out workers this was not an issue, but for live-in servants, it made life uncomfortable, cramped and restricted. "Emancipated," writing in 1927, complained that a resident employee had "no place to see her friends, no time for improvement, and in the new apartments has to enter her kitchen, after an evening out, through a long courtyard that any respectable woman is afraid to be seen going through."[30]

Because they had so little time off, servants' social lives centered upon activities within their ethnic groups. There were immigrant neighborhoods in New York City: the Swedes lived on Manhattan's East Side from about 20th to 57th Streets or in Brooklyn's Bay Ridge, while the Irish favored the West Side of Manhattan. African-Americans congregated first on the West Side and then in Harlem. If they lived in, they often maintained an address in the area, in care of a friend or relative.[31]

At times, because room and board were included, a live-in servant actually made more money than her factory counterpart, a fact noted by sociologist Lucy Maynard Salmon in her pioneering 1897 study of domestic service. In New York City just before World War I, kitchen maids, chambermaids, and general houseworkers earned about $35 cash a month. Cooks averaged about $40 a month, as did waitresses, who were in the public eye and therefore more valuable. Wages for laundresses varied, ranging from $35 to $45 a month. The latter figure was what ladies' maids and general purpose "useful maids" earned. They were often able to save money because they had so little time for social life and opportunity for spending, but the isolation increased the distance between them and their employers and reinforced the unequal relationship.[32]

A DECLINE IN THE NUMBER OF SERVANTS

Beginning with the First World War, several demographic factors enabled domestic workers to start successfully competing for control in their workplaces. First, the supply of domestic workers dropped. The outbreak of World War I in 1914 and subsequent legislation restricted immigration. The war had also brought with it job opportunities for women, most prominently clerical work. This field continued to expand during the 1920s, as did sales and some factory work. Other sectors of the economy, then, siphoned workers out of domestic service.

The number of private household workers declined absolutely and as a percentage of the female labor force, both nationally and in New York City. From 1900 to 1920, there was a drop from 141 servants for every 1000 New York households to only 66. The number of female domestics in New York dropped 20 percent, from 105,000 to 85,000, between 1900 and 1920. There is also evidence that in the mid-1920s there were fewer servants in New York than in 1920, and that it was because they had left for other occupations, not because there was less demand. This is important because a shortage gave workers leverage to demand higher wages and shorter hours, both of which they gained during the 1920s. And although there were more workers in 1930 than ten years previously, the proportion of workers to households remained about the same. The unemployed had also swelled the ranks of domestics since 1928. Therefore, the crucial period was prior to 1928.[33]

The perception of a shortage was perhaps more important than the fact of it. From the National Women's Trade Union League to local employment agencies, to newspapers (particularly *The New York Times*), New Yorkers heard throughout the 1920s that there was a servant shortage. Even when the U.S. Department of Labor denied that there was an actual shortage, saying that there were slightly more workers than jobs, employers did not believe it. And the reality was that there was a shortage

Table 9. U.S. Women Working in Occupations, 1900–1930

	1900	1910	1920	1930
Total (by Number)	5,319	7,445	8,637	10,752
Prof'l	434	726	1,008	1,482
Clerical	212	688	1,614	2,246
Sales	228	379	541	736
Operatives	1,264	1,702	1,748	1,870
Domestic Service	1,526	1,784	1,360	1,909
Service	359	629	703	1,045
Farm	697	895	892	645

Source: U.S. Bureau of the Census, *Decennial Census of the Population*, 1900, 1920, 1930; David Katzman, *Seven Days a Week: Domestic Service in Industrializing America* (Urbana, IL: University of Illinois Press, 1981): 56, 60, 290, 291, 292; "Facts About Working Women," *Bulletin of the Women's Bureau* 46 (Washington, G.P.O., 1925): 2, 23; Allyson Sherman Grossman, "Women in Domestic Work, Yesterday and Today," *Monthly Labor Review* (August 1980): 17-21; Janet M. Hooks, "Women's Occupations Through Seven Decades," *Bulletin of the Women's Bureau* 218, U.S. Department of Labor (Washington, D.C.: G.P.O., 1951).

Table 10. Private Household Workers, New York City, 1920–1930

Year	All Employed Women	Private Household Workers	
		Total	As percent of all employed women
1920	692,000	85,000	12%
1930	863,000	105,000[1]	19%

Source: U.S. Bureau of the Census, *Decennial Census of the Population* 1920, 1930.

[1]In 1930 in New York City, there were about 161,000 women in domestic and personal service, a very high number that includes beauty parlor workers and the like. I will assume that the number of household workers increased along the lines of the general population, or about 23 percent. This is a generous number and leaves us with an estimate of 105,000 female private household workers in the five boroughs, roughly similar to the 1900 number. In both 1920 and 1930, roughly 60 percent of all New York servants were white, and 40 percent were nonwhite. *Decennial Census of the Population*, 1900, 1920, 1930; Katzman, *Seven Days A Week*, 56, 60, 290, 291, 292.

Table 11. Women's Occupations, New York City, 1920–1930

Total Numbers	1920*	1930*
Employed Females*	691,727	862,860
Managerial and Professional	68,854	103,331
Technical, Sales, Administrative Support	261,707	363,059
Farming, Forestry & Fishing	345	175
Precision Production, Craft and Repair	—	—
Service	156,667	219,728
Private Household Workers	84,615	105,000
Operators, Fabricators, and Laborers	204,130	176,567

* These categories have been standardized according to the modern census. Public and professional service make up the Managerial and Professional numbers; there was no "precision production category": manufacturing & mechanical and extraction of minerals were combined into "operators, fabricators and laborers." Trade and Clerical Occupations were combined into Technical, sales and administrative support, as was Transportation & Communication, since it was mostly telephone and telegraph operators. Finally, the only service category was "domestic and personal service," of which "servants" was a sub-category. See footnote 33 for a discussion of the 1930 number.

Source: U.S. Bureau of the Census, *Decennial Census of the Population*, 1920, 1930.

of the kinds of workers—live in and docile—they wanted. Domestics and employers were on opposite sides of a growing chasm. Their perceptions of what domestic service should be began to diverge during this decade, the ground rules changed, and each side began to jockey for position.[34]

REDUCED IMMIGRATION

A second factor in the servant shortage was, many New Yorkers believed, decreased immigration. *The New York Times,* responding to its readers' interests, reported one-quarter fewer foreign-born servants in the country in 1920 than in 1910. New Yorkers could no longer go down to Ellis Island and easily pick up newly arrived immigrants who would be glad of a home.

Immigration did shrink dramatically after 1910 (by two-thirds to New York), first because of the war and then because of immigration restrictions. World War I's cost in lives and money had caused many Americans to retreat into isolationism, and anti-immigrant sentiment was on the rise. Then a sharp recession hit the country in 1919–1921, which exacerbated prejudice against unskilled workers.

A panic set in when more than 800,000 immigrants arrived between June 1920 and June 1921. Ellis Island was so badly jammed that ships had to go to Boston instead. Afraid that new arrivals would take jobs away from needy Americans, Congress passed "emergency legislation to restrict the flow of immigrants . . . in eight hours" in April 1921. Three years later, the National Origins Act was passed, formalizing the quota system, and it was followed in 1927 by a law limiting total immigration to 150,000 a year. All the laws favored northern and western Europeans—65,700 Irish were allowed in, but only 5,000 Italians.[35]

Middle-class New Yorkers were alarmed at the imposition of quotas, even though they favored precisely those groups most likely to become servants (Irish, Germans, Scandinavians). Indeed Robert L. Bacon, a Congressman from Long Island, pointed out that "the present immigration quotas permit the present immigration of quite a number of domestics. This is especially true of Southern Ireland, England and Germany. The English and German quotas are quite large, and the Free State quota is far from being filled." But these were now the nationalities least likely to emigrate. Many young women who before the war would have come to New York to work as maids now stayed in Europe, where servants were in short supply and earned good wages.[36]

Grace Harriman of the New York City Travelers Aid Society blamed European housewives and high wages for the servant shortage.

The women on the other side of the water go down on their hands and knees to them. To get any girl who will do any kind of housework to stay at home, they will pay her any kind of a price, will make any concession, and there is no one of the few girls who are coming over here who wants to do housework. Do housework? Why, just the other day we sent twelve girls on to California, each of them paying her full fare through. It costs something to go to California. You may say that the $7 a week domestic servant is wintering in California.[37]

NEW EMPLOYMENT OPPORTUNITIES FOR WOMEN

A stronger and permanent threat to the continuation of the servant class in America was the opening of other employment opportunities for women. Although domestic and personal service was still the number one occupation for American women in 1920, other occupations were growing in importance. For example, the number of American female office workers rose 500 percent between 1910 and 1930. In New York, office workers now accounted for 42 percent of all employed women. New Yorkers were aware that their erstwhile servants were "all at work in occupations they like better than being in a family and not of it."[38]

Women's economic opportunities had burgeoned during the war. Despite a temporary retrenchment afterwards because of men's return to their factory jobs and a recession, occupational variety continued to flourish. A booming mid-twenties economy and the resulting demand for workers made occupations other than domestic service respectable for young women. New technology—factory and office machines, communications devices like the telephone—also created new jobs for women.[39]

Ethel M. Smith of the U.S. Department of Labor's Women's Bureau concluded that "while immigration undoubtedly affects the supply of domestic workers temporarily,

> the chief cause, the big migration, is not a geographical shift from one location to another, either of European and Asiatic peoples to America, or of negroes out of Southern agriculture into Northern industry. It is the movement of women, in great numbers now instead of the former few, out of their historically allotted *sphere* into other fields of the world's work."[40]

Not only native-born white women gravitated toward non-domestic occupations. According to *The New York Times,* there was a drop of 100,000, or one-quarter of all foreign-born servants in the country between

1910 and 1920. "Distaste for domestic service is plainly not confined to the native born," said one observer. Moreover, after the 1924 law was passed, literate immigrants opted for factory or clerical work, and illiterates were barred from entering the U.S. It was only when no other jobs were to be had that there was a surplus of servants, as during the recession of 1919–1921.[41]

The joys of other occupations were not unmitigated. Some young women in other occupations looked wistfully at domestic service. For all of its vaunted advantages in terms of independence and earnings potential, office work was not always cherished. The changes that New York women were experiencing were difficult. More of them were in the work force and although they may have enjoyed the idea of taking care of themselves and casting off Victorian constraints, reality could be harsh. Laura Clark, an office worker, wrote bitterly that she and her fellows had to "dress beyond our means, pay board and carfare and struggle along from hand to mouth, when all the time we hear the rich people complaining that they cannot get enough help in their homes."[42]

Still, reduced immigration and the increase in other job opportunities joined to create a shortage of domestic workers, at least of those willing to work solely on employers' terms.

The balance of power was shifting, based in part on that shortage. Also, beginning in the 1920s, the composition of the labor force changed, which also affected the relationship between domestic employer and employee. The same forces that caused a shortage of workers helped make African-American women primary actors among servants. Their needs

Figure 3. "They aren't ready to be employed on your terms, but, oh, how they want to be employed on their own!" Illustration for Helen Bullitt Lowry, "Turning Tide in the Domestic Service Market, *The New York Times*, December 5, 1920.

and desires were markedly different from immigrants and brought about changes in their occupation.

THE SHIFT TO AFRICAN-AMERICANS

In New York, 1920 marked when the servant population shifted from a white immigrant base to a black native-born base. Migration from the South combined with the exodus of white women from the domestic class to cause both a numerical and a proportionate increase in black servants. There were 153,088 African-Americans in New York in 1920, an increase of 66.9 percent over 1910.[43]

African Americans flooded into the North. Between September 1922 and September 1923, almost 500,000 blacks left the South for the North, many of them brought up by employers. If they were going to work as domestics, better in New York than in the South, where "work or fight" laws compelled them to stay in jobs and with employers they may have hated. New York at least offered the chance to do something else. The laws were also not so specifically oppressive.[44]

Nineteen-year-old Virginia Johnson knew that she could get a job in New York as a maid, so she moved from rural North Carolina in the early 1920s and took a live-in position. Black West Indians, Barbadians prominent among them, joined her and other African Americans in the New York domestic job market. These immigrants used their European colonial powers' quotas to enter the United States.[45]

Paule Marshall, whose Barbadian mother worked as a maid in this period, wrote,

> the only work available to these earlier arrivals (as well as to their African American counterparts from the South) was as domestics—or as the women in Brown Girl, Brownstones termed the work they were forced to do: 'scrubbing floors.' These jobs were often sleeping-in arrangements which saw these young women overworked, underpaid, and given only every other Thursday off.[46]

Employers viewed the latter as preferable to African-Americans, since they were foreign and fit into the idea that newcomers had to work extra hard to establish themselves in the United States. But overall, mistresses tended to prefer European maids and cooks. There was widespread prejudice against black women servants. Employers of household help felt that the curtailment of white immigration struck at the heart of their domestic arrangements.

Mrs. Louis A. Jaffer of Cedarhurst, L.I. begged the President and Congress to amend the law to allow more Europeans in if they promised to be servants. She wrote,

> You perhaps do not feel so poignantly the real distress and suffering that we undergo. . . . Certainly something should be done, and be done immediately, to . . . permit healthy women of the white race who are suitable for or trained in domestic service to immigrate into this country, for a number of years at least.

Although he sympathized with Mrs. Jaffer, Congressman Albert Johnson, Chairman of the House Committee on Immigration and Naturalization, replied that no one could be forced to work as a domestic.[47]

Mrs. Jaffer and others' objections highlighted the difference between African-American and immigrant servants.

Immigrant women had used service as a stepping-stone from which they or their children moved. There was no white "servant class" in the United States; foreign-born women worked as maids or cooks because they did not speak English, or they were too timid to venture into factory work, or they enjoyed domestic work.

A native-born black houseworker's presence, however, brought housewives face to face with the fact that there was indeed a class of Americans relegated to servitude. It was difficult to believe that African-American women chose to do domestic work because they liked it. They simply were not allowed to do much else, particularly in the South, but in New York as well. Their almost complete absence in occupations other than private household or farm work affirmed this. This entrapment, which was no doubt resented, made it more likely that black women would resist long hours and low pay.[48]

African-American women in domestic work were also older than their counterparts in other occupations. There were more women aged 45 years and above in private household labor than in any other job. Beginning with World War I, without great quantities of young immigrants to fill their ranks, domestic workers grew to be comprised of the aging foreign-born and African-American women. The latter stayed employed the longest. At age 65, when most white women retired, more than one-quarter of all black women were still working in 1925. Over fourteen percent of New York State domestic workers were above 55 years old in 1940 (four percent were over 65), and African-American women over the age of 55 still dominated the field in the 1960s. Domestics thus had more life experience and self-confidence, making them more likely to confront whatever injustices they saw. This was something young, newly arrived girls were unlikely to do.[49]

The changing nature of workers' expectations forced employers to confront some of their assumptions about the extent of service to which they were entitled. When immigrants dominated the field, employers could justify their demands for long hours with the knowledge that their servants would move on into marriage or another occupation. Since until the late 1960s black women were not likely to go into other occupations, that rationale for poor treatment of workers no longer made sense. In fact, African-Americans felt that their white employers simply wanted to exercise their superiority. The latter, of course, did not agree. The battle lines were drawn. And since private household work became linked more strongly to African-Americans, an element of racial prejudice emerged.[50]

WAGES

One front of the war concerned wages. The immediate result of the servant shortage, both during and after the war, was that servants could command higher pay. Wages rose swiftly during the war. In 1918, cooks commanded between $50 and $60 a month, laundresses up to $60 a month, chambermaids and waitresses $45, and the day rate for cooking or waiting went from $1.50 to $2.50, and cleaners were up to $2.00 a day. Highly experienced workers like Anna Bjorklund of Anderson Avenue in the Bronx, could earn an average of $65 a month as a full-time waitress. On one job, she got $75 a month. This compared favorably with clerical wages.[51]

Even during the postwar recession (1919–1921), when, as one employer said, "the closing of factories is washing [cooks] out," wages did not drop tremendously. Andrew Lazare, who ran a domestic employment agency for white workers, reported that wages for untrained workers had dropped by 10 percent, but that first class cooks were still getting between $75 and $90 a month, and housemaids between $55 to $70, which still favorably compared to clerical wages.[52]

By the time the economy recovered, the "dear old $35-a-month figure" from before World War I was gone. Wages settled down, so in 1921 the average wage for most white workers was between $60 and $70 a month. Cooks made $70 or $80 a month. Some employers paid top dollar. Anna Rundquist earned $90 a month from Mrs. A. Hayman of Oyster Bay, Long Island, who paid her laundress $70. For day work, cooks like Alma Jorgenson earned $5.00, and chambermaids made between $3 and $4 a day. Mary Wynn, who had 20 years of housekeeping experience, would do "anything" for $3.10 a day. That was also the daily rate for laundry, the most arduous task.[53]

Men, of course, made more money since so few worked in domestic service, and they were assumed to be the family breadwinners. Butlers averaged between $100 and $110 a month. Their wages had not risen as quickly as women's, however, because their labor pool had been small to begin with and was not drastically affected by the decrease in immigration.[54]

African-American women earned less than whites. An observer noted that during the 1919–21 recession, "[N]orth of Mason and Dixon's line the negro women have been the first to lose their high-priced places. And employers, who have known the negro servants for the first time at their very worst period, in the first flush of high wages, seem only too glad to go back to the whites." One black woman stopped Helen Bullitt Lowry (a reporter for *The New York Times*) outside of an employment agency and said, "Yes'm, I'll work for $12 a week. It ain't what I been gittin,' but I wants a good home for Winter."[55]

This was a precursor of the Bronx Slave Market (discussed in the next chapter). African-American women, barred from other occupations, had to accept what they could get in domestic work. The gains they made during good economic times could be erased immediately during a recession.

White women, on the other hand, resisted wage erosion. Employers preferred them, and they, more than their African-American sisters, had tasted occupational freedom.

Henrietta Rothstein, Superintendent of the New York State Employment Bureau, reported, "People seem to think that there are so many servants out of work they will be glad to take anything from $25 a month up. This is not the case. The high wages of the last few years have made the girls very independent. . . . We have been able to place a few maids for general housework at $40 a month, but the cheaper help does not give satisfaction." She added, "The factory worker rarely becomes a good servant. . . . Most of these girls had rather starve than work in a kitchen."[56]

By 1925, the recession long over, cooks' monthly earnings had risen between 14 and 38 percent, to between $80 and $110 a month. Laundresses earned $70, general houseworkers $80 and kitchen maids $60 a month. Domestic work looked more attractive to some clerks. One, Laura Clark, was starting to feel that "she would rather hear the birds singing in the country for $125 a month than to earn $20 a week to the music of the elevated."[57]

Yet despite some benefits, domestic work demanded a dedication that few young women wanted to give. They were too used to being independent, and employers did not necessarily want them. This being the case, a temporary surplus of workers meant only that household labor was a last resort job. The same problems that kept the labor supply low during good times—isolation, stigma, and onerous supervision—were still there. Desperation caused by massive unemployment did not cure these ills; it merely made them more tolerable than many of the alternatives.[58]

FEWER LIVE-IN SERVANTS

The second result of demographic changes was that there were fewer live-in servants. This was a major step forward in the restructuring of the occupation's power relationship.

Although it is difficult to estimate how many servants lived in, anecdotal evidence suggests that fewer servants did so at the end of the 1920s than at the beginning. Several factors pushed servants out of live-in work.

Servants had three major objections to living in: they were essentially on call twenty-four hours a day, were under the family's eye almost constantly, and were subject to social stigma. Although the servant herself could not erase the stigma, she could resolve the first two by living out.

The employer's demands on live-in servants were often unrealistic. One maid complained about an employer who

> used to call me about an hour before dinner was to be on the table and say she'd changed her mind about dessert. Instead of fruit whip she'd like to have one of my 'lovely steamed puddings.' And when I'd try to tell her that steamed pudding took a good three hours to make, she seemed to think I was just trying to be disagreeable.[59]

Another deterrent to living in was the problems it could cause within he servants' families. Paule Marshall, the daughter of a Barbadian immigrant, wrote, "I remember the trauma I would undergo on those occasions when I was left with a neighbor while my mother disappeared for the day to scrub some stranger's floor." Virginia Johnson, who came to New York from the South during the 1920s, was single when she arrived, but married soon thereafter. However, she continued to live with "her" family, and she regarded her employer's children as hers, too. This caused resentment among her own children, resentment that did not fade with the years. Fifty years later, they still had hard feelings toward the white family's children.[60]

If these reasons were not enough, there was also the way living in expressed a lopsided power relationship. For black women, living out was a form of resistance, to employers' wishes. It also gave workers the opportunity to create what bell hooks has called "homeplace," a "safe place where black people could affirm one another and by so doing heal many of the wounds inflicted by racist domination." Hooks continued, "We could not learn to love or respect ourselves in the culture of white supremacy, on the outside; it was there on the inside, in that 'homeplace,' that we had the opportunity to grow and develop, to nurture our spirits."[61]

Hooks' mother was able to return home to her children at night and "rejoice with us that her work was done, that she was home, that there was nothing about the experience of working as a maid in a white household, in that space of otherness, which stripped her of dignity and personal power."[62]

After the postwar recession ended, then, there was a shortage of live-in waitresses and laundresses in New York. The latter, largely African-Americans, had begun doing day work in the early 1920s because they could not find full time positions. Having realized the freedom that came from living out, few wanted to go back to live-in work. Like their counterparts in Washington, D.C., they were examples to other women seeking day work.[63]

When office and shop work had become respectable in the 1890s for young native-born white women, Lucy Maynard Salmon attempted to prove that maids actually made more money per hour by living in than by working in a factory and paying room and board. Clearly, however, payment was not the issue, as Salmon's work failed to convince women to stay in the occupation. Even the possible benefits could not sway workers. As one contemporary reporter noted, "the fourteen-hour day of the domestic servant has long been defended with the counter-argument of a pleasant home and good food. But this no longer lures the girl whose eyes are fixed on a well-paid factory job with shorter hours."[64]

Based on their experience with factory work and exposure to live-out arrangements, domestics began to demand industrial conditions in the home, just as housewives had begun to do. The eight-hour day was the first target, since some industries already had it. To domestics, living out represented a way to control their own lives. Employers knew this. *The New York Times,* essentially an employer mouthpiece, reported:

> A chance advertisement in a daily New York paper twelve years ago started the ball rolling. The woman who placed the advertisement asked for some one to assist with the housekeeping for eight hours each day. She received 200 replies. Being an inquisitive woman, she questioned the girls and women who came to see her. Why did they no longer want to share a home with the family for which they worked? Nearly 90 per cent of them made the same reply:
> 'We want more freedom.'[65]

In the middle of the decade, at least one placement agency responded to servants' desire for live-out work. The Bureau of Household Occupations (267 Madison Avenue), had opened before World War I as the Household Service Station and shortly thereafter took on supplying part-time and day workers (for an eight hour workday). In 1921 a client related her successful experience with it, stressing that she and her employees each had a responsibility for efficiency. The bureau analyzed the job needed, and sent out the appropriate worker for the appropriate amount of time. If necessary, two or more workers were sent out.

> There are both advocates and adverse critics of the eight-hour day sys-
> tem. The antis have a long list of reasons, arguing a servant who 'lives
> out' to be no servant at all. But the average apartment dweller blesses
> the day the home assistant, with her two, four and eight hour day, hove
> in sight to lessen household cares.[66]

Employers still resisted, believing as Henrietta Rothstein of the New York State Employment Bureau did, that "[t]he best satisfaction is given by the servant who lives in the house." But because they could not force workers to live in, they had to change their expectations, at least as far as scheduling went.[67]

AN ATTITUDE SHIFT

Bowing to reality in terms of higher wages and live-out situations was one thing, but the key to the unequal relationship between worker and employer was the latter's attitude toward housework and houseworkers.

Attempting to explain the servant shortage, a servant who called herself "Emancipated" said:

> The American housewife has only herself to blame if she cannot get
> servants, as every industry has bettered conditions except the very old
> industry of housekeeping. . . .
>   Restriction of immigration is not the reason for the help shortage.
> There are hundreds of fine young women coming now the same as ever,
> but they will not go into what is virtual slavery.[68]

Old ways of thinking about service were hard to dislodge. Domestic work had been one of the few acceptable jobs for women, and the fact that there were now other ways to earn a living took a long time to sink in. Employers did not yet see themselves as competing for workers. Servants learned this first, but even so, they rarely confronted their employer, preferring to vote with their feet and leave jobs when they could.[69]

It was not until the very end of the decade that employers began to see the need for reforming domestic service, and even then their attempts were lukewarm. Slowly, household workers became part of the feminist struggle for women's rights, embodied in their quest for fairer pay and better working conditions.[70]

Yet the social stigma, the most serious disadvantage of service, remained. Feminists "rebelled against the age-old household roles of women; before long, even a woman contented with her familiar role felt called on to apologize that she was 'just a housewife.'" How much worse was it for those working for the housewife?[71]

From being one of the only respectable occupations open to women, it became scorned. Service was difficult work, as we have seen, and in a society that professes egalitarian ideals, like the United States, service often connoted subservience. There was little pride to take in such a job. Employers' constant complaints about the quality of their maids (or even their bragging about them as though they were prized possessions) did not help the image of the occupation. In addition, the fact that the job in many places was dominated either by immigrants or African Americans reduced its status even more. Undoubtedly, the loss of status accelerated as more black women moved north to replace white foreign-born women.[72]

THE ELECTRIC SERVANT

But the nature of housework was beginning to change, partly due to the emergence of household appliances. The spread of electricity in urban areas like New York City and concomitant manufacture of electrical appliances reduced families' dependence on hard-to-find servants.

Before electrification, maids in middle- and upper-class households woke while it was still dark to light the coal stove or turn on the gas in the cold house, cooks made breakfast while their employers slumbered, and waitresses served the meals. Beds had to be aired every day and linens kept fresh and in order. The laundry took an entire day to do, as it had to be done by hand, with water that had first to be heated. There were washing machines, but they were cranked by hand, not by a motor.[73]

The installation of electricity into private dwellings revolutionized housework. "By 1926, 16 million homes were wired for electricity," which they wanted to use. A lack of servants also served as an impetus to buy appliances. "Thirty-seven percent of those households had a vacuum cleaner, 25 percent a clothes washer, 80 percent an electric iron. Refrigerators replaced the ice box and made the 'cool cellar' obsolete." All were things that made housework easier to handle alone.[74]

Electricity and appliances went hand in hand, and housework was the connection. "There was a time," read an United Electric Light & Power Co. trade advertisement, "when all household work was drudgery. The advent of electrical labor saving appliances and adequately wired homes has changed all that." Two maids, one leaning over a steaming laundry tub and the other bent over a broom, illustrated the backbreaking nature of housework. Two people were needed to do the work of one household; with modern appliances, a woman could cope alone. In fact, electricity was the new servant.[75]

Electric companies capitalized on this and on the servant shortage, adjuring landlords to provide electricity for their prospective tenants. A May 1927 ad for The United Electric Light & Power Company warned,

> You show prospective tenants through your apartments. The impression seems to be favorable. Just as you think the whole thing is settled, the woman objects. 'But I need more outlets!' she says. 'Where would I attach all my pretty lamps? My vacuum cleaner, iron, cooker, toaster, percolator . . . ?'[76]

Builders responded to the growing need for appliances, installing electricity routinely into new developments. With new building, appliance sales climbed, as families replaced human with mechanical help.[77]

Ironically, the use of appliances did positively affect the supply of servants, albeit to a limited degree. Some European immigrants had heard that America was "the land of hope and glory for the housemaid, where the electrical appliances turn kitchen drudgery into play and where servants are paid big wages and get numerous holidays."[78]

In addition to appliances, the proliferation of available services, such as laundry and prepared foods, altered the way household chores were accomplished. Electricity made it possible for laundries like the Carolyn Laundry Company (104–110 East 129th Street) to increase output and operate on a large scale. Not only did laundries lure clothing out of private homes, but they hired women who would otherwise be working in private households.[79]

Appliances and services could not fully replace servants, however. And the perception that they could was dangerous, according to Eleanor Roosevelt. In January 1930 she wrote that it led employers to avoid addressing the conditions of the job that made it so unattractive: "Families have moved into compact modern apartments and made use of every facility for keeping

Figure 4. September 14, 1925. Used with permission of Con Edison.

house without servants, and yet found that some one had to be engaged to run the machinery which should simplify housekeeping." And if that person were not trained, the machines broke. Mrs. Roosevelt endorsed training programs with diplomas and employment contracts, which national and state industrial bureaus would disseminate and help enforce. She had a chance to see some of her ideas put into practice before five years had gone by.[80]

SMALLER HOMES

Use of appliances was one permanent change in the way women did their housework. Another was the growing realization that maids did not want to live in. In response, fewer buildings had servants' quarters built in.[81]

There was a real estate boom in New York between 1922 and 1927. By the end of the 1920s, Manhattan and Bronx had practically no open areas left, and Brooklyn and Queens had little left, helped along by highway and parkway development. Only Staten Island remained to be conquered.[82]

In all of these places, there was a trend toward smaller, easier to care for, dwellings. According to the New York real estate trade publication,

> Within less than twenty years the average number of rooms in apartments in New York City has been reduced from 5+ to 3.37. Eleven years ago small apartments constituted only 33.6 per cent. of the total, but in 1928 more than 77 per cent. of all apartments in the city contained only one, two or three rooms.[83]

Apartment living was part of a revolution. Private houses made way for large blocks of dwellings. There was no room for servants in most of the new apartments. And there was less need, or at least so employers hoped. *The New York Times* reflected employers' rationalizations:

> Families that have taken to apartment life are not so seriously inconvenienced by the shortage of men and women who will do domestic work as are those living in private houses. Cooks and maids may still be greatly desired by the apartment dwellers, but they are not an absolute full-time necessity.[84]

The structure of the servant occupation was changing, and it was reflected in the growing differentiation between social classes, which was in turn reflected in their dwelling's accommodation for servants. Only the most luxurious buildings had servants' quarters. In middle-class buildings, there were service halls and entrances, maid's toilets and other adaptations for non-residential workers. The least expensive dwellings bore no physical indications of welcoming help at all.[85]

New buildings also offered different kinds of jobs. The new apartment hotels provided maids with regular live-out hours. The Oliver Cromwell at 12–18 West 72nd Street, designed by Emery Roth, was typical. Instead of kitchens, its apartments had serving pantries to which hotel food could be delivered.[86]

200 East 16th St.

In the fine old Stuyvesant Park Section

OVERSIZED APARTMENTS OF

1½ and 2½ Rooms

Also a Few 3-Room Terrace Apartments

READY FOR OCCUPANCY JUNE 1ST.
at the Most Attractive Rents in the City

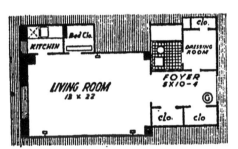

TYPICAL

1½ ROOM

APARTMENT

featuring outside kitch-
enette, large foyer,
living room, In-a-Door
bed in separate closet,
dressing room, bathroom
and four large closets.

$70 Monthly up

Figure 5. 1931 advertisement.

This solved the problem of any building with kitchens in the individual units being classified as a tenement, a label many developers feared. Increasingly, however, the attitude of the owners of 12 East 86th Street—actually on Madison Avenue between 85th and 86th Streets, on a site formerly occupied by street car barns—became prevalent. The directing operator, I. Fluegelman, directly addressed the issue of household help.

> Tremendous progress has been made in the apartment house field within the past decade and it has in a measure solved many of the problems of living, *particularly as it applies to the servant question of the present day.*
>
> Every apartment will have a completely equipped kitchen so that the families can live from one extreme to another. The housewife may do her own cooking and when she desires will be able to have her house work done by trained servants on a per hour basis. She can also have

meals or portions of meals served in her own apartment or the family
can dine in the main dining room on the ground floor.[87]

Ten years earlier, domestic service had been an occupation in which
the most common arrangement was that the servant would live in the
household and follow orders. Now, maids wanted to live in their own
homes—and there was no room for them in their employers' homes!

Maids and mistresses were beginning to agree that increasing independence from each other might be the key to maintaining domestic service as a
viable occupation. First, however, they had to get through the Depression.

Chapter Two
The Bronx Slave Market: Depersonalizing Domestic Service

As the 1920s ended fewer immigrants were arriving in New York. Instead, newcomers included young African-American women like Virginia Johnson, who migrated from the South to New York City. Virginia was lucky; she found fulltime live-in work in Brooklyn and was able to hold on to it. For others, times were harder.

By 1930, the relationship between maid and mistress had begun to change. The Depression forced a major shift in it. The connection between employer and employee grew more impersonal, which had the short-term effect of creating an atmosphere that encouraged worker abuse. In the long run, however, the loosening of personal bonds gave workers more leverage in the relationship.

Because of a glut of workers and housewives' reduced ability to pay for full-time help, a new kind of market developed. It went from employment by the month or week to work done by the day. During the 1930s domestic employment became in many cases true day work, a one shot deal in which there was no ongoing relationship. Hourly wages became more popular, too.

Initially, this market restructuring increased the employer's control over the relationship. However, as time went on, the new market validated the living-out model and encouraged part-time work. This gave private household workers the opportunity to have multiple sources of income, which increased their bargaining power.

To get there, they had to go through the depths of the Depression.

* * *

In October 1935, journalist Marvel Cooke and aspiring political activist Ella Baker traveled from *The Crisis* office in Harlem to 167th Street and Westchester Avenue in the Bronx. It was not a long journey in space or time, but they went to another world.

In Harlem, they were respected members of the community, work-ing for a brilliant editor, W.E.B. DuBois; in the Bronx, they became some-thing like slaves. They joined the line of African-American women standing patiently on a two-block stretch, waiting for white housewives to come and look them up and down and see if they were strong enough to scrub floors for a pittance.

First described in New York City in 1933, there were over 200 such marts in the five boroughs and hundreds more across the United States. Lined up on designated street corners, usually in the Bronx or Brooklyn, black domestics waited for white women to hire them for a few hours' work at 35 cents or less an hour. Such "slave markets" yielded barely enough money to survive, and maids were often the sole wage earners in their fami-lies. The Bronx Slave Market became a symbol of the Depression, of racial oppression, and of domestic service itself, as desperate women were at the mercy of employers.[1]

Cooke and Baker were angry and came to see for themselves.

> Rain or shine, cold or hot, you will find them there—Negro women, old and young—sometimes bedraggled, sometimes neatly dressed— but with the invariable paper bundle [containing their work clothes], waiting expectantly for Bronx housewives to buy their strength and energy for an hour, two hours, or even for a day at the munificent rate of fifteen, twenty, twenty-five, or, if luck be with them, thirty cents an hour.[2]

The Depression slowed the occupational diversification for women that had begun in the 1920s. Some women moved into new fields during the 1930s, but growth was nowhere near what it had been before 1930. For example, the number of female office workers rose only 25 percent between 1930 and 1940, compared to 500 percent in the previous 20 years. Simi-larly, the number of women sales workers increased only slightly between 1930 and 1940. Many female typists, stenographers, store clerks and fac-tory workers lost their jobs. They, along with those whose husbands were out of work, were attracted to domestic service. It seemed that "in a pinch any one can do housework."[3]

Thus the 1920s shortage of servants did not last. With the beginning of the Depression, many of the material gains of the 1920s faded. The ratio of applicants to domestic jobs offered at the New York State Employment Service rose by more than ten percent from 1926 to 1927. This pattern continued. When women suffered layoffs and "drifted back" to domestic

Figure 6. Bronx Slave Market workers in 1941. *The Daily Compass,* January 9, 1950.

work, white and black women competed for jobs. Over 90 percent of new entrants into private household work were women, and domestic servants became a larger proportion of working women than they had been ten years previously.[4]

For African Americans, the situation was especially bad. Guichard Parris of the Urban League related that by the winter of 1928, "layoffs of black workers and rise of black unemployment were what today's economists would call 'leading indicators.' They pointed to worsening business conditions—and they were deadly accurate."[5]

Nationally, there were about 2 million private household workers in 1930, up 550,000 from 1920, or a 40 percent increase. They now accounted for about 18 percent of all working women, up from 16 percent. In New York, however, the proportion of women in the occupation grew by 50 percent, from 12 to 19 percent. Clearly New York City's poorer women were bearing an enormous burden during the Depression, and housewives who wanted household help were able to take advantage of the situation.[6]

RESTRUCTURING: LOWER WAGES

By 1936, twice as many women sought domestic work as in 1930. Unemployment was even higher in other occupations than in service, an indication that women had turned to household employment from other fields.[7]

The growing oversupply of workers led to wage degradation. Wages had dropped the most sharply at the beginning of the Depression—between one-third to one-half for general live-in work. Household staffs got smaller, too—one person did the work of two and sometimes more. Some employers lowered their servants' wages to be able to keep them on when the family income dropped. There were more venal considerations, too.

> . . . [O]ne woman at a party confesses that [she] thought she was a
> fool to pay her maid $60.00 a month. If she cut her, say to $35.00, she
> could get the new antique table . . . or that trip to Florida . . .[8]

Lucy Randolph Mason of the National Consumers Union wrote a pastiche of things she had heard women say:

> "But, my dear," said Mrs. Jones, "you don't mean to tell me you are
> still paying your maid $10 a week when you can get a perfect treasure
> for $5 and a good enough person for $3? Why pay more than you have
> to? It is silly. I only pay $5 to that splendid girl I got last spring, and she
> does all the cooking, housework and part of the laundry, and takes the
> baby out besides. I don't even give her a room, just her meals."[9]

Such reasoning had its roots in a new consumer culture, which blossomed during the 1920s. "From a *moral point of view*," wrote Frenchman André Siegfried in 1928, "it is obvious that Americans have come to consider their standard of living as a somewhat sacred acquisition, which they will defend at any price. This means that they would be ready to make many an intellectual or even moral concession in order to maintain that standard."[10]

Wages were one symbol of dominance. When employers gave gifts in lieu of or in addition to cash, it was another way of asserting superiority. In the same way, accusations of theft established a hierarchy.[11]

To be sure, some women felt driven to theft. Fats Waller's sister Naomi remembered her reaction to low wages.

> I lost my job during the Depression, but I did okay playing numbers
> and with the gambling. One day, I looked in the paper, and this place
> wanted a houseworker. I hated housework, but I figured I'd try it. I

answered the ad, and the house was nice and clean, and I said to her,
"How much do you pay?"

She said, "Five dollars a week."

So I'm looking around the room, and she said to me, "What are you
looking for?"

I said, "I'm looking for what I can steal. You must expect me to steal
something if you're gonna give me five dollars a week."[12]

Low domestic service pay also made prostitution attractive to some
women. Afro-Caribbean immigrant Bernice (who asked that the WPA
interviewer not use her last name) worked as a domestic and also threw
rent parties at the beginning of the Depression. One night, her female part-
ner asked her to "take care" of an extra man.

> Well, that was the last of days-work (domestic work) for me. I figured
> that I was a fool to go out and break my back scrubbing floors, wash-
> ing, ironing, and cooking, when I could earn three day's pay, or more,
> in fifteen minutes. Then I began to understand how Hazel got all those
> fine dresses and good-looking furs.[13]

Indeed, domestic work was very poorly paid during the Depression
years. The average white maid earned at most only five-sixths of what
she needed to sustain herself. African-American domestics earned less
than that.[14]

RESTRUCTURING: FROM LIVE-OUT TO HOURLY

For what they earned, servants worked long and hard. Live-in domestics
still regularly worked 72 or more hours a week, and those who lived out
often worked that much or more to make ends meet. Mildred King of Louisville, Kentucky, was typical. She began work at 6:45 a.m. and stopped at
8:00 p.m., with the customary Thursday and Sunday afternoon off. Tina
Hill, who worked in Los Angeles, had similar hours, except she had just
every other Sunday off.[15]

In contrast, women in factories worked 44- to 50-hour weeks for
about twice the wages of domestics. Even black women in laundries in New
York City could make $10 a week for only 50 hours work. For domes-
tics, part-time work was no guarantee of shorter hours. One employer said
about her maid, "I want her to come at 11 to get the children's lunch, to
clean and make the beds, cook and serve dinner. She can get away around
8. . . . It's only part time."[16]

There was a "strange paradox of oversupply and overdemand" in domestic service. Employers continued to want servants who would live in. Indeed, employers failed to understand that the days of the live-in worker were largely over. The Brooklyn Catholic Big Sisters employment agency reported, "Women applying for 'living out' positions are in far greater number than can be absorbed," yet "the majority of requests in New York are for workers at $25 to $30 monthly, working early and late."[17]

New York employers still wanted live-in maids, even though maids' quarters were in short supply. The new Multiple Dwellings Law (1929) and economic necessity combined to make apartments and houses smaller than ever.[18]

Oddly enough, the shrinking apartments and disappearing maids' rooms did not dissuade housewives from wanting live-in help. One domestic worker, Gertrude King, noted, "Knowing that space is limited in most city apartments, one might expect to learn that the houseworker for whom a room did not have to be provided would be the more desirable; requests prove otherwise."[19]

No matter how desperate, domestics continued to reject live-in work. Independence was more important to them than the "$50 a month with pleasant room and excellent board gratis" offered by bewildered employers.[20]

The influx of white workers did not alter the situation. Now, like their black colleagues, many white domestics were married and thus did not want to live in, despite high demand.

> [They] have been forced to seek work because of their husbands' long
> enforced idleness; naturally enough, they are hoping they can hold out
> a little longer and that the pressing emergency will not bring about a
> disruption of their homes and families.[21]

Live-in work became less and less attractive, because it, even more than the Bronx Slave Market, degenerated so much that even white servants termed it "slavery." Servants who spoke to the New York Women's City Club in March 1935 deplored "low wages, long hours and inadequate living quarters." A cook said that her days had a "rushing tempo" and that she knew "women who have been so strenuously overworked that they have been carried out of homes to physicians' offices. For fear of losing their jobs, they have been afraid to complain of their long hours."[22]

Because live-in, and even full-time, work became so undesirable to maids, and because employers were pinched financially, part-time arrangements became common. By mid-decade, *The New York Times* could note,

"Fifty cents an hour and carfare is the customary pay, as fixed as though a union existed. . . . The tendency is growing for the houseworker to go to a home of her own when her work is finished."[23]

Especially early in the 1930s, the huge number of available workers stimulated the shift to casual labor. In 1930, for example, there was a 6 to 1 ratio of job seekers to job openings in *The New York Times* classified ads, where the vast majority of employers and employees advertised.[24]

Payment patterns reflected this shift, too, as the norm moved from monthly wages to weekly or daily. Part-time workers were usually paid on an hourly basis. Hourly pay scales could benefit workers if schedules expanded. But during the Depression, when wages dropped, hourly work was often a disadvantage. Indeed, in the Bronx Slave Market, housewives cheated workers out of hours by setting their clocks back. Workers responded by carrying their own clocks. It was a battleground, and workers learned to fight strenuously for their rights.[25]

RESTRUCTURING: SLAVE MARKETS

The markets brought African-American women into the forefront of the domestic service struggle. They were at the bottom of a two-tier labor market in domestic service in New York, with white women on top and black women on the bottom.[26]

The Depression widened the white/black wage gap. White women moved back into domestic service, forcing black women out. This created a pool of workers on the lower level (houseworker as opposed to cooks and nurses). That they were black and denied full rights of citizenship made them vulnerable to the logic of the market. They and their labor were both commodities, indistinct from each other.[27]

Why did women turn to the street corner markets?

For black women, classified ads were unlikely to bring much work. Advertisers specified "must speak French" or other requirements unlikely to be met by African-American women.

Employment agencies helped little. Dr. Anna Arnold Hedgeman of the Harlem YWCA noted that they coded their application forms to make it easy to determine who was white and who was not. Private agencies were allowed by New York City's 1926 regulating law to be segregated. This meant that state agencies could, as one historian puts it, "deter black women from using their services [by referring] them to 'agencies for blacks.' . . . Even New Deal agencies that were supposed to get unemployed workers back in the job market reflected state agencies in their discriminatory practices."[28]

Even when agencies had jobs for black women, they were not always taken because working conditions were so bad. In New York, Marvel Cooke reported,

> [T]here have been many more jobs for domestic help coming in to Harlem agencies than could possibly be filled. The reasons for this are obvious—relief, starvation wages and miserable working conditions, with the cost of living remaining high.[29]

Even worse, unscrupulous agencies lured African-American women from the South with the promise of jobs that evaporated when they arrived. Othella Brown arrived from Baltimore for a sleep-in job for $25 a month. After two days, her employer fired her because her children were not used to "colored help." The article continued,

> Ask the Y.W.C.A., ask the Urban League, ask the churches. There are a thousand cases of girls sent North to jobs which at times don't exist, or to sleep-in jobs paying often less than $25 a month. It's all a racket. Brooklyn, especially, seems to be the dumping ground for this cheap southern help, as both white and Negro maids here refuse to take sleep-in jobs.[30]

Most African-American women avoided agencies, unless they were sure that the employer would have to pay the fee. Employers also made illegitimate claims against maids' wages, charging them for transportation and other incidentals, and agencies did nothing to prevent it. Moreover, many rural migrants did not know there were agencies, so they had to improvise means of obtaining employment. Ethel Morris, who arrived in New York during the Depression, "believed the best way to find work in the thirties was simply to walk down the street in any white neighborhood. Someone would invariably call out the window and hire [her] on the spot."[31]

With all its faults, the slave market was a viable alternative. However humiliating it was, it was nearby and efficient, and women could walk there from Harlem when they couldn't afford a nickel for the subway.[32]

Vivian Morris, a WPA writer, visited the slave market at 167th St. and Girard Ave., Bronx, New York City, in November, 1938. Like many such neighborhoods, it was Jewish, lower middle-class, and well-kept. Residents lived in 5 or 6-story walkup apartments, and there were many small storefront businesses on the ground floors. One observer noted, "The depression is not evident as a coloring factor to the casual observer. The clothes worn is uniformly good stuff, latest style. . . . Relief recipients keep it quiet."

Employers here wanted to keep up appearances, and having household help was part of the façade. As standards fell, how they got that help became less important.[33]

The joining together of two worlds was evident in Minnie Marshall's story. Minnie had arrived in Harlem from the South two months earlier. Her circumstances were not unusual. [Note that the author transcribed Minnie's story in colloquial English.]

[Minnie] arrived with about six Dollars and paid four for a room, leaving two, and though, very hungry, was afraid to spend money for food that night. Early next morning, Minnie went to an Employment Agency. "Yes, they had jobs at Forty Dollars, sleep in or out." She almost shouted for joy—that was more money than she could make in Norfolk in two months! But this was New York. The Employment Agent signed Minnie up as a good cook-houseworker, etc., then he proffered her a card, saying: "Four Dollars, please."

Minnie said, her 'shoulders sagged!'

"Fo' Dollas fo' whut?"[sic]

"For the job; ya dont think I run this Agency for my health, do you?"

"No, suh, no suh, Ah only got two Dollas 'tween me an de Lawd. Ah clare, Mistuh, ah'll give you de res' fus' week ah woks, hones' Mistuh."

He tore up the slip, saying: "Ya'll pay me when you get paid—That's a hot one—keep your two Dollars, lady!"

Minnie tried agency after agency but the results were the same. They wanted their money in front. She couldn't get day's or part-time work because the agents had special cliques to whom these choice jobs went. It was rank folly for any outsider to think of getting one of these jobs. After many days of trying, rent due, money gone, a sympathetic girl in one of the Agencies, told Minnie that, "when she was out of money, she stood on one of the corners in the Bronx, where women came and hired you."

"Next mo'nin' Ah gut up prayin' that de lan lady woudn' heah me and walked de fifty-some blocks to dis place, an' I saw Othah gals standin' heah-so Ah stood wid dem.[34]

Desperate, Minnie took twenty-five cents an hour for her first job, in a seven-room apartment that was not "fitting' fo' hawgs to live in. Dey was sume doity!"

A typical abuse of workers occurred that day, too. Minnie's employer said, "Your time begins now. You vill be pait by dot clock. See—nine-forty five?" Minnie related, "Dat dam' clock sed de same time dat she said, so Ah tho't mah clock was wrong. . . . 'Bout six o'clock, ah tol' huh, 'Miss Gol' blatt, ah's thru." "She sehs, 'bout time,' . . .

> "Den she gi' me mah money—dollar, eighty-seben cent.
>
> "Ah sehs: 'Miss Gol' blatt, ain' you' miscalc'late? Ah wukked eight hours—tu'k fifteen minutes fo' lunch?'
>
> "'Listen' dear goil, Hi neffer cheat hany body. You voiked seven hours—fifteen minutes, vich giffs you vun dollar—heighty-two sants, hand hi took hout fife sants for bringink you here, vich makes hi should giff you van eighty seven, [sic] bud hi giff you, per agreement, a nize fat tip of tan sants—van eighty sefen. Goodby!'
>
> "[A]h was mad den, but when ah got out an' foun' dat it wus eight o'clock and dat ole heifer done cheat me out of two hours, ah cou'd a kilt huh. Well, ah at leas' had sumf'n fo' my lan'lady.[35]

The work was crushing and sometimes hazardous. Women reported that they washed windows in the cold or cleaned up years' worth of accumulation of clutter in attics or basements in one day. Washing windows inside and out was dangerous in a high-rise city. Black women told of sexual harassment and being given heavier work than advertised. In addition, the markets were demeaning. White housewives would inspect the black women's knees. "If they had crust on their knees, they'd hire them," for that indicated they were accustomed to scrubbing floors.[36]

Not only were the women themselves inspected, but so was their work. Minnie Marshall's first employer looked in the corners for dust, checked her husband's shirt collars to see if they were adequately starched, and peered nearsightedly at the floor to see if it was clean enough.

Minnie said, "Ah hates the people ah Wukks for. Dey's mean, 'ceitful, an' ain' hones'; but whut ah'm gonna do? Ah got to live—got to hab a place to steh—' dough my lan'lady seys ah gotta bring huh sumf'n or ah can' stay dere tonight. . . ."[37]

RESTRUCTURING: THE LOOSENING OF TIES

All of this—the glut of workers, the trend toward live-out work, wage degradation, and the market restructuring embodied in the Bronx Slave Market—added up to a loosening of ties between employers and employees. Before the Depression, there had been a shared relationship. Employers had felt some sense of responsibility for their workers.

Figure 7. Marvel Cooke washing windows as part of her slave market exposé. *The Daily Compass,* January 9, 1950.

The Depression helped to depersonalize the occupation. Before, there could be ties of affection, arising out of familiarity. Now, there was a market transaction.

Moreover, housework itself continued to be transformed. Americans bought more appliances during the 1930s, especially refrigerators, sewing machines, vacuums and washing machines.[38]

The resulting alteration in the ethos of housekeeping contributed to the devaluation of the maid in the 1930s. The advent of widespread availability of electric appliances helped to shift responsibility for the performance of housework from maids to mistresses. It meant that only the really unpleasant jobs—scrubbing floors, washing windows and the like—were left for household help. The distaste with which these jobs were held rubbed off on workers.[39]

Employers' unscrupulousness worsened the situation. In the Slave Market, they sometimes pitted workers against each other.

> "A weazened little woman, with aquiline nose, thick glasses, and three big diamonds which seemed to laugh at the prominent-veined hands which they were on passed down the line, critically looking at the girls. When she reached Minnie, she stopped peering: "Can you do woik-hart voik? Can you vash windows from de houtside?"
>
> "Ah c'n do anything—wash windows, anywhere." Time was passing, she had to get a job or be put out.
>
> "Twenty-fife sants an hour?"
>
> "No ma'am; thirty-five."
>
> "I can get the youngk goils for fifteen sants, and the old vimmen for tan sants." She motioned toward the others who were eagerly crowding around.
>
> "Yas'm; ah' llgo," said a frog-eyed, speckle-faced; yellow gal, idiotically smiling.
>
> "Me. too," chimed a toothless old hag with gnarled hands—a memento of some days in Dixie.
>
> "See!" said the woman.
>
> "But dey caint do de wokk Ah kin do," rebutted Minnie defiantly.
>
> "Thirty-sants," said the bargain-hunter, with an air of finality.
>
> "Le's go," said Minnie flashing me a gold-toothed smile.[40]

There was only so long that these employer tactics could work, however. As abuse grew worse, workers grew bolder in protecting their own interests. The Bronx workers often banded together to run off women willing to work for less than 30 cents an hour, and once demanded and received 35 cents an hour. Three black workers fed up with abuse founded a Domestic Workers Union in 1934. By 1937, it had its main office at 112 E. 19th Street, and a branch office at 2705 White Plains Road in the Bronx. An affiliate of the A.F. of L. Building Service Union, it had 350 members, 75 percent of them African-American.[41]

There had been unions before. A domestic worker union in New York City formed in 1901, but it lasted at best a few months. In 1915, Washington, D.C. domestics formed the Association of Women Wage-Earners, and

Figure 8. Negro maid. Washington, D.C., Farm Security Administration—Office of War Information Photograph Collection, Library of Congress Prints & Photographs Division Washington, DC.

by 1920, there were 10 southern black domestic worker locals affiliated with the Hotel and Restaurant Employees' Union (American Federation of Labor or A.F. of L.). Unfortunately, these locals were for women working in public places, not private homes.[42]

Primarily African-Americans populated most unions—they needed more help than white workers. A better known Domestic Workers Union was begun in Harlem in 1931 by a group of Finns and African-Americans. Dora Jones, the black Executive Secretary of the DWU, explained to Vivian Morris, a WPA writer,

> Until 1935 the office was located in the Finnish neighborhood [120th to 128th Streets, east of Lenox (Sixth) Avenue], but the hunger riots of Harlem on March 19, 1935 marked the demolishing of the office by the rioters. In 1936 we set up the Domestic Workers Union Local 149 A. F. of L. in this building (241 West 84th Street). We have grown not spectacularly, but at a steady clip. The members we get—we hold.[43]

At its peak the union reported 500 members, but by December 1949, it was down to 125 members. It was now independent of the AFL-CIO and focused on African-Americans. It sponsored black history programs to attract newcomers and organized among the regulars at the Bronx Slave Market.[44]

In 1936, the 100 members of a Washington, D.C. domestic workers union formed under the auspices of the Women's Trade Union League succeeded in getting their weekly wage up from $3.00 to $10.00.[45]

But there were problems with unions. The maternalistic YWCA encouraged domestics to organize, but leaders noted that there were obstacles to affiliation with traditional industrial unions. To industrial workers, domestics seemed sheltered and a threat to them. Their presence in the YWCA meant that industrial organizers might keep away, reducing other workers' chances of being unionized.[46]

Domestic workers lacked most of the attributes typically viewed as necessary for successful unionization. There was little occupational identity, because there were so many types of servants, each with distinct duties. More importantly, there were too many workplaces to allow workers to truly band together. And they were expendable. The bad economy and oversupply of workers exacerbated the situation. Battles could be fought and won, but with a few exceptions, individual situations were precarious enough to demand the workers' full attention. The re-emergence of the slave markets during the 1949–1950 recession shows how vulnerable workers were. A union could certainly have benefited them, but few had the time or the energy to devote to one.

Ironically, the same thing that prevented unionization and slowed improvements in material conditions—the private nature of the occupation—was attractive to many workers. They liked negotiating on their own, or choosing for whom to work (when they had a choice). Some would say that they had more control over a relationship with a household employer than if they worked for a large company. In booming times, domestics were sought after and had demand-associated leverage.

Nevertheless, all organizational efforts on the part of workers increased their distance from employers. And in New York, there was another advocate for domestic workers, who in his own way contributed to the widening gulf.

Father Divine, a religious cult leader, had many domestic workers among his followers. He used this to give the wealthy what they wanted—docile, competent, cheap help—and he got his followers jobs. But it was very different from a union. His followers' "claim that they 'did not need a union' had its basis in the fact that they were already organized in defense of their rights—with Divine as their labor leader." "Father" was outraged at the Bronx Slave Market. He told his followers to insist upon $10 a week and no less, calling the dollar a day wage "an outrage. It is ridiculous."[47]

His motives were not entirely altruistic, however; he collected his followers' paychecks. Since the workers had room and board as part of his community, they could wait out the downturn. Despite their docility and willingness to live in, Father Divine's followers were aligned with him, not their employers.[48]

The police chief in Sayville, Long Island, a suburb of New York City where Father Divine had a large house, reported,

> The fact is, the religious satellites, who called themselves by such funny names as "Happy Boy Job," "Patience Delight," "Eternal Faith" etc. were honest as the day is long and were excellent servants in every other respect. In addition to that, they could be hired for half the price of the lazy, sullen, shiftless Niggers [sic] who were natives of the town.[49]

They also received domestic training, so they were desirable workers. They worked harder than other servants, employers concluded, and were less expensive.[50]

These workers protected themselves from feeling the indignities of household service by placing their faith somewhere else, and by placing themselves on a different spiritual plane from their employers. The latter did not matter; the Kingdom of God—or Father Divine—was of sole importance to them.

Workers in general dreamed of better conditions. In the late 1930s, the *New York Amsterdam News*, a black paper, began running a cartoon called "Tisha Mingo." It featured the exploits of a beautiful, elegant African-American domestic who worked for an idealized white mistress. When she begins work for this new employer, we learn that "Tisha's new missy wants Tisha to be the sharpest thing in Harlem, so, she gives Tisha a double century note and tells her to shoot the works." Of course, the strip had to maintain some believability, so Tisha wore a uniform and called guests "Miss——" while they called her "Tisha." But how many real mistresses would wake up their maid in the morning and go biking and to a nightclub with her while they were vacationing in Bermuda?[51]

Such dreams were in sharp contrast to realities like the Bronx Slave Market. During the same months the strip was running, Myrtle Taylor, a Harlem resident, wrote to the *New York Amsterdam News* editor, "At least twice a day I pass the corner of Westchester Avenue and 161st street, in the Bronx, and see a fairly large group of Negro women waiting there to be

Figure 9. *Tisha Mingo*, by Jay Jackson, *The New York Amsterdam News*, September 4, 1937.

inspected and chosen, like the slaves of the pre-Civil War period." Gloria Langford, a young black woman, wrote to Eleanor Roosevelt in 1936:

> You will find us in the employment agencys [sic] trying to 'sleep-in' for thirty dollars a month or 'sleep out' for eight dollars a week. You will find us sitting on boxes on corners of the Bronx waiting for a perfectly strange woman to take us into her home to wash blankets floors windows dogs or children for from fifteen to twenty five cents an hour and a lunch of mouldy cheese half-spoiled fish stale bread and leftover tea thrown in for good measure.[52]

RESTRUCTURING: THE TIDE TURNS

The relationship between maid and mistress was changing. The hardships and abuses of the Depression were real, but they also had a sort of silver lining. The growing distance between maid and mistress and resulting depersonalization of their relationship actually made workers more likely to

Table 12. U.S. Women Working in Occupations, 1900–1940

	1900	1910	1920	1930	1940
Total (by Number)	5,319	7,445	8,637	10,752	12,574
Professional	434	726	1,008	1,482	1,608
Clerical	212	688	1,614	2,246	2,700
Sales	228	379	541	736	925
Operatives	1,264	1,702	1,748	1,870	2,452
Domestic Service	1,526	1,784	1,360	1,909	2,277
Service	359	629	703	1,045	1,422
Farm	697	895	892	645	351

Source: United States Department of Commerce, Bureau of the Census, *Decennial Census of the Population*, 1900, 1920, 1930, 1940; David Katzman, *Seven Days a Week: Domestic Service in Industrializing America* (New York, 1978): 56, 60, 290, 291, 292; "Facts About Working Women," *Bulletin of the Women's Bureau* 46 (Washington, G.P.O., 1925): 2, 23; Allyson Sherman Grossman, "Women in Domestic Work, Yesterday and Today," *Monthly Labor Review* (August 1980), 17-21; Janet M. Hooks, "Women's Occupations Through Seven Decades," *Bulletin of the Women's Bureau* 218 (Washington, D.C.: G.P.O., 1951).

see themselves as independent actors. Emotional ties were severed, removing some of the leverage mistresses had previously had. The slave markets helped make the hourly wage and intense negotiations commonplace.

These changes made it possible for workers to capitalize on World War II. By 1940 domestic service was no longer the single most important female occupation in the United States. Only one-fifth of all American women worked in domestic service in 1940, down from one-third in 1930. And although the number of servants in New York remained fairly constant, the ratio of female domestic servants to families in New York City went from slightly less than 1 in 10 in 1930 to 1 in 16 in 1940, because of overall population growth.[53]

World War II ended the Depression abruptly. Like other women, maids, cooks and laundresses went into war work. One observer estimated that the supply of workers in New York City went down 10 percent in 1940 and another 20 percent by April 1941. Moreover, whatever immigration there had been to New York was sharply lower because of the war; not even refugees could fill the need for servants.[54]

Table 13. Private Household Workers, 1920–1940, New York City

Year	All Employed Women (000)	Private Household Workers	
		Total (000)	As percent of all employed women
1920	693	85	12 percent
1930	863	161	19 percent
1940	875	116	13 percent

Source: United States Department of Commerce, Bureau of the Census, *Decennial Census of the Population*, 1920, 1930, 1940; Kenneth T. Jackson, ed., *The Encyclopedia of New York City* (New Haven: Yale University Press, 1995).

And need there was. Between 1940 and 1945, the female labor force in the United States grew by more than 50 percent, from 12 million to 18.5 million, until women comprised 36 percent of the civilian work force, and 37 percent of all women worked outside the home. Three-quarters of all new female workers were married, so that by 1945 almost one-fourth of all married women worked, up from 14 percent in 1940.[55]

Although nationally there were more domestic workers, in New York the number fell 28 percent between 1930 and 1940. Shortages like these gave domestic workers real bargaining power.

They also spurred reformers to deal with the Bronx Slave Market, as it was bad for the image of domestic service, and with the war on, it seemed ever more crucial to recruit new domestic workers. Because of reformers' attempts to end the Bronx Slave Market, public views about domestic service also changed. Sentiment began to turn against abusive mistresses.

REFORMING THE SLAVE MARKETS

There were many efforts, particularly on the part of African-Americans, to dissuade both employers and employees from using the Bronx Slave Market. The *Crisis* article cited at the beginning of the chapter was just one example of journalistic exposure.

The Domestic Workers Union took action as well. Dora Jones, its president, said in February 1939 that the Union asked clergymen to discourage their congregants from patronizing the slave markets, and encouraged synagogue and church members to supervise an employment center in their neighborhood where women could wait for jobs. The union also lobbied for a minimum wage law for domestics, and asked the market habituées' clergy to "impress upon these women the direct harm they do to themselves and others by going to these slave marts; and accepting the low wages that these heartless employers offer them." *The New York Times* took up the cause, publishing a series of articles about the markets. These articles emphasized the damage the markets did to the occupation's prestige (thus threatening the supply of workers) and called for the markets' elimination.[56]

With the increasing publicity about them, the markets became embarrassing to upper-class reformers and to government officials. The city administration and the white press finally began to pay attention to the slave market situation in the late 1930s, but it was slow going to effect change. Dorothy Height of the Harlem YWCA testified in May 1938 before the City Council against the markets at the Grand Concourse and Highbridge Road, Bronx and Prospect Avenue near Prospect Park, Brooklyn. "Councilman Charles Keegan objected to the term 'Bronx slave market.' But Miss Height said: 'The expression is as well known as Hi-de-ho,'" the refrain of a popular Cab Calloway song.

The Women's City Club, after a March 1939 study of the Bronx markets, recommended more publicity of the free state employment bureaus and a law prohibiting "street-corner bargaining for labor." And in December 1939, the Bronx Citizen's Committee for the Improvement of Domestic Employees called for educating Bronx housewives as to the evils of ad hoc hiring and advocated opening hiring agencies near the mart corners that could provide both shelter and aid in negotiating wages and hours.[57]

In 1941, New York City finally began "to remove unemployed women from street corners and thus eliminate the Bronx 'slave markets' that have fostered the sidewalk hiring of day workers." The City Council had begun studying the problem in 1939, but it took two years for them to act. In fact, officials believed that workers were on relief and only supplementing their income on the street. This was not true, as it was mostly women too proud to go on relief who resorted to the markets.

In early 1941, representatives of the city Department of Welfare took three buses to the Bronx and brought back 85 women to make voluntary statements about conditions. (They probably received lunch and a day's wages in return for their help.)

On May 1, 1941, less than three months after the bus trip, Mayor La Guardia marked the opening of the Simpson Street Day Work Office, a domestic employment office at 1029 Simpson Street in the East Bronx. It was open from 7:30 a.m. to 4 p.m. five days a week, and between 7:30 and 11:00 a.m. Saturdays. It was free of charge to both employees and employers, unlike normal employment agencies, and was funded with money from the Federal Social Security Board administered by the New

York State Employment Service. A second office opened in July 1941 at 12 Elliott Place in the West Bronx, near the most notorious slave market at 167th Street and Jerome Avenue.

Sixty African-American women showed up at the converted storefront on Simpson Avenue on May 2, and one-quarter of all who turned up got work. *The New York Times* reported, "The domestics were highly pleased with the new set-up and said they would appreciate it even more in bad weather." The Bronx Committee on Street Corner Markets announced that by September 1941, 6,000 black women had gotten jobs. Though the workers now had additional dignity, the main beneficiaries were housewives, who could phone in their job orders, and the city, which had gotten rid of an embarrassment.[58]

Despite this momentary glow of satisfaction, conservative attempts at ending the markets failed. By the eve of America's involvement in World War II, slave markets were still rampant in New York City and elsewhere, and they were visible signs of African Americans' subservient position in American life.

Indeed, after the May 1 opening of the Simpson Avenue center, ten workers took up their positions on the street corner, since the center did not begin actual operations until May 2. And the free employment agencies run by the New York State Employment Service were in employers' neighborhoods in Manhattan, Brooklyn, Queens and the Bronx, to which workers still had to travel. Marvel Cooke, writing in 1950, said that the Simpson Avenue hiring hall had "merely put a roof over the Slave Market. Bidding for labor at depressed rates was more comfortable than heretofore, but other evils of the market remained." Others agreed: Mayor LaGuardia remarked in May 1941, "Nothing to date has really been solved here on this question of the domestic here, if we are to be perfectly frank." The conditions and attitudes that led to the formation of the marts had not abated.[59]

The Bronx Slave Market reoccurred even after World War II caused an irreversible decline in the number of domestic workers. In the late 1940s, appliance mania was at its highest level, largely because manufacture and sales of such durable goods was driving the economy. Part of the excitement was the assumption that a machine could replace human labor. This depressed the worth of a servant. And since black women were still relegated to menial jobs, they were still vulnerable to exploitation. Thus, when a recession hit the country in the late 1940s and created a pool of jobless workers, the conditions were again ripe for slave markets.[60]

In the fall of 1949, during a recession, Marvel Cooke went back to the Bronx with a paper bag, to a market she felt never went away and was now enjoying a resurgence. She joined a group of women who had domestic jobs that did not pay enough, so they turned to the market to augment their incomes. Despite housewives' complaints about high wages, they were clearly not high enough.[61]

Figure 10. These women waited on a street corner, holding paper bags containing work clothes. *The Daily Compass,* January 8, 1950.

Comparing 1950 and 1938, Marvel Cooke wrote,

> There is no basic change in the miserable character of the slave market. The change is merely in the rate of pay. Ten years ago, women worked for as little as 25 cents an hour. In 1941, before they left the streets to work in the factories, it was 35 cents. Now it is 75 cents.[62]

All the worst elements of American private household work coalesced in the Bronx Slave Market: racism, chiseling, grinding labor, mistrust and theft. Yet it also represented a turning point, and it was an icon that could spark resistance among black women. Ironically, one of the reasons the Bronx Slave Market was so abusive—the hourly wage—became an advantage for many workers during and after World War II. So many private household workers left the field during the war that pay rates went up. The hourly system, which was exploited by employers as a way to control costs and avoid obligations to workers, wound up being a tool for workers looking to regulate their own schedules. Abuses also led to some public outrage, which helped fuel reform efforts and lay the groundwork for later positive shifts in attitudes toward the domestic service occupation.[63]

Despite some of the positive outcomes related to the market restructuring, the Bronx Slave Market endured. The failure of the effort to end the Bronx Slave Markets was a failure to act upon the root causes of it, particularly housewives' sense of entitlement to help and the lack of value placed on housework itself. There were many other attempts to reform the occupation through the postwar years; they failed for the same reason. Although some groundwork was laid, the time was not yet ripe for major changes.

Table 14. Average Monthly Wages for Live-In Household Help (Room and Board Included), New York City, 1917–1995 and 2003 Equivalents

	1917–18	Mid-1918	1919	1920–21*	1923–25*	1930s *$	Early 1940s **	Late 1940s**	Late 1950s **	1963	1995 ***
Kitchen-maid	$35	$40	$60	$50–60	$60	$30–50	$60–70	$100–120	$150–200	$200–225	$1500–1950
2003 $	503.41	489.03	637.87	458.47–617.00	647.25–628.75	425.93–651.08	637.87–744.18	764.11–916.93	954.03–1272.05	1202.54–1352.85	1811.72–2355.24
Cook	$35–40	$50–60	$70	$70–80	$80–110	$50–85	$100	$140–180	$250–350	$300–350	$1750–2150+
2003 $	503.42–575.33	611.29–733.55	744.18	641.85–822.67	863.00–1152.72	709.88–1106.83	1063.11	1069.76–1375.40	1590.06–2226.08	1083.80–2101.44	2113.68–2596.80
General House-worker	$35–45	$45–50	$50–70	$60–70	$70–80	$30–55	$80	$120–150	$200	$250	$1750–2150
2003 $	503.42–647.25	550.16–611.29	531.56–744.18	617.00–719.84	755.12–838.34	425.93–716.18	850.49	916.93–1146.17	1272.05	1503.17	2113.68–2596.80

(continued)

Table 14.—(continued)

	1917–18	Mid-1918	1919	1920–21*	1923–25*	1930s *§	Early 1940s**	Late 1940s**	Late 1950s**	1963	1995***
Chamber-maid	$35	$45	$60–70	$60–70	$70–80	$30–50	$60–70	$120	$160–180	$240	$1750–2150
2003 $	503.42	550.16	637.87–744.18	617.00–719.84	755.12–838.34	425.93–651.08	637.87–744.18	916.93	1017.64–1144.84	1443.04	2113.68–2596.80
Waitress	$40	$45	$50	$60–75	$60–70	$30–50	$60–70	$120	$170	$250	$1750–2150
2003 $	575.33	550.16	532.56	617.00–771.25	647.25–733.55	425.93–651.08	637.87–744.18	916.93	1081.24	1503.17	2113.68–2596.80
Laundress	$35–45	$45–60	$50–70	$65–70	$70	$35–60	$70–80	$120–140	$200	$200–250	$1950–2400
2003 $	503.42–647.25	550.16–733.55	531.56–744.18	596.01–719.84	755.12–733.55	496.92–781.29	744.18–850.49	916.93–1069.76	1272.05	1202.54–1503.17	2355.24–2898.76
Couple			$70–80			90–150					$3500–6000+

2003 $					641.85–822.67		1277.79–1953.23			4227.35–7246.89
Butler	$70	$80	$100	$100	$110	$40–90	$130	$180+	$300+	$400	$2150+
2003 $	1006.83	978.06	1063.11	916.93–1028.34	1186.62–1152.72	567.91–1171.94	1382.04	1375.40	1908.07	2405.07	2596.80

* The real value of wages shifted during these intervals. The recession increased purchasing power by as much as 12 percent between 1920 and 1921. Inflation eroded purchasing power by 3 percent in 1925, although it recovered by 1928. Purchasing power also declined over the course of the 1930s, by 9 percent between 1933 and 1938, for instance. The range presented here is for the lowest wage equivalent in the entire period to the highest wage equivalent in the entire period.

§ The low end of the scale was for black workers, the high for whites. Wages are based on what agencies and employers offered; workers generally asked for 20 percent more. Figures are for the years 1933 and 1938.

** For comparisons to 2003, the year 1943 stands for the early 1940s, 1948 for the late 1940s and 1958 for the late 1950s.

*** These are high-end numbers. Illegal aliens could make as little as $540/month for live-in general work. "For Immigrant Maids, Not a Job but Servitude," *The New York Times*, February 25, 1996.

Sources: A.E. Johnson Agency placement books, 1917–1963, held at the Lindquist Group offices, Greenwich, CT; A.E. Johnson Agency Wage Sheet, 1995; *The New York Times* "Household Help Wanted" classified advertisements, 1938–39; "Fewer Domestics Found in Survey," *The New York Times*, November 17, 1946; "Household Employment Wage Sampling," April 1946, Women's Bureau Records, Box 298 (1946), 1946 (Memoranda); "What Is Its Relative Value in US Dollars?," Economic History Services, http://eh.net/hmit/compare/. The last is based on the Bureau of Labor Statistics' Commodity Price Index (CPI).

Chapter Three

From Condescension to Recruiting: Household Service Reform Efforts from WWI through Korea

"Domestic Help: A National Issue," fretted Catherine McKenzie, writing in *The New York Times* women's pages in 1938. She described the loss of the turn-of-the-century's "hard-working Katy or Hilda or Annie"; they were young and grateful for the work they got. These days, "Annie, new style" or "dusky Blossom" made demands—and there were not enough of them. McKenzie echoed the thoughts of many in saying that perhaps putting more young women through training programs would solve both the shortage and lack of skill of household workers.[1]

Such training programs were part of conscious efforts to reform domestic service at a time when demographic and economic forces were restructuring it. Like the attempts to end the Bronx Slave Market, such undertakings largely failed. However, reform did move from efforts based on an assumption of employers' superiority to those based on an assumption that domestic workers deserved the same rights as other workers.

Reform came from two sources: workers and employers. This chapter will focus on both. However, workers themselves continued to act in an atomized fashion: They focused on gaining ground in their one-to-one relationships by demanding better wages, hours and conditions primarily on an individual basis.

Reform came in three waves. The first started a little before World War I. Efforts were purely voluntary and largely unorganized. In a period when maids were making strides toward better working conditions, employers, even if they were involved in organizations like the YWCA, were concerned with retaining servants and improving their performance. Reform, to these employers, meant reforming workers.

The second wave began just before the Depression and continued into the years of the Second World War. During this period, abuse of domestics was rampant, and reformers on both sides of the fence called for regulation. Much of the regulation was to be voluntary, but, for the first time, there was a call for government intervention. The idea that private household workers were entitled to equal treatment with other workers began to gain ground.

The third period was when reformers actively sought government intervention. It peaked after World War II, when the servant shortage, begun during the war, continued. Most occupational reform centered on attempts to pass protective legislation (i.e., wage and hour laws) and to include domestic workers under Social Security. This, reformers felt, would help attract workers to the occupation by standardizing and regulating it. Ultimately, legislation helped to distribute power more equally in the worker-employer relationship.

After domestics were covered under Social Security in 1950 (more fully in 1954), the steam went out of reform efforts. By that time, however, a sea change had taken place.

Domestics were now legally entitled to many of the same rights that other workers had, which gave them leverage. Indeed, the decision whether or not to file social security payments became one that employee and employer made together. Employers suffered the legal penalties for non-compliance, but evasion was usually the workers' choice. A continued shortage of workers gave them additional bargaining power. No longer was the relationship built on the power of the mistress—the maid had power, too. The balance had shifted.

THE FIRST WAVE: THE STIRRINGS OF REFORM

During the 1920s, domestic service reform was purely voluntary, for two main reasons.

First, government intervention into employer-employee relations was new, dating from the early years of the century. Because it was new, the right of the government to regulate even "public" activities was still very much in dispute. In a series of Supreme Court decisions beginning with *Hammer v. Dagenhart* (1918), the power of Congress to regulate the workplace was called into question. Too, industrial unions wanted to keep government out of labor relations. They espoused their own brand of voluntarism, "a policy under which workers were to be schooled to rely exclusively on their trade unions for promoting and protecting their interests as wage earners . . . Above all, no positive aid from the Government . . . was to be sought or accepted."[2]

Second, household employers were largely condescending to their employees. Their maternalistic attitude made it impossible for them to see workers as their partners in a relationship. Voluntary reform efforts were therefore tinged with *noblesse oblige*. Employers, individually or in groups, often had the best of motives. But they were convinced that they deserved help in the kitchen and laundry room *on their own terms*. Most employers were white and native born, which gave them higher social status than their help. They reinforced their sense of entitlement in the way they treated household workers.

During the 1920s, for example, employers refused to accept the fact that there were now fewer white, European servants who were willing to live in and work for pre-World War I wages. The head of a New York City domestic employment agency expressed the hopes and attitude of his clients when he predicted in 1920 that "in three or four months, . . . we will have almost the old conditions back—girls willing to work for $7 or $8 a week instead of 'highty-tighty' dusters, willing to assist in housework for $15 a week."[3]

The 1919–21 recession seemed to prove him right. Anecdotal evidence suggests that New York City wages dropped in 1920–1921. After having to pay higher wages and be nice to their help during WWI, housewives were determined to regain the upper hand. During the postwar recession, it seemed they could, since jobs were scarce for all ethnic groups. To African-Americans, the situation was familiar. As Nettie Bass, a black Washington, D.C. domestic, put it, employers "know'd you was never getting store, factory, or government work. You was there for life." Employers felt, "[W]ork isn't as plentiful as it used to be and the house servants will have to get in tune with the mistress or take the air."[4]

Essentially, employers wanted to return to prewar conditions when most servants lived in and worked long hours for little pay. Employees, on the other hand, had no intention of going back to the bad old days. As noted in previous chapters, domestics increasingly insisted upon living in their own homes, and they pushed for shorter hours. They wanted "the democratization of the kitchen and the abolishing of the more or less feudal relations of domestic service."[5]

Yet reform was hindered by the realities of domestic service. It had been the dominant field for women's employment for so long that women had few other jobs with which to compare it. Only 20 percent of American women had been in the labor force in 1900. Fully 40 percent of those were in private household employment. Another twenty percent took in boarders or were prostitutes, leaving only 40 percent doing factory, clerical or shop work. Before the First World War, even though domestic service was arduous, its conditions were similar to and in some ways better (equivalent pay, room and board included) than these other occupations.[6]

This neat, cheerful
kitchen scene may
be duplicated in your
own home at a sur-
prisingly moderate
outlay. The kitchen
furnishings can be
obtained on the Sixth
Floor, the curtains
on the Fifth and the
Linoleum on the
Eighth.

Figure 11. McCreery's advertisement, *The New York Times,* June 17, 1923.

During the war, more women than ever had worked in standardized industrial conditions in offices and factories. Women who had experienced better working environments during the war and who then returned to private household duty wanted comparable circumstances in the home.[7]

Industrial conditions meant regular hours, decent pay, living in their own homes, freedom from a mistress's demands, and impersonal and predictable supervision. Women in industry also had standardized wages and hours, thanks to new protective legislation. By the early 1920s, only in domestic service were 14-hour days still normal. It was no longer similar to other jobs, and the negative contrast with other occupations made it seem abusive to its practitioners.

WORKERS' COPING STRATEGIES

Within the confines of their occupation, domestic workers coped through resistance and direct action. The essence of resistance was encapsulated in a New York City domestic's belief: "One very important difference between white people and black people is that white people think you *are* your work. . . . Now, black people think that my work is just what I have to do or what I do to get what I want." The status of the job did not affect the status of the jobholder. As Sharon Harley has noted, even if domestics did not like their jobs or the people for whom they worked, they felt good about themselves.[8]

This was true for immigrant servants as well. Since most young new-comers—Irish, German, Scandinavian, Japanese and Mexican—worked as domestics, the job could not demean them within their own communities. It was a temporary position, something they expected to leave upon marriage. At the very least, they could reasonably anticipate that their children would not continue in the occupation.[9]

As such, domestic service was something that could be celebrated. Henry Crookhorn's Swedish parents worked as live-out help in New York City from the teens through at least the 1930s. They "imitated the rich people they worked for" in clothing, food, and manners. Imitation extended even to Henry's father tipping the children five dollars for rubbing liniment on his back after his twelve-hour work days. Mr. Crookhorn, like most other household workers, was not owned by his job or his employer. He made choices about what he valued. Living out was one of them.[10]

All of the ways in which domestics approached their jobs were geared toward creating and maintaining their own independence. Even if they acted the role of servant on the job, they did not internalize it. They resisted being identified with their work. Instead, the job was a means to an end.

One direct action some domestics took was to simply leave household employment. Native- and foreign-born white women left for clerical and sales jobs, and some African-American women went into non-domestic personal service jobs in beauty parlors or commercial laundries. Irish-born Mary Casey stopped working as a domestic in 1922, after she had 19 years experience as a cook and chambermaid. She switched to office work, at the A. E. Johnson Agency, which had placed Casey in many of her domestic jobs. Casey earned only slightly more than she had made as a cook, but she apparently was in the process of making substantial changes in her life. She was between 35 and 40, and had recently moved from East 52nd Street, an Irish enclave, to East 214th Street in the Bronx, near where the IRT subway line and the Third Avenue El had recently been extended. It is likely Casey had recently married and wanted more independence. Working for the agency was a good transition for her; she worked there for five years and then moved on.[11]

Workers' second direct action strategy was to maximize their wages. Servants had always gone from job to job in search of better pay, and that process seemed to accelerate during World War I and the 1920s. When they could, black women alternated between factory and household work, seeking the highest earnings. Other domestics learned how to work the agency system to maximize their earnings. Mary Casey went through 13 positions in a 28-month period, beginning as a $55 per month chambermaid in March 1918 and ending as an $85 per month cook in July 1920. In March

1919, she took a dip in salary in two stopgap jobs, but they lasted only a few days each and then her pay resumed its climb. Agnes Dunn, who used the same employment agency, went from a waitress position in 1917 to a $40 per month cook in April 1918. She stayed longer at her positions than Casey did, presumably learning her craft. By April 1920, she was earning $70 a month as a cook in Bedford Hills, a suburb of New York City.[12]

These types of individual actions constituted most of workers' activity in the early part of the century. Workers themselves were not organized apart from a few mixed-class and race organizations like the YWCA. These were employer-dominated organizations; as such, they were not likely to encourage unionization. Workers did in fact spend time together, primarily in their own ethnic enclaves or in clubs, but they tended not to organize unions. The very few exceptions were short-lived.[13]

THE FIRST WAVE: EMPLOYERS ORGANIZING FOR REFORM

While workers in the 1910s and 1920s acted on their own, the employing class tended to organize. Ironically, for the most part it was the presence of servants at home that allowed them to join activist clubs and associations.

In 1915 the new Young Women's Christian Association (YWCA; founded 1906) organized the Commission on Household Employment (soon the National Commission on Household Employment, or NCHE). The subject was of great interest to both the employers and employees who were YWCA members. A new American focus on labor issues was behind it as well, along with middle-class women's role as "public housekeepers" and their need for household help so they could maintain their public role.[14]

Intended to serve both workers and employers—the former by improving work conditions and the latter by raising work standards—the NCHE advocated purely voluntary reform of the occupation. It relied on the good will of both parties, a strategy the YWCA continued to advocate through the 1940s.

The National Women's Trade Union League (WTUL; founded 1903), which advocated protective legislation for women in industrial occupations, also favored voluntary adherence in the home to industrial "standards of hours, wages and working conditions."

During the 1920s, the WTUL focused on women factory workers. It was not until they were covered under minimum wage, maximum hour and other social legislation that their champions moved on to deal with servants.

Members of the WTUL included Mary Anderson, later the New Deal-era Director of the U.S. Department of Labor's Women's Bureau and, briefly, Frances Perkins, Franklin D. Roosevelt's Secretary of Labor. These women believed in the power of "state action" because the United States government had been able to help labor so much and so quickly during World War I. They would bring this point of view to bear on household service during the 1930s and 1940s.[15]

It is remarkable how much organizing employers did. So threatened were middle-class women by the shifts occurring in the structure of household work that they banded together to defend themselves from both the realities of the present day and those they dreaded for the future.

The increasing discord in the 1920s between maids and mistresses embarrassed the latter: surely newly enfranchised women should be able to keep the peace at home. Therefore, employers and their advocates studied the situation, holding meetings and publishing articles. Investigations began with the assumption that employers were reasonable in their expectations. This prevented them from noticing much that could be altered about the job itself. They did address some issues immediately (such as wages) but only because their hand was forced by a dearth of workers and a need to attract more to the occupation—whether to fill an actual need or to enable them to depress wages is an open question.[16]

The "servant problem" was not new, but its terms had changed. In the nineteenth century, the main complaint had been the help's competence, particularly when the help was Irish (as was true for much of New York City). Hasia Diner has noted that "the bulk of the material describing and detailing the 'Doings and Goings of Hired Girls' lamented that Irish servants were: terrible cooks, poor house cleaners (having been born and bred in the mire of the bogs), temperamental if not violent, and clumsy and awkward in handling the family's precious china and crockery." Employers also lamented servants' drinking and propensity for quitting jobs.[17]

Now in the 1920s, there were fewer immigrants, more African-Americans, and altogether fewer servants. The endless supply of cheap, docile labor that had made complaining a sport dried up. Because employers were seriously alarmed at the servant shortage, workers gained a voice. Some employers even tried to understand their maids.

Many New York City women who were accustomed to having servants had never done housework. One New York matron's attitude changed only after several workers quit in quick succession.

The trouble, I decided, couldn't be all with the maids. Something must be the matter with the mistresses. . . . I found out by not trying to get any help for three months. In those three months I did every bit of the work of my house of seven rooms and for my family of four myself. At the end of that time I knew better than I had ever known before what I wanted of a maid and wherein my former demands on her time and strength had been unreasonable. With that actual experience of general housework as a background, I hired Susan. That was five years ago. She is still with me.[18]

The YWCA in 1924 sponsored a more organized effort at creating understanding. Funded by the YWCA, a group of college girls worked (for free) as domestics for six weeks in order to study the occupation. Their goal was to gain more insight into the workers they would someday hire, "the other half."[19]

These efforts were few and far between. Because household appliances were in their infancy, there remained in the 1920s a real need for help in doing housework. Those who could not afford paid helpers relied on neighbors and family members to get the job done. Since the work was done in the home, a private space, it was natural for housewives to want to exert some measure of control over the circumstances under which they employed help. They reasoned, "Shouldn't the worker be inconvenienced rather than the person who was paying her?"

Thus, to employers any change that gave more power—whether in the form of money or time or the ability to negotiate for either—to the worker was a bad change. Mistresses resisted all adjustments except those they themselves suggested and controlled.

Most employers believed that the root of the problem was their servants' recalcitrance. Workers thought employers made unreasonable demands, and these opposing stances made it difficult to accomplish any substantial change in the occupation. It was only when they had no choice that employers looked at their own part in the problems of domestic service.

For the most part, employers decided that workers did not know what was expected of them. In 1924, an employment agency, Scientific Housekeeping, Inc., conducted an experiment. Located at 138 East 47th Street in Manhattan, Scientific Housekeeping was essentially a conservative, employer-driven organization backed by some of New York's most prominent women. Its goal, according to president Dorcas Boardman, was not simply to supply houseworkers. They wanted to ensure a supply of workers with "skill, deportment, finesse" and began a training school. To their credit, they saw the employment relationship as two-sided. Only in making both parties aware of their responsibilities, and by professionalizing the occupation could that goal be reached, for suitable employees would not otherwise be attracted to the job. To that end, they proposed six-day weeks, eight-hour days, regular meal hours, pay for overtime and the proper tools. Their proposals largely fell on deaf ears.[20]

Home economists weighed in, saying that housekeeping itself needed to be elevated. Part of the problem between maid and mistress was the conflict between housewives' knowledge that housework was important and their imbibed notion that it was valueless. It was difficult to value workers who performed the tasks for them, even more so because if one did the work oneself, it was without pay.[21]

A shift in thinking about housework did not occur in the 1920s. Neither was there a significant alteration in most employers' views of their service relationships. Events overtook them, however. So many young women were leaving the occupation that those who remained demanded shorter, live-out hours and higher wages. The power relationship was altered. Employers began to cast about for a way out.

THE FIRST WAVE: VOLUNTARY CONTRACTS

Rather than let workers dictate the terms of the relationship, employers in the 1920s advocated a contract between housewife and servant. It emerged in Washington, D.C., when prominent women formed the Housekeepers Alliance in 1920 to protect their interests. They adopted an employment contract that specified the amount of notice to be given on either side, with penalties for failure to comply. "Worthy" maids would receive a bonus and a wage increase after the first year. This incentive would protect employers, because it was much more likely that a servant would leave than be fired.

As the decade progressed, things worsened for employers. Mary Hubbard, a domestic service agent, cast a cold eye on her clients, who concealed "beneath their admirable surface affectation of blithe sovereignty, a latent ripple of agitation. (Wages had doubled and the query in all minds . . . , "What are we all coming to?" was answered only by the still more morose conviction that we Had Come.)"[22]

Employers had begun to see that the major problem was in attracting workers to the job. The editors of *The New York Times* scolded, "Regular hours, more freedom and a better industrial standing are the lures. Householders are themselves somewhat to blame for not having taken what steps they could to improve conditions of domestic service. Letting the help share the radio and the Ford is a belated attempt at appeasement."[23]

In response to the changing times, the YWCA and National Coalition on Employer-Employee Relationships in the Home (NCEERH, fd. 1928, successor to the 1915 Commission on Household Employment) also promoted the contract idea. Among other things, it provided for 48-hour (live-out) and 54-hour (live-in) weeks, vast improvements over existing 72- or even 84-hour weeks.[24]

The idea did not catch on before the end of the decade, however. Mistresses thought the contracts were too lenient—they needed help more than eight hours a day!—and maids thought them too harsh, since they wanted five-, not six-day weeks. Few wanted to live in. The contracts that proposed eight or nine hours a day incorporated the detested (by maids) "on-call" time. During on-call time, a servant was technically not working, but she had to be available to answer the door or telephone. Two hours of on-call time equaled one regular work hour. Therefore, if there were two hours of on-call time each morning and each afternoon, an 8-hour day became a 10-hour day. It was very likely that this would occur, since a main object with employers was to maintain "the old-fashioned American home . . . with all its storied atmosphere and hospitality . . . the unit of American civilization." This meant help at breakfast, lunch and dinner.[25]

In response to employer criticism, the YWCA produced a revised model contract in 1929; it was adopted at the National Committee on Household Employment conference in 1931. This contract called for 60 "actual working hours."[26]

It was almost impossible, however, to gain employers' agreement even to voluntary contracts. They wanted to dictate the terms of the relationship. Despite the national leadership's championship, almost no YWCA branch officially adopted a voluntary contract. If a large organization failed to win over its own members, there was little hope for the rest of the employing class. Throughout the 1920s, they felt little need to change themselves. They grudgingly paid higher wages and put up with live-out help; it was more than enough.[27]

THE SECOND WAVE: THE GROWING NEED FOR INTERVENTION

When the Depression struck, employers quickly embraced the return of plentiful servants willing to work for little money. Surely now the upper hand was again theirs.

And it did seem possible that things would go back to pre-World War I standards. Real changes in domestic service had just begun by the end of the 1920s. Women were still responsible for cooking, cleaning, laundry and childcare, and they wanted help with those tasks. Experts saw no reason that they should not have it. Coming from the employing classes, reformers continued to assume that "happy and smooth-running homes" required at least some paid workers.

But if the home was the bulwark of the American nation, the deterioration of the domestic service occupation during the 1930s put it in jeopardy. Homemaking itself began to be tainted by abuses like the Bronx Slave Market. By 1937, the Women's Bureau was concerned: In order for homemaking to be truly respected, it observed, "household employment [had to be] raised to the status of a dignified and self-respecting occupation, with limited hours, clearly defined tasks, and human relationships which are socially and economically sound and compatible with mental health and membership in a democratic society."[28]

How were they to accomplish this?

By 1937, everyone agreed on the drawbacks of domestic work as described by the Young Women's Christian Association (YWCA) sub-committee on household employment: "long hours, low wages, lack of opportunity for social life, uncontrolled labor supply, the difficulty of covering household employees in existing laws, such as workmen's compensation, minimum wage, [and] social security."[29]

Still, most legislators and middle-class white women saw domestic service as a purely personal relationship, in which there should be no outside intervention. For example, the New York City Women's City Club was strongly against unions. The few members who favored some kind of collective action did not advocate strikes or traditional unions. Rather, they recommended clubs for domestics and signed employment agreements. A typical housewife's attitude was, "My husband has enough troubles with unions in his business without having union troubles at home." Reformers were well aware of this prejudice. In 1937, the Women's Bureau noted of a potential speaker on "What the Worker Wants": "She is a member of the Washington union of household workers and could refer to its standards for employment. She is not a radical person, and if she mentioned the union would do so in an unobjectionable way."[30]

Ultimately, reformers followed a middle course. The abuses of the Depression and the stream of New Deal protective labor legislation made them realize that some government intervention could be useful. The compromise position was for voluntary agreements governing conditions and hours and for government provision of old-age pensions and minimum wage standards. While affording workers some protection, this would still give the housewife plenty of leeway and put her first in the relationship.

Voluntary agreements grew in popularity in reform literature through the 1930s: they provided a minimum of guidelines for both parties and assigned responsibility on both sides (albeit lop-sided in favor of the employer). Such agreements enjoyed support from the National Council on

Household Employment, the YWCA, the Women's Bureau, the Presbyterian Church U.S.A., and other women's organizations.[31]

Workers, particularly African-American women, were more cynical and felt that unions could do more than voluntary agreements. Even in 1943, with a wartime labor shortage going on, Geraldine O'Connell, president of the New York Domestic Workers' Union, an AFL local, needed to point out how voluntary efforts failed.

> When the employer is hiring you she will say you are just to help with the cooking; soon you find yourself making the meals alone. You might be hired to do just her personal laundry; soon you're doing the tablecloths, towels and curtains besides. . . . Although the union makes clear that the ten-hour day prevails, . . . women still tried to fix the maid's time from 8 a.m. to 8:30 p.m., with never a thought of overtime. The shortage has taught women nothing. . . . They still consider free time Thursday afternoons and every other Sunday ample recreation periods.[32]

Government studies bore out O'Connell's assertions. The New York State Department of Labor found in 1946 that average working hours for full-time workers were 10.5 hours daily in a 5 ½ or 6-day week. Part-time workers averaged 5 to 8 hours a day.[33]

Voluntary contracts were not enforceable in law, and there was no suggestion to make them so. Domestic arrangements were considered private and informal and as such were not legally covered by implied contracts, either. The mistress-maid relationship was "terminable at the will of either party, exercisable without any previous notice to the other."[34]

Nor were any work conditions stipulated by law. Conditions were generally so bad during the Depression that the Women's Bureau felt it had to include this reminder in its proposed voluntary employment agreement: "Comfortable living conditions include: (1) adequate food, (2) private room, or one shared by another employee if necessary, (3) access to bath, (4) adequate heat and light, (5) a place to entertain friends."[35]

Voluntary contracts failed to dramatically alter the occupation during the 1930s. The campaign for them did, however, serve to raise employers' consciousness about the value of household help. By the end of the decade, reformers were making vague recommendations for women to "realize the economic value of domestic worker" and end the social stigma of being servants. They even began to use the term "household assistant." Many agreed with Eleanor Roosevelt, who said, "We have a whole field for employment here, if we put it on a professional basis where it will appeal to Americans with professional standards."[36]

THE SECOND WAVE: TRAINING

Many reformers believed that training houseworkers could raise occupational standards—still putting the burden for change on the worker. Training became extremely popular during the Depression. The YWCA had sponsored training for houseworkers in the 1920s, and it picked up the pace in the 1930s. The Women's Bureau supported training programs throughout the decade. Eleanor Roosevelt, already a prominent reformer and, after 1933, First Lady, strongly encouraged local training programs.[37]

A typical program was six to eight weeks long, for five part or full days a week. Its topics included meal planning, preparation and service; cleaning; sewing; laundry and ironing.[38]

Many local YWCA's sponsored their own training programs. Its 137th Street (Manhattan) and Ashland Place (Brooklyn)—both African-American—branches had their own employment agencies. During the Depression, when black women lost department store and other non-household service jobs to whites, most of the Y's placements were for domestic service. The Harlem Trade School (137th Street YWCA, fd. 1912) began to train workers for this occupation. The school affected only a small number of women, however, about 400 in 1937.[39]

Government agencies emulated voluntary organizations. In December 1935, the Federal Emergency Relief Agency (FERA) allocated $40,000 to New York so the WPA could start a "household science training" program for 600 girls on relief. The course of instruction, said Mrs. Sarah S. Dennen, director of the WPA's women's division, "would include marketing, table service, laundry, cooking and job applications."[40]

The following year, the New York City Board of Education, in conjunction with the WPA and the Girls Service League (a voluntary organization), provided a free 6-week household training course. This was an excellent example of federal-local and public-private partnership. Enrollees sought the higher wages they could command if trained, and graduates did get jobs. In 1937, 500 women from this program were placed in domestic jobs paying $35 to $75 a month. This was the going rate for good jobs and vastly better than Slave Market wages. Unfortunately, after spending $500,000 to place 5,678 trained workers nationally, the Household Workers' training project ran out of money in 1937 and had to wait for re-funding.[41]

At the 1938 discussions over funding for the WPA training courses, some Senators laughed at the notion of spending money to teach women how to keep house, but "there was no serious objection to a proposal which would take nearly half a million unemployed young people—'especially colored girls and women'—off the relief rolls."[42]

Figure 12. Poster for the Household Service Demonstration Project, WPA, 1939. Work Projects Administration Poster Collection, Library of Congress, Prints and Photographs Division Washington, DC.

This was an unrealistic estimate, given that the number of centers and their enrollment was small. The WPA's 1938 training program, the Household Service Demonstration Projects, had only six centers in New York (a city of 6 million). Just two were for African-American young women, even though they accounted for over three-quarters of all employed black women in New York, and roughly 50 percent of all its servants.[43]

Figure 13. Attempts to train domestics were still being made in the 1950s. "Training Mature Women for Employment," *Bulletin of the Women's Bureau* 256 (Washington, DC: U.S.G.P.O., 1955).

By the early 1940s, training could be seen as a failure, too, along with voluntary contracts. Relatively few women had been trained, and workers were not particularly interested in the courses. For example, the WPA domestic training center in Manhattan had only half the students

it could handle in November 1941. Aside from the few successful placements made, training's major impact—like the contracts'—was to raise
awareness that domestic service was a real occupation. Because Congress
was involved in funding the WPA projects, domestics had finally gained
visibility among its members. This would help in the final wave of reform,
the one that succeeded in obtaining some parity before the law for household workers.[44]

THE THIRD WAVE: TOWARD EQUAL TREATMENT

Starting in the mid-1930s, sentiment for equal legal treatment of domestic
workers grew. The Women's Bureau took the lead during this period, push-
ing for inclusion of domestic workers under Social Security and labor laws.
Through its research reports and Congressional testimony, the Women's
Bureau argued that private household employees comprised a significant
group of American women workers and as such deserved to be protected
by legislation. In the Social Security fight, their main ally was the Social
Security Administration itself, joined by groups like the YWCA.

By the 1940s, the YWCA was concerned about race relations, specifically its own segregationist policies. It was an interracial organization
(10 percent of its members were African-American), but its activities were
largely segregated. In 1940, 73 of 417 branches (18 percent), like the 137th
Street branch in New York City, were designated as African-American only.
The efforts of black leaders within the YWCA, like Dorothy Height, who
had strongly criticized the Bronx Slave Market, led to the Y's self-integra-
tion. The Y also affected its younger members by encouraging interracial
experience and education of white women about antiracism.[45]

Because a growing proportion of domestic workers in New York were
African-American (43 percent in 1940, and 56 percent in 1950), the YWCA
lobbied for the 60-hour week in New York State, and it heeded its members
who were domestics when they said they wanted social security coverage.
YWCA leaders saw legislation as a way to improve black women's lives.[46]

Female labor leaders chimed in for legislation for domestic service.
In 1941 Cara Cook, secretary of New York Women's Trade Union League
(WTUL) said, "Because antiquated notions about conditions of domestic
employment cannot possibly compete with hours, pay and standardization
of even unskilled factory jobs we say defense should begin at home with a
minimum standard of decent working conditions." Rose Schneiderman of
the WTUL recommended social security coverage, workmen's compensation and unemployment insurance—in short, affording servants the same
protection as other workers.[47]

The problem was that they may have misread the situation, putting words into workers' mouths. Most government workers and labor leaders came from an industrial reform background. Mary Anderson, Director of the Women's Bureau during the 1930s and 1940s, had been a dishwasher in a boarding house, but had quickly moved on to the boot and shoe industry. Before being appointed to government service, she was an organizer for the WTUL. Frances Perkins, the New Deal Secretary of Labor, came to Washington from an industrial commission background in New York State. By its very nature, the WTUL was oriented toward factory workers. Also, what would benefit women in industrial settings would not necessarily do the same for household employees. The latter's wages were very low, so any government program that took money out of their pay could be seen as detrimental to them.[48]

Moreover, there was no single voice—or even just several definable voices—for domestic workers. While most domestic workers agreed that conditions, including hours and pay, should be regulated, there were differences of opinion about programs like Social Security, which involved pay deductions. In the early days, these doubts were shared by much of the nation.[49]

Moreover, neither workers nor employers could agree about the type of regulation: should it be governmental or voluntary? How was it to be enforced? It was hard to see how millions of individual homes could be policed, and the very notion of it went against the grain of American culture.[50]

The dilemma was whether to rely solely on the parties' mutual good will or enact laws to try and coerce at least a change in behavior, if not of attitude, on the part of employers.

In the 1930s and 1940s turning to the government—particularly state and federal government—for codes of behavior and help in solving problems was still new. It was applied first to business activities *outside* the home. The bifurcation between the public and private spheres was still very much in evidence.

Although it was a government agency dedicated to promoting women's welfare in the U.S., the Women's Bureau relied on persuasion, not legislation. Its leaders deplored low wages on humanitarian grounds, but did not successfully or even energetically push for wage regulation. Instead, during the 1930s they tried tactics like attempting to convince employers that paying paltry wages undermined the American economy.

> While it may seem of little importance whether Mary or Jennie or
> Bridget get five or eight or ten dollars a week, just multiply Marys'

and Jennies' and Bridgets' wage situation around 700,000 times until you face the problems of wages for some two million women workers in the field of household employment and you will find a situation of national significance. Just a dollar more a week added to the wages of the country's domestic workers would mean two million dollars a week or more than one hundred million dollars per year of the Nation's purchasing power.[51]

To attract workers, the Women's Bureau also attempted to recast household employment. Perhaps doing away with the name "domestic service" would help. "What's in a name?" asked the Women's Bureau in 1937. "How to make household employment attractive to women preparing for or seeking new jobs—through new names for occupations, new approaches, elimination of social stigma, etc." Along with training, through the 1930s the Women's Bureau also sought the "standardization of the household employment vocation so that intelligent high-grade and potentially competent workers will want employment in the field." Standards would include minimum wage protection, maximum hours of 60 per week, a week's vacation, overtime pay or compensatory time, and "suitable living conditions." The Bureau also supported including domestics under Social Security.[52]

All the Women's Bureau could do, however, was provide information to interested parties. It organized and supplied material for domestic worker study groups, patterned after YWCA summer conferences for domestics. It supplied studies to legislators. With no authority, the Bureau saw little concrete accomplishments. By the end of the Depression, the central conundrum remained:

> One of the most acute and widespread labor problems facing our country today has to do with household employment, in which field there is a marked shortage of skilled workers though at the same time able young women refuse to consider domestic work as a possible vocation.[53]

It was a long road to legal protection for domestic workers. Until 1937, no state covered domestic workers under maximum hours legislation. And when Washington State enacted such a provision in June 1937, its 60-hour a week limit was repeatedly violated.[54]

Despite pressure by the YWCA, the Women's City Club of New York City, the Citizens Union and other New York organizations, New York State legislators pointed to that example of unenforceability when they declined to pass bills to set maximum working hours at 60 per week and to extend workmen's compensation to servants in 1938, and again upon reintroduction in 1939.[55]

Neither were domestics covered under the 1938 Fair Labor Standards Act (FLSA), which established minimum wages. (Because they were not engaged in interstate commerce, domestics had also not been covered under the 1933 National Recovery Administration (NRA) wage and hour codes.) Such codes would have been of little help in raising wages in any case, since their recommended wage scales adhered as much as possible to prevailing wages. They were not meant so much to advance wages as to prevent further degradation.[56]

Congress and the President made industrial occupations their top priority as they struggled to improve the United States economy. But domestic workers faced another obstacle: Southern members of Congress. They opposed legislative change for two reasons: first, they saw governmental intervention as federal domination of the states, and second, they construed the regulation of household and farm labor as a challenge to the existing racial system. In general, regulators were hesitant to enter the private home even in spirit. Since most lawmakers were in the employer class, they naturally saw things from that perspective and believed that voluntary efforts were sufficient. And as Southern Democrats controlled Congress, their legislative agenda prevailed.[57]

By the opening of World War II, then, the domestic service industry was one of the few (along with agriculture) that were completely unregulated. Abuses were rampant, and the stigma was still there.[58]

World War II brought workers welcome changes. They went in droves into defense jobs, and wages went up for the domestics who remained. The servant shortage was of crisis proportions. One woman "estimated that she was paying one-third more than she formerly did. The girls can ask more money, she asserted, because 'if they're not in defense they think they can get into it and they tell you so.'"[59]

She was correct—full-time (60 hours a week) workers' pay had risen almost 50 percent, up 7 cents an hour by 1944. Permanent part-time workers (35 hours was considered part-time for domestics) earned 10 cents more an hour. Hourly workers got a minimum of 60 cents an hour (for 1 to 8 hours), according to the U.S. Employment Service. This meant all workers earned between $3.00 and $4.20 a week more than they had in 1940, when the average was $9.00. And even with a slight increase in the number of day workers in 1944, perhaps some of them women with children who could not make a factory schedule work for them, demand for help had also increased. Women were paying "black market" wages and/or stealing servants from each other. Domestics made only roughly half what factory workers made, but their pay was equivalent to waitresses.[60]

But even though domestic work was no longer the worst-paid job in town, high pay could not make domestic work more attractive. "[J]obs that offered more status or freedom" were more desirable than household employment.[61]

An obstacle to true reform was that many middle- and upper-class women did not want to give up their domination of the maid-mistress relationship. Mrs. Grace Loucks Elliott of the National Board of the YWCA feared that when the war ended, conditions and pay would deteriorate. In 1944 she said, "Now is the time to set [new] standards, not when the war is over and the domestic market glutted." Mrs. Elliott expected "a great many changes in attitude all around after the general shake-up of the past two years"—both on the part of workers and of their employers.[62]

Circumstances proved her only partially right. As extraordinary as they were, the relatively short war years provided little impetus for employers to change. As World War II ended, former servants, especially black women, assumed they would be going back to other women's homes. According to an April 1945 survey, 81 percent of those who had left household labor for war work planned to return to their old jobs after the war.[63]

Moreover, those who worked in hotels and laundries had discovered that if domestic work was hard, it was even harder when one did it for dozens, if not hundreds of families instead of just one. Typical statements were:

—Prefer to return to domestic service. Anything but laundry work.

—Want to be maid in private home. Don't have to work as hard as in the laundry.

—Am janitress in an office building. Prefer to be a private-home cook.

—Prepare vegetables in a restaurant. Want maid work. Can't stand on cement floors. My feet are killing me.[64]

Workers, however, were different now. They had grown to expect better things during the war. So even though they stayed in domestic service, workers attempted to gain more control over their own jobs. They refused to do certain kinds of work. Employers complained that their household help seemed "allergic to cleaning windows" and to scrubbing floors "on their knees." Workers had not liked doing these chores before the war, but they had felt they had no choice but to do them. Employers thought they could force these tasks on them again. They truly thought they could go back to prewar habits. They were wrong, and it proved to be a crucial turning point in the relationship between employers and employees.[65]

THE THIRD WAVE: LEGISLATIVE ACTION FOR DOMESTICS

If it did not change employers much, World War II was still a watershed in terms of legislation. Having failed to cover domestics under workmen's compensation from 1935 through the war, New York State finally passed such coverage in 1946. Part of the reason for previous failures was that organizations like the League of Women Voters, the Women's City Club, the Consumers League and especially the Women's Trade Union League had linked workmen's compensation to minimum wage and maximum hour provisions. In 1946 they separated workmen's compensation out from the other, more controversial proposals.[66]

The new law covered full-time (at least 48 hours a week) workers in cities of 40,000 or more residents. During the first year, $263,300 was awarded in claims, and 1948 saw that sum doubled to $535,429. By the mid-1950s, disabled domestics received almost $1 million a year in benefits.[67]

There was not just coverage. New York State waged a public relations campaign to encourage employers to obtain the necessary insurance. It could be very expensive not to do so. One example was the case of Mary, who was injured when "young Johnny came home from school one afternoon . . . and playfully pulled the rug from under" her. Her back was broken, and she was so traumatized, she spent several months in a mental institution. By the time she was well, her employer, who had not bought insurance to cover his liability, had spent over $30,000 on her medical bills. For $50 a year, he could have bought a New York State Workmen's Compensation Law policy.[68]

The law had passed because it benefited both workers and employers. Though limited, it was a step forward for workers' rights.

THE THIRD WAVE: THE SUCCESSFUL BATTLE FOR SOCIAL SECURITY

While coverage under workmen's compensation was a step forward, it was still something that was easy for employers to deal with. They had to purchase just one insurance policy and pay only a yearly premium for it. The benefits far outweighed any inconvenience.

Coverage of household workers under Social Security was a much more significant step in evening up the scales in domestic service. First, it was a national program. Second, it inserted the government squarely within the household. And finally, it entailed major inconvenience to employers,

Table 15. U.S. Women Working in Occupations, 1900–1950

	1900	1910	1920	1930	1940	1950
Total (by Number)	5,319	7,445	8,637	10,752	12,574	16,507
Professional Workers	434	726	1,008	1,482	1,608	1,976
Clerical	212	688	1,614	2,246	2,700	4,408
Sales	228	379	541	736	925	1,418
Operatives	1,264	1,702	1,748	1,870	2,452	3,287
Domestic Service	1,526	1,784	1,360	1,909	2,277	1,459
Service	359	629	703	1,045	1,422	2,073
Farm	697	895	892	645	351	481

Source: David Katzman, *Seven Days a Week: Domestic Service in Industrializing America* (New York, 1978): 56, 60, 290, 291, 292; "Facts About Working Women," *Bulletin of the Women's Bureau* 46 (Washington, G.P.O., 1925): 2, 23; Allyson Sherman Grossman, "Women in Domestic Work, Yesterday and Today," *Monthly Labor Review* (August 1980): 17–21; Janet M. Hooks, "Women's Occupations Through Seven Decades," *Bulletin of the Women's Bureau* 218, (Washington, D.C.: G.P.O., 1951); U.S. Department of Commerce, Bureau of the Census, *Decennial Census of the Population,* 1900, 1920, 1930, 1940, 1950.

since the onus for reporting and withholding contributions rested solely with them. In all these ways, social security coverage represented a sea change in the perception of the occupation and its practitioners.

The 1935 Social Security Act had provided for three programs: "1. Unemployment Compensation and Old-Age Benefits. 2) Public Assistance to Needy Aged, Needy Blind, Dependent Children in Their Homes. 3) Health and related programs." For the purposes of this discussion, the first two are the most important, as health care was not very large. The key differences were between the first and the second programs. Unemployment compensation and old-age benefits operated on the insurance premise. People paid money in to secure their comfort if laid off and when they retired. It was the old age pensions that concerned reformers.[69]

Female servants' wages were so low that it was obvious they could not save for their own retirement. Yet they were not covered for a number of reasons. It was an unproven program, designed for industrial occupations. Relatively few people were expected to enroll at the outset, out of fear that

Table 16. Percent of U.S. Women Working in Occupations, 1900–1950

	1900	1910	1920	1930	1940	1950
Professional Workers	8.16	9.75	11.67	13.78	12.79	11.97
Clerical and kindred	3.99	9.24	18.69	20.89	21.47	26.70
Sales and kindred	4.29	5.09	6.26	6.85	7.36	8.59
Operatives and kindred	23.76	22.86	20.24	17.39	19.50	19.91
Domestic Service	28.69	23.96	15.75	17.75	18.11	8.84
Service (Non-Household)	6.75	8.45	8.14	9.72	11.31	12.56
Farm Laborers	13.10	12.02	10.33	6.00	2.79	2.91

Source: Katzman, *Seven Days a Week*: 56, 60, 290, 291, 292; "Facts About Working Women," 2, 23; Grossman, "Women in Domestic Work, Yesterday and Today," 17–21; Hooks, "Women's Occupations Through Seven Decades"; *Decennial Census of the Population*, 1900, 1920, 1930, 1940, 1950.

they would overwhelm the system. Both the large numbers of domestics (over 2 million nationwide) and the non-industrial nature of their work helped disqualify them from OASI.[70]

These were actually secondary considerations in the exclusion. The roughly equivalent numbers of workers and workplaces was the primary reasons legislators gave for not covering domestics. To collect payments from such a vast number of people who were scattered so widely seemed to the framers of the law to be an administrative nightmare. Domestics and agricultural workers were stereotyped as uneducated blacks who floated among a number of employers whom they could not remember accurately. Legislators therefore exempted both domestics and farm workers (also very numerous and in many establishments) from OASI and unemployment coverage.[71]

Another consideration was Southern legislators' fear that a federal program that provided income to blacks would disrupt both the wage and racial structures of the South. Since over three-fifths of Southern African Americans worked either in agriculture or domestic service, the Southern bloc engineered their exclusion from the federally-administered Old Age and Survivors Insurance (OASI) provisions; they were covered only under state-controlled Old Age Assistance (OAA), which provided funds to the aged needy who were not covered by OASI.[72]

Participants in OASI contributed to their own retirement fund, giving them a feeling of independence and freeing them from charity. OAA came out of general funds, and Southern blacks' fears were realized when local administrators distributed fewer funds to blacks than to whites. They thus reinforced the existing social structure.[73]

Despite these obstacles, many reformers had felt since Social Security's 1935 enactment that a key way to protect workers was to cover them under the Old Age and Survivors Insurance (OASI) part of Social Security. Because there were so many African Americans in agricultural and domestic jobs, organizations like the Urban League and the NAACP pushed to have those occupations included in 1935. The latter's motivation was to afford domestics equal treatment. Because domestic service was such a dominant occupation for women in 1930—it had over 2 million women, or 15 percent of all working women—organizations like the YWCA and Women's Bureau also wanted coverage.[74]

After their failure in 1935 to win coverage for domestics, the Women's Bureau continued to lobby for their inclusion under OASI. Throughout the second half of the 1930s, the Women's Bureau staff placed articles in magazines, gave radio speeches, wrote letters to and attended meetings of clubs, local YWCAs and national organizations, all stressing the need for Social Security coverage for maids. Mary Anderson, Director of the Women's Bureau believed there were administrative problems only because of the lack of occupational standards. If these could be resolved, there should be no problem in covering domestics.

The reasons for The Women's Bureau's support were varied. Coverage would help the occupation, not only in benefits but also with added prestige. The Women's Bureau tried to convince employers, would help attract and retain good workers. It would also be a way to make the occupation more attractive to skilled workers and put it on a more industrial footing.[75]

The Women's Bureau also wanted to aid African-Americans, who comprised about one-half of all American domestics, but they realized this was a hard sell in Congress. Perhaps in an attempt to appeal to legislators' fiscal sense, Anderson pointed out that "the inclusion of household employment in the social security program would be an important factor in giving more security to the Negroes and in taking many of them off relief." In 1937, there were 175,000 domestics on relief.[76]

To Mary Anderson, the exemption of domestics was "one of the serious gaps left in the social security program as first established." The advisory council to the Senate special committee on social security and the Social Security Board agreed; both recommended extension of old-age and unemployment benefits to private household workers.[77]

How many domestics agreed is unclear, although the Women's Bureau reported that they complained about the matter. Certainly workers wanted unemployment insurance and job standardization, along with higher wages and better working conditions, but when domestics wrote to the Women's Bureau, few mentioned legislation, much less specifically the old-age insurance laws.[78]

Some domestics were expressly against old age coverage. A New York City maid writing in 1946 wanted only disability and/or health insurance. She wrote, "I wish somebody would do something about sickness insurance. Old-age pension does not bother us. Very few maids live to be 65 anyway, so why worry about that?"[79]

In contrast, a 1940 Women's Bureau report on "Domestic Workers and Legislation" quoted a song "[w]ritten by domestic workers at a YWCA Industrial Conference and sung lustily and feelingly on many occasions."

> Social security we need!
> Social security indeed!
> March we forth two million strong
> Workers all, but stand alone
> While all legislative measures pass us by![80]

The Women's Bureau and YWCA assumed these latter domestics were in the majority, as did their allies at the new Social Security Board (later Administration). To answer objections to coverage on administrative grounds, the SSB staff spent enormous time and energy setting up regional and local offices, devising systems for processing the taxes to be collected and for dispensing benefits. Everyone involved in the original law had expected such problems that the first social security benefits were not to be given until 1942.

Yet things ran so smoothly that the date for benefit distribution was pushed up by 2 years in the first set of amendments. As early as 1941, the Social Security Administration (as it was now called) felt it was "administratively feasible" to cover domestics, unlike the self-employed, a much larger group. "[B]ecause of controversy," the SSB did not then aggressively pursue the extension of the unemployment tax provisions to domestics. They proposed a system of books for which stamps could be purchased. When the book was full, the employer would mail it in to the Social Security Administration.[81]

Merely tackling that issue did not win the day. Despite the Social Security Board's (SSB) spectacular success in managing the social security programs, the first major amendments (1938) to the Social Security Act passed domestics by. Clearly, the Women's Bureau and Social Security Board needed to take another tack. They turned to the shunting of domestics into OAA.

The states' control of OAA remained, but over the course of the 1940s, it became clear that OAA was too expensive to fund. Congress had prevented the use of general funds for OASI because of cost. Why then, several Congressmen reasoned, did it make sense to leave 2 million workers outside of OASI just so they would be dependent upon general revenues through OAA? Actually, it was worse: the Social Security Administration estimated that 2.9 million of the 23.4 American workers not covered by OASI in 1945 were domestics (28.9 million Americans *were* covered by OASI).[82]

This argument swayed the American Federation of Labor, which in 1941 encouraged coverage of "farm, domestic and other workers not now covered."[83]

In the end, although the Roosevelt administration saw expansion as a way to control inflation, Social Security was not expanded during the war. A 1941 bill failed because critics decried it as an indication that America was turning socialist through social welfare.[84]

The next great hope, the Wagner-Murray-Dingell bill, was proposed in 1943 and supported heavily by the Social Security Board and the Women's Bureau. The latter was concerned about women who were able to contribute because they worked in covered industries during the war, but who might not have accrued the minimum time required to receive benefits. Such women could lose their entire investment unless traditionally women-dominated occupations—domestic service, farm work, and non-profits—were covered. Despite bipartisan support, this bill, too, failed to win passage. Lawmakers were too preoccupied with the war and the problems of an enlarged labor force to focus on Social Security.[85]

With the war just behind them in 1946, Congress did pass a limited extension based on another Murray-Wagner-Dingell bill. It extended coverage only to veterans. It was limited in this way because Congressmen were worried about the costs to small employers and farmers. Some argued that it would be "cheaper to provide public assistance." Another argument was that it would be "impossible" to accurately determine farm laborers' income. Indeed, many agricultural workers were paid in kind, not cash, which did make it difficult to estimate income.[86]

Proponents of expansion could not persuade Congress that it was cost-effective. They even argued that OASI would help maintain "a high level of employment" by increasing the amount of money available for consumer spending.[87]

Even the eloquence of domestics' supporters could not sway legislators. Mrs. Bertrand Bakonyi, a Washington, D.C. domestic worker, said,

> I am a domestic worker, having come to this country 20 years ago, and I should like to be included in the social security program. My wages are too low to permit me to save anything for my old age even though I have not had serious illnesses or unemployment. If I had lost time I would have had to ask for charity.[88]

Another witness, Miss Ruth Liseren of the YWCA's Industrial Assembly (which represented 27,000 industrial workers), pointed out,

> I am a domestic worker but I represent the Industrial Assembly of the National YWCA, which has just met in Atlantic City. The idea of social security was to do away with charity but many persons are excluded. Domestic workers number 1,700,00—the largest group of women in any occupation. Our wages are low and we cannot save for our old age; moreover, we receive no unemployment insurance if we are out of a job. Many women have to continue working at 65 and 75, which is harmful not only to them but to American family life. Some domestic workers took jobs in industry during the war and after paying social security taxes, they must return to domestic work where they are not covered. But according to a recent survey of the Women's Bureau, most of them do not want to go back to their old jobs. The scarcity of domestic workers will continue unless something is done.[89]

And Vivian C. Mason, Executive Director of the National Council of Negro Women, said,

> Negroes are relegated to the lowest level of employment and particularly need security because their wages do not permit them to lay aside anything for a rainy day. They entered industrial work during the war and many are now compelled to return to noncovered employment. They need the protection of OASI.[90]

While domestics were again excluded in 1946, it was probably because they were lumped together with another African-American-dominated occupation, agriculture. This was actually a hopeful sign, because it meant there were few specific objections to covering domestic workers.

During the next few years, Americans slowly came to the realization that domestic service was, whether they liked it or not, competing for workers with other occupations. The Women's Bureau, Social Security Administration, YWCA, Presbyterian Church U.S.A., NAACP, Urban League and other organizations all kept up a steady barrage of lobbying for federal action, particularly for inclusion of domestics under social security.

There was still a sense of noblesse oblige on the part of reformers. They had decided for them that OASI coverage was one of the things that would "professionalize" the occupation. Whether servants earned enough to be able to afford a percentage of their wages being taken out, whether employers would decrease their wages to offset their own contribution—none of that was seriously considered. Instead, debate centered on the inconvenience to the employer, the need for expansion of coverage, even racial inequality vis-à-vis social security. After inclusion, some observers believed that Social Security did not have that positive an effect on any black workers.[91]

By 1949, "coverage of domestic workers [was] still one of the lively questions," according to Frieda S. Miller, the new Director of the Women's Bureau. As he had in previous years, President Harry S Truman again had encouraged expansion of coverage in his post-1948 election Economic Address (as the State of the Union speech was then known).[92]

In their renewed lobbying, the Women's Bureau stressed that the original exclusions were "a matter of expediency" because of the newness of the program. That reason no longer applied. Moreover, the nation was in a recession, and the Social Security Administration advised expanding coverage to encourage spending. Probably most importantly, Social Security needed a wider base of contributors to keep paying for itself. It made more fiscal sense to include more people in OASI than OAA, too, since the latter was taxing already strained public coffers.[93]

In fact, OASI was in more than financial trouble. Proponents of the so-called Townsend Plan had several bills pending in Congress. Each was a variation of the theme to provide $200 a month annuities for every American over age 60. This money would have to be spent in full in the thirty-day period before the next check arrived. Compared to this incredibly expensive plan, expansion of Social Security suddenly looked great.[94]

In addition, Southern Democrats no longer controlled Congress. This made the hearings' tone very different. For the first time, Ways and Means Committee members asked questions of witnesses who supported domestic worker coverage. Race relations were a political issue, so covering black-dominated occupations was now attractive. And again, the SSA stressed that coverage was administratively feasible. Now, there seems to have been no question that domestics would be covered.[95]

In 1950, legislators were saying things like, "[T]he social security bill . . . is long overdue. . . . I am in favor . . . of covering all persons in the United States . . . whether he is a farmer, an agricultural worker, a self-employed businessman, or professional person, or domestic employee." (Rep. Hugh Mitchell (D, Washington)).[96]

Southerners still objected: Rep. William Colmer of Mississippi said, "I do not want to see remain in this bill the provision about domestic servants. Every one of you is going to hear about this when you get home."[97]

But concerns about the economic viability of OASI and the need for an expanded contribution base won the day. Finally, in 1950, social security covered domestic servants under Old Age and Survivors Insurance (OASI). Not every private household worker was covered, however. In conference committee, Congress changed coverage to non-farm household workers employed at least 24 days in a calendar quarter for one employer, who received at least $50 in pay for that work. The compromise bill was passed August 17, 1950 by the Senate and sent to President Truman.[98]

The bill comprised 30 major changes in social security law. The most significant change was the extension of OASI coverage to almost 10 million people. Domestic workers accounted for one million of these.[99]

The social security law took effect January 1, 1951, and it immediately affected domestic service relationships. For the first time, housewives had to file quarterly reports and pay taxes on their household help payrolls, using a one-page form. They were officially employers.

The Social Security Administration, the Internal Revenue Service, and the Advertising Council joined together to educate women as to their new duties. New York women who resided on or near Park Avenue snapped up the fifteen-page booklet, "Household Employer's Social Security Tax Guide," which many women found useful. Housewives were not happy about paying taxes, although many soon realized that 1 1/2 percent of a maid's pay was such a small amount it would not force them to "drop having a maid."[100]

By the end of January 1951, over 9,000 housewives had filed applications for social security at the First District income tax office in Brooklyn, and 7,000 plus had filed in the Third District, Manhattan. There was a shortage of forms in New York, and housewives were allowed to simply request Form 942 before the deadline, April 30, 1951 at midnight. Roughly 20,000 people filed the form in the First District, which comprised Kings, Queens, Nassau and Suffolk counties, and about 40,000 in Manhattan. Though less than the total employed, it was a good start.[101]

Many maids registered for social security numbers for the first time, never before having worked in covered employment. Some, like Josephine Condon of New York City, were happy to be included. However, others may not have been pleased with their inclusion under social security, feeling that participation would open the way for their having to pay federal income tax. And some also may not have liked having *any* money taken out of their pay.

There were unforeseen obstacles, too. Father Divine, an African-American religious cult leader who had been active in New York City and its environs since the Depression, barred his followers from participating in the social security program, saying that insurance was "against our religion." This presented a problem for the social security office, for there were many housewives who had to put pseudonyms like "Angel Marie" on their applications. The agency insisted that they be filed, according to the law. The Baltimore social security office kept a file of Father Divine followers under these names; if they ever wanted to collect on their social security, they could.[102]

Despite the initial success of the program, it rankled some employers that they had to include the government in their domestic relations. On April 30, 1951, a group of Marshall, Texas women refused to pay social security tax, saying, "There's nothing in the constitution that says anyone can be forced to buy insurance—either for himself or for his employes [sic]. . . . We contend that this law would put us in involuntary servitude, in direct violation of the Thirteenth Amendment. It would make us, against our will, tax collectors and insurance salesmen for the Government. In good conscience, we cannot comply."[103]

They fought for three years, suffering the seizure of their personal property—$44.23 in taxes and penalties. They hired former Congressman (and chair of the House Un-American Activities committee) Martin Dies to represent them. In 1954, the Supreme Court declined to hear their case.[104]

These housewives had an extreme reaction, but it pointed up the difficulty of getting domestic workers better conditions. There was still enormous resistance to regulation of the mistress-maid relationship.

As time went on, however, people became more familiar and more comfortable with paying Social Security. The law was again amended in 1954. About 250,000 more domestics were included under Social Security when the requirement for 24 days' work a quarter was dropped. Now, anyone who worked in a household and received at least $50 in cash wages in a quarter, or about $4 a week, was covered, and the tax was raised to 2 percent from both employer and employee.[105]

Indeed, paying the tax could be seen as a positive: it meant that one had a servant. For far from ending after World War II, the servant shortage had worsened in the decade since. In 1955, *The New York Times* reported that "the problem of acquiring skilled domestic servants . . . was as acute as in World War II." The 1952 immigration law had reduced European

Table 17. Domestic and Other Service Workers in New York City and Nearby Counties, 1930

		Other domestic and personal service	Laundries, cleaning and pressing	Hotels, restaurants, boarding houses, etc.
New York State Total		420,199	59,782	209,647
Bronx County	M	13,575	5,502	11,320
	F	13,319	1,361	4,368
Kings County	M	25,597	9,872	18,950
	F	36,615	4,985	8,894
New York County	M	50,816	7,699	60,596
	F	93,781	7,853	26,539
Queens County	M	10,622	2,786	10,610
	F	14,801	1,405	3,685
Richmond County	M	1,242	3400	809
	F	2,101	284	366
Nassau County	M	5,366	576	1,914
	F	10,986	482	871
Westchester County	M	7,646	1,266	3,443
	F	21,643	1,225	1,741
Bergen County (N.J.)	M	2,443	627	1,812
	F	6,568	379	737

Source: U. S. Department of Commerce, Bureau of the Census, *Decennial Census of the Population*, 1930.

immigration "to a trickle," according to Philip Faingnaert of the Mme. S. Jacquin agency, one of the oldest in New York City. And New Yorkers were better off than the rest of the nation, reported Ted Warburg of the United Employment Agency, which supplied workers in 32 states. He "observed that sleep-in help, while difficult to obtain in New York City, was almost nonexistent in other parts of the nation. Despite the fact that apartments and homes are smaller than in pre-war days, homemakers' demands for sleep-ins far outnumber those available."[106]

Table 18. Ratio of Female Servants to Families, New York City and Individual Boroughs, 1930

	Servants	Families	Ratio S/F
New York City	160,617	1,722,954	0.09 or <1/10
Bronx	13,319	321,270	0.04 (1/25)
Kings	36,615	616,875	0.06 (1/16)
New York	93,781	468,956	0.20 (1/5)
Queens	14,801	280,064	0.05 (1/20)
Richmond	2,101	35,789	0.06 (1/16)

Source: *Decennial Census of the Population*, 1930.

Social security coverage, despite the Women's Bureau and YWCA's hopes, did not fulfill the promise of attracting workers to a more professional occupation. Nor did it benefit the large part of workers who worked part-time, a proportion that grew over time. The law also did not take into account that many workers did not earn enough to allow them to easily set money aside. They therefore began to collude with employers to avoid paying social security, a form of cooperative activity that would have been unheard of even twenty years earlier. The law thus affected the dynamics of the employer-employee relationship, albeit in an unplanned-for way.

The other lasting impact of Social Security coverage was that finally, domestics were accorded equal treatment under the law. The occupation's profile rose, even because of the housewives' battle against Social Security. Domestics finally had some protection, which gave them more self-confidence. The next step was to change employers' attitudes.

Table 19. Ratio of Female Servants to Families, New York City and Individual Boroughs, 1940

	Servants	Families	Ratio S/F
New York City	116,226	2,065,900	0.06 (1/16)
Bronx	9,183	380,660	0.02 (1/50)
Brooklyn	29,205	725,560	0.04 (1/25)
Manhattan	63,662	550,820	0.12 (1/8)
Queens	12,667	365,720	0.03 (1/32)
Richmond	1,509	43,200	0.03 (1/32)

Source: *Decennial Census of the Population*, 1930.

Exhibit A Proposals for a Volutary Agreement in Household Employment
National Committee on Household Employment
525 West 120 Street, New York, N.Y.

Preamble	Household employment, the oldest type of employment known, is the last to become modernized. . . . Tensions have long existed between employer and employee, with the strange paradox of oversupply and overdemand. . . . If the employer is to have satisfactory help she must compete with industry on a business basis. Recognizing that the spirit is more important than the form, the committee submits the following agreement which will not become a panacea, but a device by which groups of enlightened employers and employees may work out standards of performance and security, laying a foundation for such legislation as may be necessary to make it attractive to the best type of worker, so that it may no longer be, as Jane Addams said, "the belated industry."
Working Agreement	A definite written agreement between employer and employee should be made at the time of employment. It may be signed or unsigned and should be subject to periodic review to meet changing conditions.
Duties	Regular duties shall be clearly defined based on an analysis of the job to be done within the hour limit agreed upon. A high standard of work shall be expected in return for good wages and satisfactory working conditions.

Hours

1. *Actual working hours* shall be defined as hours of duty during which the worker is not free to follow her own pursuits.

2. *Total actual working hours* shall not exceed 60 hours within the week. A schedule of less than 60 hours is desirable.

3. *Time on call* is that time when the worker is not free to leave the house, but may rest or follow her own pursuits, being available for emergencies. Two hours on call shall be equivalent to one hour of working time. Overtime may be adjusted by extra time off or extra payment on rate per hour basis. Frequent overtime should be avoided.

4. *Time off* shall include two part-time days each week beginning not later than 2 p.m. on weekdays and immediately after the midday meal on Sundays, or one whole day each

week, or its equivalent. In the 60-hour week some evenings will be free. Four out of eight holidays shall be given during the year and some adjustment made for church attendance. Free time shall be defined as hours when the worker is free from all responsibility to the employer. Meal time cannot be considered free time if the telephone must be answered.

Vacation   One week with pay shall be given after one year of service, two weeks with pay after her second year.

Termination   Notice of one week or one week's pay shall be given on
of Services   termination of service by either party.

Wages   For full-time employment the scale of wages will range from the minimum wage for the unskilled worker with a rising scale for increasing skill and experience. We urge fair and adequate wages based on the local Community Council on Household Employment wage scale or comparable to that paid in the local industries. Payment should be made weekly or bi-weekly on the day due. If the employee wishes a monthly wage, 4 1/3 weeks should be calculated as one month.

Living   Comfortable living conditions include: (1) adequate food,
Conditions   (2) private room, or one shared by another employee if necessary, (3) access to bath, (4) adequate heat and light, (5) a place to entertain friends.

Source: National Committee on Household Employment, "Proposals for a Voluntary Agreement in Household Employment," Women's Bureau Unpublished Materials. 1956: "Domestic Workers. Household Employment (1912–1956)." Box 286.

Chapter Four
Seeing Similarities: The Happy Housewife and New Respect for Domestic Servants, WW2 and Beyond

Consider this 1945 cartoon from *The New Yorker:* A maid sat in the kitchen, reading the newspaper. Her employer poked her head in the door and asked, "Did you ring, Nora?"[1]

Now consider that a young mother in the 1990s called her housekeeper her amanuensis, meaning she gratefully felt her housekeeper had taught her just about everything she knew about keeping house and taking care of her children.[2]

There was a sea change in that 50-year period. The 1945 cartoon captured a lack of respect for household help in its snide suggestion that maids took advantage of their employers. In the 1990s, the employer truly respected and depended upon her help.

* * *

For the domestic service relationship to be based on something other than one party's subservience to the other, employers had to stop taking for granted the services performed. After World War II, changes in homemaking itself, along with a sustained shortage of help, caused housewives' attitudes to alter significantly. Women began to value housework itself more, along with its practitioners. Employers' growing respect for workers, however grudging, shifted the balance of power in domestic service.

By the 1950s, consumerism and a revival of "traditional" mores joined to fuel the idea that it was not just the housewife's responsibility but her joy to keep her own house. Appliance manufacturers urged women to replace scarce servants with machines. Trapped alone in their (often suburban) homes, housewives became frustrated with their roles in the 1950s and 1960s, and there were new debates about women's role.

The employer class, now doing much of their own housework, struggled to assign their tasks real value. In so doing, they helped to raise houseworkers' position in relation to them. If the work was good enough for housewives, then it had to be worthwhile doing. Because there continued to be relatively few of them, workers capitalized on this sense of value. By the 1970s, it was less socially acceptable to take housework for granted and treat its practitioners poorly. The women's liberation movement and its mantra that "the personal was the political" accelerated this egalitarian trend.

DEMAND AS A FACTOR IN SHIFTING ATTITUDES

To understand this shift, we first need to look at housewives' reliance on domestic help. If demand continued to be high, then there was a shortage of workers. They could expect concessions, which employers expected to make.

It is difficult to gauge demand. Many observers have noted that everyone wants a maid, but not everyone in fact hires household help—usually for financial reasons, or because they cannot find anyone to hire. Estimates vary as to how many families relied on maids, cooks and/or laundresses. Anecdotal evidence suggests that domestic help was widespread: Prior to the second World War, when the American middle class was fairly small, many middle- and upper-class families had domestic help—a maid, a cook, or perhaps just a once-a-week laundress. Others believe that very few—perhaps only five percent—Americans hired help.

This lower percentage derives from dividing the number of servants into the number of households, something that would hold true only if all domestics worked full-time (five days a week for at least 40 hours, for only one family). Historian Phyllis Palmer disputes this, saying that dividing the number of servants by households is "a ludicrous method because it implied that all households, including those of servants, had access to hired domestic labor." In his 1946 monograph on domestic service, Nobel Prize-winning economist George Stigler supports her argument for the pre-World War II era.

Palmer separates employers by economic class and calculates that domestic help was very widespread. She relies in part on a 1937 *Fortune* survey that reported that about 70 percent of the rich, 42 percent of the upper middle class, 14 percent of lower middle class and six percent of the "poor" hired household help on a regular basis. Palmer also cites a 1929 study of families (including African- and Mexican-Americans) with incomes between $2,000 and $3,000 or above, which accounted for 41 percent of the US population in that year. Many of these families hired help—almost a majority in some parts of the country. It seems then that at least 15 percent (and probably more) of American families hired house-hold help, and it was quite common for the middle class to hire help in the interwar period.[3]

George Stigler looked at income levels, too, along with general popu-lation increase. He concluded that "the more than doubling of the num-ber of families between 1900 and 1940 implies a vastly increased potential demand for servants," and that "the net effect of wives into the labor mar-ket has been to increase the demand for servants more than the supply."[4]

Stigler cited 1935–1936 family expenditure surveys that reported that higher income families had more domestic help than others, and that urban families availed themselves of paid help more than rural fami-lies. He further noted a study of 16 urban areas in which 36.1 percent of childless families and 50.6 percent of those with children who had incomes of $2,500—3,000 employed some kind of domestic help. The respective percentages for those earning $5,000—7,000 were 89.9 per-cent and 90.9 percent.[5]

Additional, anecdotal evidence includes *Ladies' Home Journal* arti-cles published in 1941, which suggest that $3,000 in annual income was the cutoff point for those hiring domestic help. The Alden Griffins earned $2,000 a year and did not have household help, a change from their pre-Depression situation. The Thomas B. Wrights, on the other hand, brought in $5,000 a year and spent $455 of it on household help and laundry. And although the *LHJ* stated that 95 percent of American women did not have paid help, they pointed out that it was because two-thirds of American families earned between $1,000 and $3,000 a year. "If she had a little more money," concluded the author, "this young Mrs. America would do things a little differently."[6]

Estimates could only suggest demand. Roughly four percent of New Yorkers who were employed for 12 months in 1939 earned between $2,500 and $3,000. Seven percent earned $2,500 and above. Using the proportions listed above, approximately 10,000 New Yorkers would employ servants. But there were about 140,000 domestic servants (female and male) in New York City in 1939, over 120,000 of who reported annual incomes of $100 or more. Clearly, the use of domestic help was more widespread than indi-cated by income surveys.[7]

It was also more variable. In 1965, the U.S. Department of Labor sur-veyed households and estimated that one-twelfth of American families (or about 8.5 percent) hired help on a regular basis, that is, at least once every two weeks, much of it on a part-time or irregular basis.[8]

As late as 1997, *The New York Times* reported that 10 percent of American women used domestic help for cleaning, and 20 percent of New

Yorkers used such help for spring cleaning. If previous surveys were any indication, this estimate, too, was on the low side.[9]

The per capita amount spent on domestic workers was low enough to indicate that many families, even the well-to-do, had only part-time help throughout the century. This supposition is supported by a review of the records of a New York City domestic employment bureau that catered to the upper class. The Mrs. A. E. Johnson Agency had a large number of day workers listed in 1920–21. It was a desirable category for workers: most of them had between 20 and 40 years of experience, and all the women had at least 10 years of experience. They and their live-in colleagues changed jobs frequently. And while many employers were repeat customers or had a house full of servants, there were a larger number of one-time only or occasional patrons.

This was also true of the Johnson Agency placements in the late 1950s, with one significant difference: there was only a small fraction of the number of live-in positions. In January 1965, the U.S. Labor Department reported that three-fifths of all regular private household jobs were for a day or less a week, and only a fourth were full-time positions, meaning that irregular jobs would likely be also for a day or less.[10]

Therefore, it appears that the number of employers was probably higher than simple division of the number of servants into number of households would imply. Assuming that people's desire for help remained the same, overall demand must have stayed at least constant and probably expanded as the population grew.[11]

Even as the United States population increased, however, the number of servants in the country remained fairly constant.

In 1940, about five percent of all employed American workers had been domestic servants and there was one servant for every 17 families. In 1944, there was only one servant for every 20 American families. In New York City, the ratio of female domestic servants to families went from slightly less than 1 in 10 in 1930 to 1 in 16 in 1940.[12]

During and after World War II, there was a decrease in the number of domestics. By 1947 the number of domestics had *decreased* by one-third while the number of women in the work force had *increased* by more than one-third since December 1941. More than six million women entered the work force, and almost two million working women shifted industry nationwide after Pearl Harbor. Not only were servants the largest group of job changers, but domestic service was the only occupation to lose workers. In all, almost a third of all American domestics, 400,000, changed occupations between December 1941 and March 1944.[13]

By 1960, the number of domestic workers nationwide had plunged by over 22 percent, from about 2.3 million in 1940 to 1.7 million. Yet the decline from 1940 did not mean that demand was less. Unemployment in the nation ran about five percent in the early 1960s, and the rate for domestic service was consistently a half a point below that. There were twice as many domestic jobs as unemployed persons in 1965. This indicated that although families were making do with fewer workers, demand for their help remained high.[14]

Stable demand and a reduction in the domestic labor force, then, caused housewives to view their paid help more generously. They expected to have to negotiate with and woo them.

EXPECTATIONS REGARDING HOUSEWORK

Housewives' disillusionment with housework in the 1950s and 1960s led them to challenge its meaning and raise its value, a shift that improved their perception of domestic workers. It began in the early part of the century.

The twentieth century "happy housewife" myth was peculiarly wrapped up in the departure of work from the home except for cooking, cleaning, laundry and child care. By the 1920s, this transformation of the home from producer to consumer was largely accomplished in the United States. Of course, there was still some household-based production, in the form of sewing, gardening and associated canning, bottling and pickling, but especially in urban areas like New York City and its suburbs, families purchased what they needed.

This was apparent in the growth of other female occupations outside the home. Clerical and teaching occupations grew the fastest, but sewing, food industry jobs, non-private household domestic jobs (i.e., hotel housekeepers) were also important. In many cases, women took these jobs as a direct segue from their traditional household chores.

Most women remained at home, the "woman's sphere," and they began to be preoccupied with the business of housework.[15]

Ellen Swallow Richards, a leader in the scientific housekeeping movement, wrote of the housewife's situation: "The time was when there was always something to *do* in the home. Now there is only something *to be done*."[16]

Shorn of her productive responsibilities, the housewife needed a new role. Domestic scientists provided it.

Industrialization had led not only to the departure of production from the household. It also produced new concepts of efficiency, which women, beginning with Catherine Beecher in the nineteenth century, were eager to apply to the home. A new field of inquiry, domestic science, emerged.

The result was a new approach to housework and a new kind of housewife—the domestic scientist. By incorporating the latest scientific information into the methods for running her own home, she could change the humdrum kitchen into a laboratory. Moreover, she could view herself as a bona fide worker with a respectable career without renouncing the traditional values of wife- and motherhood.[17]

During the early years of the twentieth century, the gospel of scientific housekeeping spread. Starting with "The New House-Keeping" in September 1912, Christine Frederick wrote a series of very popular articles about it in the *Ladies' Home Journal*. The articles excited interest in the *Journal's* readers.

By the 1930s, domestic scientists "considered 'management' to be the major thrust of homemaking, practically eclipsing housework itself."[18]

FRUSTRATION WITH HOMEMAKING

Domestic scientists' efforts to make housework meaningful failed, however. As World War II began, servants got war jobs, and there was no one left for housewives to manage. Women had to care for their homes under difficult circumstances. Added to the normal cooking and cleaning was dealing with food rationing and shortages, creative trading of ration coupons, the cultivation of Victory gardens, and cutting back on nonessentials. Those who worked outside the home squeezed household duties into their time off. The U.S. government urged each housewife to be "'a general in her own kitchen,' making do with her family's rations and saving valuable resources for the war effort."[19]

For the most part, women coped alone, making a joke of the idea of household management. Most maids left during the war, like the one in the 1946 movie *The Best Years of Our Lives*, who "went out for the evening three years ago and never came back."[20]

Reformers hoped that "this absence of Nellie and Anna, and the others" would teach employers to treat their paid help better.[21]

It did teach housewives how hard it was to get along without servants. As more women poured into war work, they found it harder to do their shopping and cleaning. Turnover in war industries was very great because of housekeeping problems. Frieda Miller, Director of the Department of Labor's Women's Bureau and formerly associated with the New York City Department of Welfare, said, "The greatest problem facing the women in the factories, the laundries, the stores—and I think this applies to secretaries and professional women as well—the most difficult problem is the problem of combining home and job."[22]

ELECTRIC WASHING MACHINES

Figure 14. Vacuum Cleaner Specialty Co. advertisement, January 4, 1920.

By 1943, war industries' average workweek was between 48 and 54 hours, with Sunday the only day off. Shifts in factories were often scheduled awkwardly and shops closed before women could get to them. For New Yorkers, transportation was not a huge problem because of the city's extensive bus and subway system, but in the suburbs and elsewhere, gas rationing often made journeys to work difficult to arrange. Food rationing made shopping and cooking harder, stretching housewives' ingenuity. Worse, in September 1942, the federal government restricted production of many consumer goods, including electric refrigerators, vacuums, irons, radios, phonographs, water heaters, waffle irons, toasters, percolators, food mixers, and juice extractors. Both household appliances and parts to repair them were in short supply.[23]

There was only limited help outside the home. During the war, some factories set up laundries and groceries for their workers, but these affected only small groups of women.

The disappearance of the laundress made laundry, the most time-consuming task, more difficult. There were 43 percent fewer private family laundresses in 1940 than in 1930 (200,000, down from 340,000). There were proportionally more in commercial laundries: in 1930 67 percent of laundry workers were private family, and in 1940 only 52 percent. But there, too, workers were fewer in number than ten years previously.

In addition, although seventy percent of American women sent their laundry to commercial laundries during the war (because they had no time to do it at home), there were, according to the Women's Bureau,

> two conflicting tendencies. . . . On the one hand, those factors that have caused other household activities to shift from the home coupled

Heavy Tin Wash Boilers

Figure 15. John Wanamaker advertisement, *The New York Times*, March 1, 1923.

with the development of a high type of commercial laundry work at lower prices have furthered the rise of laundry service. On the other hand, the availability of a practical type of home washing machine and prejudice against commercial laundries have served to keep this type of work in many homes.

Indeed, because of the increasing unreliability of commercial laundries due to lack of workers, and because home machines broke down and could not be replaced, many housewives had to revert to using laundry tubs and washboards again.[24]

For the rest, running a home and managing a job got increasingly difficult. This made a desire for household help even stronger once the war ended.[25]

Americans also continued to assume that a certain level of income and sophistication in a household meant there were servants. In the 1943 edition of *Table Service*, Lucy G. Allen wrote of homes in which the lady of the house supervised a staff, including a cook, maid and at least one waitress. Allen acknowledged that there might be "households where service is limited," but that was as far as she would go. Having written the original version of the book in 1915, Allen's attitudes were old-fashioned. Her publishers were more realistic, however, pitching the book as one "which any housekeeper—with or without maid—will find invaluable."[26]

The desperation of the war years signaled the beginnings of a change in attitude. Without household help, women feared the worst for their homes and lives. Reflecting the worries of its readership, *The New York Times* reported on this growing concern:

> A [woman] expressed the opinion that it really was about time that domestic help, "the most overworked group of women," were coming into their own. "They've been taken advantage of for years," she said. "I would not care even if they had unions. All I want is some one to do the housework. I don't want to do it."[27]

Women were thus starting to make grudging concession to servants. This inclination was encouraged when housewives' troubles did not go away after the war. The servant supply did not increase appreciably, and women may have been lonely, too. There were fewer grandparents and single relatives living with families, ice and coal were no longer delivered to the house, and human companionship was harder for the housewife to come by.[28]

Postwar suburbanization increased housewives' isolation. William Whyte noted, "People may come out of the new suburbs middle-class; a great many who enter, however, are not. . . . As the newcomers to the middle class enter suburbia, they must discard old values. . . . Without those values," Whyte wrote, "newcomers are lonely. Often it is months before the people even strike up a conversation with the neighbors about them." Life in New York City was often anonymous; in its suburbs the same could be true. A houseworker enabled the mistress to socialize outside of her home, or she served as a companion. In the latter case, it was hard to maintain a strict hierarchical relationship.[29]

APPLIANCES AS THE "NEW SERVANTS"

In their desire to have help with housework, women also increasingly relied on appliances. In postwar America, household goods were a source of pride. Vice-President Richard M. Nixon used the modern American kitchen as the example of American superiority during the 1959 Moscow "Kitchen Debate."

In an appliance-filled electric kitchen Nixon argued to Soviet Premier Nikita Krushchev that America's "many different manufacturers and many different kinds of washing machines" represented freedom of choice for housewives.[30]

Appliances were the "new servants," wrote Mary Roche, the managing editor of *Charm* magazine in 1955, the same year the magazine

Figure 16. "The Kitchen of Tomorrow" was supposed to make the housewife's job easier. Libbey-Owens-Ford Glass Company postcard, © 1943. Used by permission of Pilkington North America, Inc.

published some of Betty Friedan's writing on women's frustrations. These "substitutes" had "a distinct advantage over servants in that they [could] be expected to stay a while."[31]

The hope that appliances could replace household help had also arisen in the 1930s. For example, eight architects designed houses for a fictional Mrs. Bliss, who

> does her own housework for two good reasons: first, financial circumstances preclude an all-time maid; second, she actually enjoys the work. . . . She insists on doing the housework efficiently by using the best labor and timesaving equipment. Electricity is her servant.[32]

The typical housewife probably could not afford full-time help, but she also probably did not like housework. Nor could appliances alleviate loneliness or shoulder some of the homemaking burden. Rather, their presence solidified the shifting of all responsibility for homemaking to the housewife.

Even services that used to be found outside the home were disappearing in the name of progress. Suburbanite Edith Stern wanted human help *outside* the home.

Electric Washers
AND
Vacuum Cleaners
MAKE YOU INDEPENDENT OF THE SERVANT PROBLEM

Figure 17. Vacuum Cleaner Specialty Co. advertisement, *The New York Times*, January 4, 1920.

> My former daily marketing was merely a few minutes chore of noting immediate needs and then telephoning to a paternal character who would deliver the cut he knew I always got when my Aunt Mathilda came to dinner. Today, marketing involves thinking out a long-term list, struggling for a parking place, trekking through an enormous supermarket, waiting in line until I have been checked out, and then doing a longshoreman's work when I return to my maidless home. I'll trade in all my modern mechanical marvels for two good maids and a broom.[33]

Indeed, electrical gadgets did not reduce the time spent in doing housework. Ruth Schwarz Cowan points out that women in the 1950s spent about the same amount of time doing house work as the previous generation, between 48 and 61 hours.[34]

The U.S. Department of Agriculture reported in 1953 that

> [a]lthough today's households are smaller, the housewife's duties may be heavier than in the past. . . . Decrease in family numbers has been in adults who previously could help with the housework. . . . There's a shortage of hired household help, too. . . . The report suggests that while mechanical devices have helped to alleviate some of the housewife's burdens, they also have brought some work back into the home. Laundry once sent out is now done with home equipment. Many housewives do their own preserving for the home freezer.[35]

Advertisers acknowledged this truth. One ad suggested to the housewife, "Did you *'cash in'* this Christmas? Put your *'Christmas cash'* into a gift with a *future* . . . A modern Morton DREAM KITCHEN." In that kitchen, the housewife could put a small dishwasher: "If you're a housewife you wash about 12,000 pounds of dirty dishes a year, 229 pounds a week, 35 pounds a day. You have your hands in oceans of soapy, scalding water." Another advertisement advised that "HOME can be a wonderful summer resort when it's full of help for hot housewives."[36]

As early as 1933, Hazel Kyrk had noted,

> We have shown a tendency to use the time freed by labor saving machinery not for more leisure, but for more goods or services of the same general character. . . . The invention of the washing-machine has meant more washing, of the vacuum cleaner more cleaning, of new fuels and cooking equipment, more courses and more elaborately prepared food.[37]

And for women who could not afford appliances, housework continued to be hard, backbreaking work.[38]

By the 1950s, because of the dearth of human help and the presence of appliances, domestic scientists began to shift their focus from housewives as managers to housewives as doers. They were decision makers and the primary purchasers of household goods.[39]

To cope with the servant shortage, they did not advocate occupational reform. Now the answer was to count one's blessings that there were no servants to be had. Home economists said that

> housework was becoming too scientific and complex to be performed by uneducated women anyway. . . . Thus the woman who could not afford, or could not find, a servant was not to be pitied—she had simply realized that this was a job which could no longer be delegated to her social inferiors.

They were trying to bolster women's egos by raising the level of respect for housework itself.[40]

In that spirit, Janet L. Wolf's *What Makes Women Buy* (1958) followed in the mold of Christine Frederick's landmark *Selling Mrs. Consumer.*

Wolf advised the advertising industry, "[T]he term housewife no longer carries prestige." She urged advertisers to appeal to women's selfishness, to promise the presumably dissatisfied homemaker "new ways to make herself happy: buy our soap and look young, buy our cereal and make your children into Olympic athletes, buy our vacuum cleaner and never do housework again."[41]

There was a dichotomy in the advice given to women: housework is wonderful and fulfilling, and do anything you can to get out of doing it.

QUESTIONING WOMEN'S ROLE

The sometimes confused attempts to recast housework as wonderful picked up momentum in the 1950s. Experts attempted to jolly housewives along, giving them projects to make them feel more valuable.

Lillian Gilbreth's *Happier Living through Saving Time and Energy* (1954) focused on increasing production in the household. Like Christine Frederick before her (in her 1914 book *Household Engineering*), Gilbreth stressed that household management was a full-time job. Like paid employees, housewives could take satisfaction in a job well done. Housewives were also expected to be busy, according to women's magazines of the day. Only in this way could housework "be perceived as 'real' work. . . . The net effect of the efficiency movement for the American housewife, therefore, was actually to *increase* the amount of work she did and the amount of social pressure on her to do it."[42]

And women could never catch up. Commenting about the history of the household, Angela Davis wrote,

> The cleavage between the home and the public economy, brought on by industrial capitalism, established female inferiority more firmly than ever before. "Woman" became synonymous in the prevailing propaganda with 'mother' and 'housewife,' and both 'mother' and 'housewife' bore the fatal mark of inferiority.[43]

Despite women's magazines' portrayal of housewives as happy homemakers, housework continued to suffer from low prestige. A sociologist noted that it lacked

> the basic criteria of most jobs. It has no organized social circle which judges performance . . . , no specific pay scale, and no measurement against other performers of the same role. . . . As an economic role, it is immediately placed low in that status hierarchy, because of a lack of wage or salary scale.

The low status was shared with paid houseworkers.[44]

The household was coming under greater and more negative scrutiny. Works like Philip Wylie's *Generation of Vipers* (1942, reissued 1955) took pot shots at the household, blaming mothers for their children's failings—and indeed, for the nation's failings. Because production had moved so completely out of the home, housewives were stereotyped as lazy. One advertiser noted:

Some ads talk as if there were something dirty about a woman concerned with dirty dishes. The ads burble on about sequined dresses for cocktails a deux at the Toplofty-Plaza, and tweeds as much at home at the Colony as at the Beagle and Bugle Club. The idea behind these ads is that even if you aren't a pampered plutocrat, you like to be talked to as if you were one.[45]

Growing frustration with housework led to attempts to upgrade the housewife's role. Some felt that a name change from housewife to homemaker would help. A small sample of New York women was split fairly evenly between the two terms. To some women the word housewife connoted drudgery, while "'Homemaker' implie[d] pleasant surroundings that you are responsible for." Some women associated low status with the word housewife. But to others, the word homemaker "makes our work sound like a chore. It's a Pollyanna word, and I'll stick to 'housewife.'" Another said it was an impossible standard to meet: "That word sounds like a dietician, or a psychologist, or an economist. Of course, I'm a bit of all that, but I'm tied to the house and talk children, children all day—the glamour of 'homemaker' isn't there."[46]

As during the 1930s debate about changing the name "servant" to "household help," it became clear that terminology was neither cause nor cure for the housewife's woes.

Pressure on the household mounted as social expectations rose. By 1965–66, housewives spent 4 hours a week more in housework than they had in 1926–27 (55, up from 51). Even laundry, which had been eased the most by the advent of machines, consumed more time than in previously had, because whites had to be whiter. Machines also reduced housework to mindless, rote tasks. As *The New York Times* put it in 1955, "Housework Is the Road to Boredom." Shopping in supermarkets was a more impersonal experience than visiting small shops. Women would gladly have given these tasks to servants, if they could find any. These "household managers" now managed technology instead of people.[47]

Part of women's frustration, felt William Whyte, was that women were

easily misled by the facades of those about them in suburbia and a frequent consequence is the 'superwoman' complex. Only a minority of wives are really successful at handling both a large agenda of social or civic obligations and their home duties, but everyone puts up such a good front that many a wife begins to feel that something is wanting in her that she is not the same.[48]

At the 46th annual meeting of the American Home Economics Association in Minneapolis, MN, many presenters discussed homemakers'

Figure 18. After World War II, housewives were responsible for their own cleaning. ©1945 The Clorox Company. Reprinted with permission.

predicament. One blamed homemaking education, "for it sets house-keeping standards so high that they are unrelated to real life." Other culprits were chores women didn't like doing, loneliness, feeling left out of adult life. And another expert said, "Women are frustrated because men don't give them credit for doing housework any more—they feel that equipment does all the work in the home." Finally, "in this age of cake-mixes," housework had little creativity to offer.[49]

The baby boom meant more demands on women. The birth rate rose from 18 to 19 per 1,000 persons in the 1930s to about 25 per 1,000 after World War II and for 25 years beyond. This increase was mostly attributable to younger women having children, and it was accompanied by "more exacting models of motherhood," in which women submerged their identities into those of their families.[50]

Because there were fewer household workers, women were now setting standards not for paid help, but for themselves. But even lowering standards, for example by not ironing sheets, did not help alleviate frustration.[51]

In terms of the level of that frustration, there was a class split. Middle- and upper-class women had less respect for housework than working-class women. The former were more educated, and higher amounts of education typically resulted in more dislike of housework. In 1949, "a third of the 1934 graduates of the best women's colleges confessed to a feeling of stagnation and frustration in their lives."[52]

For working-class women, on the other hand, homemaking was "a respected role for women." Those who had jobs prior to marriage gave "no indication that the transition from work to housewifery entail[ed] any loss of prestige." And they enjoyed the work, finding it to be a source of good moods. They had high standards of cleanliness and were busy all day, every day. However, both white- and blue-collar women "preferred food preparation and supervision to home care."[53]

Working-class women were not as frustrated as college-educated women, as the latter had higher expectations of themselves in terms of being involved in hobbies, reading, formal dinners or nights out. Interestingly, the chief frustration for blue-collar women was not housework itself, but caring for young children without help, which was more of a problem for the least-educated women than for high school graduates—because their husbands gave them no help, unlike more educated men.[54]

Educated women wanted household help so they could pursue other activities, including work outside the home. Working women turned to outside services, a growing number of which in turn helped make it possible for more women to work. In the 1960s and early 1970s, families with working women spent more on services than those without.[55]

When they could, women continued to hire help. The head of a New York domestic help employment agency noted in 1955 that she was "overrun with requests." The records of the Johnson agency, also based in New York City, show that business was very good in the 1950s and 1960s. It had changed, however, from primarily full-time workers to primarily part-time workers.[56]

Figure 19. Abner Dean cartoon, 1955.

Workers preferred live-out work, and many liked the flexibility part-time work offered. Wages were relatively high, so fewer families could afford full-time help. The change affected the employer-employee relationship because part-time schedules entailed more negotiation than full-time. Negotiations meant that employers could not take workers for granted. And the relative scarcity of workers overall gave them a more equal footing in bargaining.

There was still a long way to go, however. These were just the beginnings of a more equitable relationship. The household worker role—paid or unpaid—still had very low prestige. As the 1960s progressed, more women were increasingly dissatisfied with their lot, stuck at home, many with now-empty nests, looking for meaning in their lives.[57]

The time was ripe for a catalyst, and Betty Friedan supplied it.

RECASTING HOUSEWORK

In 1955, Betty Friedan wrote in *Charm*, a mainstream women's magazine, about going back to work and hiring "a really good mother-substitute—a housekeeper-nurse." This was the culmination of her decade-long look at "the dynamics of discrimination against women in a variety of institutions, including the family."[58]

Friedan viewed housework as a sacrifice, something that kept her from her "real" life. From her educated middle-class perch, however, she had little for the "mother-substitute" who would enable her to pursue her own goals. Friedan also came from an industrial union background, and women factory workers had traditionally felt no solidarity with houseworkers. They viewed them as naive and sheltered. Indeed, YWCA officials had noted in the 1930s, "[a] preponderance of household workers in the Y.W.C.A. represents a threat to those doing recruiting for industrial workers."[59]

Friedan must have shared some of these sentiments. There was a double gulf between her and household workers—that of the middle-class to the working-class—but also between industrial and household labor. To Betty Friedan, work outside the home was worth more than work inside the home.

Friedan carried that outlook into her writing. Much of *The Feminine Mystique* (1963) was an attack on housework as stifling. This was a necessary phase in the development of feminism. In the short term, however, that attack perpetuated a disregard and disdain for paid household help— based on a fear of being stuck doing housework—and in fact amplified it. If there was no value in the work being done, why should the worker be treated well?

But Friedan struck a chord with other women of her class. Starting in the early 1960s, women began to question their social role. One author wrote,

> Not long after she masters the Three R's, the average American girl learns to think one way and to act another in the presence of a man. If she tends to like books and to think for herself, she soon learns to cloak her personality in the garb of a clinging vine.
>
> Sooner or later, she acquires a husband (the purpose of the disguise, after all, is to please and attract a man) and maybe she lives happily every after. Or perhaps, three children later, she begins to wonder if she has become a chauffeur and a household drudge and she casts about for some form of creative self-expression.[60]

Not surprisingly, psychologists found that women, especially those who were college educated, wanted a more active role for themselves. They wanted to work outside the homes and be successful mothers. They wanted an equal role in family decision-making. But they believed society, and their husbands, wanted them to be passive.

As a result, said sociologist Dr. Anne Steinmann, "Today, women's creative work must be done outside the home, making it difficult to combine their need for self-realization with their roles as wives and mothers. . . . Whenever you educate women, you get this problem of conflict."[61]

And yet more education seemed to be the answer for "bored housewives." In the mid-1960s, a group of California women who felt "displaced by automation" created Every Woman's Village, a cooperative "university" that within two years became a school of 800 with 55 faculty members.[62]

Education also influenced women's employment choices. College-educated or politically active women like Ruth Friedman, a committed leftist in the 40s, found it hard to stay at home.

> There was no discussion about which one of us would go on for further education. It was just taken for granted that it would be Ben—taken for granted by both of us. It wasn't until some time around the late fifties that I began to feel unhappy about being at home alone with the kids and seeing that Ben was advancing himself intellectually and in every way. He was *out there* and I was *in here*. . . . I started to think about going back to work.[63]

Experts felt that the housewife needed to be trained in how to make her work more enjoyable. This was an extension of the scientific housekeeping movement, which had inspired so many training classes and attempts at reform for paid household service. As there grew to be fewer and fewer servants upon which to practice, the housewife herself became the focus of reform efforts and study.[64]

Now appliances became villains. Dr. Roger Revelle, Director of Harvard University's Center for Population Studies told a Senate subcommittee, "One of the lost souls in our modern technological society is our American woman." Appliances made it possible for her to do her housework by herself, which made her the "loneliest, hardest-working" woman ever. With little relief available, middle-class women's frustration was coming to a head. The women's movement was being born. Another strand in its formation was the increase in the number of women working outside the home.[65]

By 1950, economic necessity and a desire for self-expression led 30 percent of American women to work outside the home, up from 25 percent in 1940. This included 28 percent of those who were married with children. The numbers kept rising. By 1960, over one-third of all women and almost that many married women worked outside the home. And in

1970, 40 percent of all women, married included, were employed. The trend continued. Fifty-five percent of American women were in the labor force in 1986. New York experienced similar growth.[66]

Women who worked outside the home in the mid-1950's, no matter their reasons, were a threat to housewives' status. Authors like Charlotte Adams (who in 1953 published *Housekeeping After Office Hours: A Homemaking Guide for the Working Woman*) were careful to stress that they "considered full-time housewives bona fide working women. They just don't get paid." The conflict between two camps of women (those who valued housework and those who did not) emerged in the women's movement, as women attempted to bring value to all their roles.[67]

WOMEN'S LIBERATION AND NEW RESPECT FOR HOUSEWORK

Someone who would not have described herself as a feminist, Clare Booth Luce, fired one of the first salvos in defense of housework's value. In 1967, she said that divorcing women deserved not alimony but severance pay. She placed the annual value of housekeeping at $10,000, an income made by the top 20 percent of households. Luce and Betty Friedan debated "full equality between the sexes," with Luce saying that there should be equal pay for equal work, and that "a vast amount of menial and routine work must be done daily or civilization would cease to function." Friedan responded, "Postpone marriage . . . or childbearing until you have established yourself in your career and are able to pay for domestic help."[68]

Their debate encapsulated a divide among women on the best way to increase women's status. On the one hand, Friedan thought housework dragged women down. Luce, however, wanted to raise the status of housework itself. Both views benefited domestic workers. To career women, household help was valuable. That value gave domestics leverage in their relationships with employers. To housewives, it was important to raise the status of housework. This in turn also positively affected paid houseworkers.

One optimistic observer wrote in 1964: "[T]he status of housework has been raised, owing to the vast improvement in home appliances and packaged services, as well as to the resulting performance of such work by middle-class wives, however unwillingly." This point of view, echoed by others, complemented Luce's argument that housework was economically valuable.[69]

The trickledown effect on domestics was reflected in books like *The Well Organized Woman* (1971), one of many such written in the late 1960s and early 1970s. The author, a Frenchwoman named Christiane Collange, advised running the home on business principles. This suggestion had roots in the early days of the domestic science movement. Collange believed it was a way to gain more respect for the home and its activities. She added some words for employers of domestic servants:

> [T]ake the trouble to follow [your maid's] suggestions and be interested in her techniques. . . . Nothing is more discouraging to the employee who is submitted to this regimentation than to feel herself relegated to the position of an instrument of execution, unable to make any suggestions about her work routine. She feels dehumanized.

Working women, Collange wrote, were more likely to leave the worker to her own devices. "Besides," she added,

> working women are much more aware of the service being performed than the wife who stays home all day. Who gives them the opportunity to collapse when they get back from the office and mutter, 'I'm absolutely dead. I can't lift a finger!' The maid![70]

Indeed, the increase in the number of working women had an effect on employers' relationships with their cleaning ladies. Workers vastly preferred to work for women employed outside the home both because there was little direct supervision, and because working women realized they were receiving a valuable service. As elderly black domestic Hannah Nelson said, "If these women did their own work, they would think just like I do—about this, anyway."[71]

She was right. Not until the 1960s, after housewives began to have their own existential crisis about housekeeping, did they really begin to look at the nature of housework and of what they asked servants to do. Workers contributed their share, using the leverage given to them by the very real shortage of workers. They were able to demand better treatment, and for the first time, the woman of the house could understand their feelings of oppression. The personal became the political—and as mores changed, women were face to face with political reality in their own homes.[72]

For example, Joan Davison, a housewife who was in her early 30s in the early 1960s, pondered the nature of housework. She concluded, "[I]t is not work, it's labor, and labor is not valued. Labor is menial, manual. You do it with your hands, not your head or your heart."[73]

No matter how it was dressed up, agreed feminist Pat Mainardi in 1972, housework still stank.[74]

Unlike Betty Friedan, Davison did not evade housework. Years later, she wrote, "Gradually, like so many of my contemporaries, I started to internalize the role of the servants I rejected, becoming simultaneously the demanding mistress who gave orders and the critical subordinate who resisted them, griping." It was self-awareness like this that paved the way to better employer-employee relationships.[75]

Faith Merrill, a professor of pediatrics, said of her life in the 1950s,

> I was never very interested in being a perfect little housewife—cleaning a house is my idea of nothing to do. . . .
>
>   I thought this job [in a nearby hospital's pediatrics department] might be fun to try. And it turned out to be great fun. By this time I'd hired a woman who came to my house every day and ended up being with me for twenty-four years. That made all the difference. No matter how helpful my husband was willing to be, and he was very helpful, if I hadn't had the security of knowing I had this surrogate at home, I couldn't have done what I did.[76]

This is not to say that housework itself was valued as highly as it could be. As Arlie Hochschild remarked in *The Second Shift* (1989), "[W]omen end up doing the second shift when the second shift is secondary. The more important cost to women is not that they work the extra month a year; it is that society devalues the work of the home and sees women as inferior because they do devalued work."[77]

In the 1970s, Joann Vanek found that women did housework in a time-consuming and ostentatious manner—on the weekends—to prove the work's value. She quoted S. Ferge, a Hungarian sociologist: "The results of housework . . . are accepted as natural and are only noticed when they are absent. It is therefore the work itself whose existence must be felt and acknowledged: working long hours and working on Sunday can serve to demonstrate this." To this end, women in the paid labor force hired no more help than women who did not have jobs.[78]

The value of housework remained a conundrum. Value it too highly, and one had to pay help so much that it became unaffordable. Value it too little, and abuse of domestic workers blossomed.

Even with the increasing perceived value of housework, household helpers were not uniformly respected. Amy Vanderbilt, who assumed her readers might be lucky enough to have household help, reflected the growing democratization with this comment: "In very formal households Mona [the maid] will call [a guest] 'Madam' or 'Ma'am' rather than Mrs. Johanson, but it is increasingly acceptable for household employees to use such titles with their employers and with guests." For hidebound traditionalists, the familiarity of using someone's *last* name was quite a step forward. And Vanderbilt did not respect workers. In an example of a reference letter, her pseudonym for the maid was "Hilde Dummkopf."[79]

Feminists' discomfort with having household help was more reflective of social change. They were now leery of subjugating anyone. Carolyn Reed, who in 1971 founded a domestic workers organization, Household Technicians of America, noticed this phenomenon.

> One of the things I encountered when I first began being involved with some of the feminist groups was that they acted like their attitude about housework was the meaning it had to have. . . . I remember that the Household Technicians were doing a party for Gloria Steinem, over on the West Side. . . . We were paid quite well, a professional fee, to cater the party. We had on black uniforms, and it freaked out some of the feminist women there. They could not deal with it. They said, 'Poor maids—they got maids here, we're leaving.'
>
> I remember having to get up and say to them, 'Hold it, cool it! First of all, I don't like you to think we're *maids*—we are household technicians; we're experienced; we are professionals. And we're being paid—that's very important. We need money, we're being paid, and we're going to be respected—so you have to get it out of your head that this is a demeaning job. If you' don't want to do it, I'm glad that you don't want to, because we will gladly do it for you—but for a salary, and with respect; the same as other people get—as a job, as a profession.' Most of my efforts have been getting that into people's heads. And I explained to them that the uniform is the uniform of my profession. It's just like a doctor wearing his white coat. . . . And I said, "So I choose to wear my uniform. I'm not gonna ruin my clothes—you may spill something on me."
>
> There was a positive reaction. I think what my speech did was relieve people of their guilt feeling that, "Oh, gee, now I don't have to feel guilty. She's feeling okay about it, so now I don't have to feel guilty."[80]

A transformation had occurred. Rather than a symbol of subservience, the uniform became an emblem of self-respect and professionalism. In addition, the guilt and the resulting self-awareness helped correct the mistaken belief that service itself was demeaning. Workers themselves had always known that. The problem was not the work; it was the way household workers were treated. Even though Betty Friedan had not specifically set out to liberate household workers—in fact, she looked down on housework—the feminist movement she helped spark contributed to domestics' ability to decry their treatment and stick up for themselves.

Another sign of an evening of the scales was the change in workers' titles. In 1948, the most common designation was "maid, general." A.E. Johnson Agency records for the late 1950s show mostly cooks, waitresses, general houseworkers, and cleaners. The majority lived out, and many worked by the day or the week on a temporary basis. There were still chambermaids, parlormaids and ladies maids, but they worked only for the wealthiest families, and these classifications were fading out. The bulk of the Johnson Agency's clients were solidly middle and upper middle class people who could not afford large households and needed general-purpose workers.[81]

By the 1990s, specialization had largely died out and titles were geared away from those denoting or connoting servitude. There were no more servants or laundresses. The correct generic term was now "household help." There were two major divisions in the positions the Johnson Agency filled, sleep in or sleep out. Now there executive housekeepers and "beginning couples." Most placements were for couples; the woman did the cooking, cleaning and sometimes laundry, and the man served as a butler, did the driving, and might also do handyman and yard work. Some jobs specified things like "childcare will do some hsk," "straight laundry" or "no laundry," new definitions that resulted primarily from employees' wishes. Employers asked for what they knew they could get.[82]

The continued participation of women in the work force exerted its own kind of ameliorative effect. As one observer put it in the early 1990s, "[T]oday's employers may have less psychic need to exact the kind of deference and subordination from domestic workers that Phyllis Palmer describes as occurring in the interwar years; their outside work brings its own rewards and they may not see their identities as being so tightly bound up with domestic displays of privilege."[83]

Maids understood. Helen, the Davison's maid, said,

> She gets nervous of me, I know. She has all these good wishes for the whole world, and she wants to 'liberate' everyone so it's embarrassing when she has to stop and think about *me!* I'm not her slave, but I do a lot of her dirty work, and she knows it. But if I was in her shoes, I'd be doing what she does—I'd be hiring myself a maid or two and doing other things with my time.

Helen perceived herself as equal to her employer, and her employer at least struggled to feel the same.[84]

Mary Romero, in her discussion of Chicana domestics in Los Angeles, listed six ways they created a more positive working environment for themselves:

> (1) increasing opportunities for job flexibility; (2) increasing pay and benefits; (3) establishing and maintaining an informal contract specifying tasks; (4) minimizing contact with employers; (5) defining themselves as professional housekeepers; and (6) creating a small-business-like environment.[85]

These women redefined domestic work "as skilled labor," and as such, they negotiated for better conditions and more control over their work. Their leverage derived from their ability to pick and choose their employers, something that became easier as more workers were able to afford cars, or lived in metropolitan areas with good public transportation.[86]

The occupation therefore received more respect in the 1990s than in the 1920s as a result of a) workers' own rising self-respect, b) the leverage workers gained because of their relative scarcity, c) the increased appreciation working women had for household help, and d) employers' need to raise the status of housework for their *own* self-respect.

The change was not complete, of course. Barbara Bergmann has noted that the "low status of paid domestics has persisted, whatever the decline in class consciousness or feelings of race superiority." However, she has suggested, "a change in the status of housework may be in the offing. It is not uncommon now for college students to do housecleaning part time. The high status that college students expect to occupy in society may reduce any anxieties that they will lose face by performing housework."[87]

A more severe constraint on the progress made in the equalizing of the employer-employee relationship was racism.

In the early and mid-1970s, Robert Hamburger interviewed a dozen African-American household workers, most of whom still had to demand "that they be treated like human beings—not like machines, not like dogs, not like servants, but like *human beings*."[88]

It was not until African-American women were able to leave the occupation that the disrespect born of racism began to lift from the occupation.

Chapter Five
A New Landscape

Gustafsa Gustafson and Marta Byrne, emigrants from Sweden and Ireland, were typical new servants in 1920s New York. Virginia Johnson, an African-American migrant, represented the middle portion of the century, when immigration was restricted. Today, a West Indian immigrant like Beverly McDonald or a Latin American immigrant like Dina Aguirre is most likely to do housework.

This last shift in nationality and ethnicity was due to events in the 1960s.

By 1965, much had changed in American domestic service. The number of workers had sharply decreased, most had part-time schedules, and wages were at an all-time high. Employers had begun to realize that their employees were valuable and deserved respect.

New changes were about to occur, completing the restructuring of the occupation. It became an immigrant's job once again, as African-Americans left and were replaced. The 1964 Civil Rights Act and 1965 Immigration Act set these changes in motion. The first allowed African-Americans more job opportunities, so they could finally move out of domestic service. Then new immigrants arrived to participate in a field greatly changed from the last great immigration influx prior to World War I. It was again a stepping-stone occupation, from which people would move up the social ladder.

Legally protected by Social Security and newly valued, domestics could enjoy a more business-like relationship with employers. To be sure, abuses remained, especially for undocumented aliens. But for the most part, domestic service had moved from an employer-dominated structure to a negotiated relationship.

This shift happened first in New York City. Its liberal government made use of all available resources to train African Americans in new occupations, and its expanding 1960s economy absorbed those workers. The city was a magnet for immigrants as well. Immigration to the United States increased sharply from the late 1960s on, and an average of 15 percent of arrivals headed for New York (when the city's population was only three percent of the nation's total).[1]

ETHNIC AND OCCUPATIONAL PATTERNS BEFORE 1965

Immigration had always been a crucial source of domestic labor in the northern United States, especially New York. As sociologist Aaron Levenstein asserted, "The virtual disappearance of domestics in this country, which makes conversation under the beauty parlor dryers, is somehow believed to be evidence of a change in the American character. It is evidence principally of a change in our immigration laws. . . ." The 1920s immigration restrictions contributed to a shortage of servants. In the 1960s, a change in immigration laws helped bring about another shift in the composition of the domestic service occupation.[2]

Before World War I, Irish, the Germans and Scandinavian immigrants dominated domestic service in New York City. A few West Indian women came from British colonies like Barbados and Jamaica, under the parent country's quotas.[3]

Many European maids were able to use "this opportunity as a springboard to better things, from marriage to office work." For example, while 60 percent of first-generation Irish immigrant women worked as domestics in New York in 1900, only 17 percent of second-generation women did. There was a similar decline for Scandinavian women. As David Katzman noted, "it is certain that no foreign-born group had formed a permanent service class in American society."[4]

African-American women could not enjoy that claim. As part of the Great Migration north, African American women streamed into New York in the 1920s and 1930s in search of jobs. The point for them was to get to New York, even though they knew they would probably have to start out working as servants. In the South, there was no hope for mobility out of domestic service. In the North, however, they might be able to work in a laundry or a beauty parlor.[5]

A shortage of servants, real or imagined, created domestic jobs in New York for black women. In the 1920s, the "servant problem" was prominent on the editorial and news pages of *The New York Times*. Sympathetic to its affluent readers, the *Times* reported on attempts to bring in more European women who would work as maids. "But," asked the *Times'* editors, "is that where the chief trouble lies? Not in the view of the Department of Labor. According to its Bureau of Labor Statistics, the real difficulty seems to be that both native and foreign-born prefer other ways of making a living."[6]

Despite generous European quotas and New Yorkers' desire for European servants, then, supply did not match demand in New York. Black women were thus able to find employment, although sometimes with difficulty, because New Yorkers were prejudiced against them. Josephine Holmes, the Harlem YWCA's Employment Secretary, told the 1928 Conference on Employer-Employee Relationships in the Home, "[A]s much as 80% of our calls demand *light colored* girls with straight hair and the fact remains that practically 80% of our applicants are *not* light colored, but various shades of brown."[7]

Black women, then, had a hard time maintaining employment even in a low-status occupation like domestic service, and they were never more than about one-half of the servant population. And although their presence in a northern city like New York meant they were poised to take advantage of opportunities later in the century, things got more difficult first with the onset of the Depression. White women were laid off from clerical and factory positions; in 1936, over 50 percent of all women seeking work sought domestic service jobs. As a result, reported slave market investigators Marvel Cooke and Ella Baker, "[w]here once color was the 'gilt edged' security for obtaining domestic and personal service jobs, here, even, Negro women found themselves being displaced by whites." All this, she wrote, for a job in which a maid had "to scrub floors on her bended knees, to hang precariously from window sills, cleaning window after window, or to strain and sweat over steaming tubs of heavy blankets, spreads and furniture covers."[8]

The YWCA reported in 1931, "Until recently household employment offered the one sure type of work for Negroes . . . but . . . it looks now as if the term 'marginal worker' will soon be applicable to all types of labor in which Negroes are engaged."[9]

Despite economic hardship, maids asserted themselves. A male representative of the New York City Home Relief Bureau complained at a 1937 conference of the "serious shortage of trained domestic workers." His fellow panelists (all women) told him in no uncertain terms that there was a shortage only of servants who were willing to work long hours in bad conditions for very low pay. More and more women domestics wanted live-out or part-time work, especially black women, who often had their own families, unlike European immigrants who came over as single women. That way, they had more control over their time and situation.

Clearly, African-American women wanted to make their default occupation more bearable. That they disliked it became apparent during World War II, when New York's Negro women flooded into clerical and semi-skilled occupations that had opened up because men were in the armed forces and European immigration had dropped because of the fighting. Although black women were compelled in large part to remain in kitchens, dining rooms and laundry rooms, more and more of those were located in restaurants, hotels and other public places. And the few remaining maids could call more of their own shots.[10]

The change was equally profound for both white and black women, although the drop in the share of African-American women who worked as servants was more significant than the corresponding shift for white women. Psychologically, too, the changes were most dramatic for African-American women. Fanny Christina Hill, who moved from domestic work in Texas to a job in a Los Angeles aircraft factory, said, "[The war] made me live better. . . . We always say that Lincoln took the bale off the Negroes. . . . Well, my sister always said, 'Hitler was the one that got us out of the white folks' kitchen.'"[11]

In 1940, two-thirds of employed New York African-American women worked in domestic service. In 1947, the proportion had dropped to one-third. New York State had fair employment laws, and so more black women there were also able to take jobs in plants with federal contracts and in clothing factories. All received higher wages than before the war, even those who remained in domestic service. They moved into semi-skilled jobs in manufacturing and laundries and into clerical positions.

Nationally, the percentage of black women in domestic service dropped, too, from 57 percent in 1940 to 43.7 percent in 1944. This was despite the Urban League's Vocational Opportunity Campaign (founded 1930) findings in 1943 that black women were not being hired "to the extent necessary and possible" in defense work. Even after the Fair Employment Practices Committee was established, the United States Employment Office was sometimes guilty of referring African-American women to domestic jobs instead of factory work.[12]

In fact, nationwide, there were 50,000 more African-American servants after the war than before, but they were a smaller proportion of all African-American women workers because of the gains in other occupations. In 1947, only 44.5 percent of employed black women were working as domestics, or a total of 928,270 out of 2,086,000 (400,000 more than in 1940). Still, "domestic service became more racially polarized as the black share of all female household employees increased from 46.6 to 60.9 percent." So even though African-American women's labor force participation changed for the better, the structure of the occupation was irrevocably altered. This, along with the new confidence black women as a whole gained from other new opportunities would increase tensions in the home as domestics chafed in their role.[13]

Figure 20. April 1943. Farm Security Administration—Office of War Information Photograph Collection. Library of Congress Prints and Photographs Division Washington, DC.

Because of layoffs of women immediately following the war, there was a surge in the number of available domestics in the first postwar years. Prices in general remained high, however, so many potential employers either did without maids or hired them on a part-time basis where before the war they would have had full-time servants. Some black women had been able to retain or return to their wartime jobs, although as a group they could not yet move out of domestic service altogether. Buoyed by their wartime experiences, black women refused to move back into their employers' homes. Therefore, when housewives and working mothers looked up a few years later and wanted old-style servants, the pool of willing full-time and/ or live-in servants in the New York area had shrunk. Some European refugees became domestics, but the Puerto Ricans who had been flowing into New York worked, by and large, in the needle trades, not as domestics.[14]

For them, and for other women, other occupations beckoned, making permanent the changes that World War II wrought. In both New York City and the nation, the amount of household help shrank. Almost one-third of all U.S. private household workers left the occupation between 1940 and

1950. While one-tenth of New York women were servants in 1940, only three percent were in 1950, and the national proportion of female workers in the field dropped sharply to 8.4 percent, a decline of more than half.[15]

By 1960, although the supply of American household employees had risen by 500,000, New York City's count fell by over 10,000. The national increase was due primarily to an influx of Mexicans in the Southwest, while New York still depended on other immigrant groups and African-American migrants from the South.[16]

The decennial increase in the national supply was also an anomaly; the downward trend in the number of domestics continued after 1960. By 1970, only five percent of employed American women were private household workers, and New York City had an even lower ratio, four percent, proportions that persisted in declining despite the migration of workers from the Caribbean and Latin America into household jobs.[17]

African-American women remained visibly dominant in the occupation. Nationally, there were now more black domestic workers than white, although the New York proportion remained about 50–50. This shift was important in light of other social changes. First, the civil rights movement was beginning and with it a growing resentment of discriminatory behavior of the kind that kept African-American women in domestic service jobs. Second, as Phyllis Palmer put it,

> [t]he changing racial composition of domestic workers occurred simultaneously with changing notions of what housework was and how it should be performed. White women sought to make housework a fulfilling position for the unpaid wife-manager, while black women sought to make it a respectable job for women workers.[18]

Because black women had so little occupational choice, the tension between these two goals did not resolve for years, if indeed it has. In 1960, black women were still more than four times more likely to be domestic servants than their share of the work force warranted. And they comprised a larger ratio of female private household workers in New York City than ever before, almost 60 percent, even though African Americans comprised only 10 percent of the city's population.[19]

The two goals of making housework fulfilling and a respectable job did mesh to a certain extent and improve the occupation, in part because the "servant shortage" continued. For example, in 1962, *The New York Times* reported on "nanny-napping" in Central Park, in which mothers offered nannies higher salaries to persuade them to leave their current job and work for them. One woman reported, "The only sure way to keep

Table 20. Private Household Workers, New York City, 1920–1990

Year	Total	Private Household Workers	
		All Employed Women	As percent of all employed women
1920	692	85	12
1930	863	161	19
1940	875	116	13
1950	1,074	75	7
1960	1,205	62	5
1970	1,293	38	3
1980	1,385	24	2
1990	1,546	23	1

Source: United States Department of Commerce, Bureau of the Census, *Decennial Census of the Population*, 1920–1990.

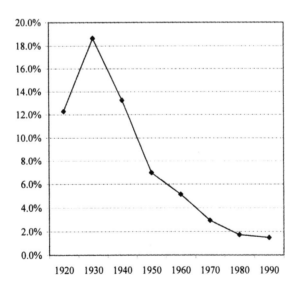

Chart 7. Private Household Workers, New York City, 1920–1990

Table 21. Ethnic Distribution of Private Household Workers, New York City, 19020–1990 (by Number)

Year	Total	White	Non-White*	Asian	Hispanic
1920	85	60%	40%		
1930	161	60%	40%		
1940	116	57%	43%		
1950	75	44%	56%		
1960	62	42%	58%		
1970	38	35%	65%		1%
1980	24	20%	61%	2.5%	16%
1990	23	**	**	**	**

Sources: Historical Statistics of the U.S., Colonial Times to 1970, Part 1, Series D182–232 (U.S. Dept. of Commerce, Bureau of The Census, 1975): 132; Decennial Census of the Population, 1920–1990.

* Nonwhite includes Asian and Hispanic until 1970. It includes Afro-Caribbeans in all years.

** Similar to 1980 distribution, but with a higher Hispanic percentage.

your nanny from being stolen is to take your child to the park yourself, and keep the nanny at home." This was only the visible sign of a shortage of household help (nannies were some of the few servants who went out of the house and were available for "napping"). And despite efforts by employment agencies to recruit foreign maids, sometimes so strenuous as to be illegal, only about 2,500 entered the U.S. in 1964. Black women, therefore, continued to benefit from generally decreased European immigration, at least as far as maintaining employment as maids and having somewhat improved wages and job conditions.[20]

ATTEMPTS TO IMPORT SERVANTS

Between 1920 and 1970, a period of reduced immigration, New Yorkers tried to bring in foreign maids, preferring them to African Americans. European immigrants, particularly the Irish, Germans and Scandinavians, had been a traditional source of domestic labor before World War I. Employers had mocked them, but when their ranks dwindled, all their faults seemed minor in the face of the available replacements. Their primary virtue was that they were white. Some New Yorkers, like Mrs. Louis A. Jaffer of Cedarhurst, L.I., felt that only "healthy women of the white race" could maintain the "real home life and atmosphere among the great majority of our people."[21]

Immigrants were also less demanding than African-Americans. The latter insisted on working shorter hours and living in their own homes, which employers found inconvenient and detrimental to their standards of living. "I still do not quite see how it would be possible to keep the true spirit of the home and still have perfectly standardized working hours for the maid," said one woman in 1928. "The members of the household who are working on schedule surely need the relaxation that comes from lack of schedule pressure when they get home." Immigrant women were more likely to accommodate employers' desires, i.e. live in and be on call.[22]

But the Depression and World War II had sharply reduced immigration. The total number of servants in New York City and the United States declined after peaking in 1930. After the war, as African-American women continued to live out, employers hoped for renewed immigration.

The 1948 Displaced Persons Act and its 1950 amendment allowed in 400,000 war victims. The bracero program, which admitted farm workers to the Southwest on a temporary basis, was enacted in 1951. The 1952 McCarran-Walter Immigration and Nationality Act reaffirmed, over President Truman's veto, the national origins quotas established in 1924. In 1953, the Refugee Relief Act permitted entry to another 214,000 newcomers. With the exception of special relief acts to admit post-Mao Chinese and Hungarians fleeing after 1956, the immigration front was quiet until 1965, when the Hart-Celler Act was signed into law. Another period of relative inactivity followed until 1980, when more refugees were allowed in the country. In 1986, Congress passed the Simpson-Mazzoli Immigration Reform and Control Act, which attempted to curb illegal immigration by providing amnesty for pre-1982 arrivals and forcing employers to police citizenship. The 1990 Immigration Act continued the welcoming trend, but the 1996 Act moved to make immigration harder, particularly illegal immigration.[23]

Prior to 1965, no law had a positive effect on the number of immigrants willing to be household workers. As a result, after World War II a shortage of workers endured. Housewives tried to cope in several ways. They cut the hours for which they sought help; they raised wages; they took on more household tasks themselves; they used more appliances and other conveniences. Still, even after the war, they could not get the numbers or kinds of workers they wanted.

During the 1950s, the burgeoning economy and fledgling civil rights movement enabled some black women to leave private household domestic work. Especially in a city like New York, African-American women moved into non-household service jobs as office building cleaners. There was also such a need for workers that companies began to hire black women for non-public-facing clerical positions. All of this reduced the ranks of servants.[24]

With employment and government agencies working on their behalf, women tried to hire young workers from the American South and from Latin and South American countries who were not subject to immigration laws. They would also, employers hoped, be docile, working long hours for low wages.

In 1948, the New York State Department of Labor, working with its Puerto Rican counterpart, brought up 30 Puerto Rican women between the ages of 18 and 35 to take part in a three-month domestic service training and placement program. Later that year, a Florida agency flew a planeload of housemaids from St. Thomas (U.S. Virgin Islands) to the mainland. Both these groups had the appealing characteristic of U.S. citizenship, which meant they were not subject to Labor Department certification or quotas.[25]

Puerto Ricans did not take to domestic service, however, and instead gravitated to the needle trades, which gave them more personal freedom. Nor was the U.S. Virgin Islands' population large enough to satisfy demands.[26]

The 1948 Displaced Persons Act raised hope and provided some workers. However, it provided only a trickle of a supply of domestics. In fact, in 1946, while the exact numbers were still being worked out, former New York City Mayor Fiorello LaGuardia (now head of the United Nations Relief and Rehabilitation Administration) urged Congress to triple the number of admissions from 50,000, saying, "We can employ [that number] as housemaids in New York City alone."[27]

The enactment of the 1952 immigration law offered employers a way to bring in domestic help, but it reaffirmed the quota system and allowed domestics entry only for a year. Employers could sponsor an alien employee outside quotas and preferences for that period of time, but since the workers presumably did not meet permanent immigration criteria (skill set and/or quota inclusion), the law did not allow them to stay permanently. The quota system and the preference it gave to highly skilled immigrants made it nearly impossible to bring in even Southern European maids.[28]

Around the country, there were various efforts to bring in foreign workers and get around immigration restrictions. In 1953, El Paso, Texas housewives formed the Committee for Legalized Domestics. They wanted to have the informal shopping pass system formalized, so domestics from Juarez, Mexico could work in specific U.S. neighborhoods. These employers also wanted formalized contracts so that sponsored maids could not leave their employ after immigrating permanently.[29]

Southern African Americans were a potential alternative to Europeans. Yet problems arose here, too, because agencies looking for live-in workers preyed upon naive teenagers. In 1957, one 14-year-old African-American girl came from Georgia to Long Island through the offices of the Gem Agency of Roslyn and Great Neck. Upon her arrival with two other girls, she was told she would have to pay the agency $47 out of her expected $60 earnings (for two weeks' work). Though the girl was the wronged party, because she was a minor alone, she was arrested as a juvenile delinquent after "her second employer within a week called the police to report that the agency had sent a minor for a domestic job."[30]

Despite a 1958 law preventing such activity, the agencies defrauded workers in other ways, including "seizure of the worker's luggage; billing her illegally for food, lodging and other services required by law to be provided by the agency, and providing inadequate food and lodging." All of this discouraged Southern migration to New York.[31]

Even the importation of servants under the one-year contracts allowed by law did not work well because there were unscrupulous employers. As with African Americans, minors came from Europe and were arrested as juvenile delinquents. The number of incidents was large enough that the home countries of foreign servants expressed alarm at their citizens' working conditions.[32]

In the absence of European workers, agencies then turned to a new source of labor—South American immigrants. Open immigration was still allowed for Western Hemisphere countries, and enterprising agencies and employers took advantage of this. Intercontinental Maid Service, Ltd., based in Hartsdale, New York, brought about 500 young women, mostly Colombian, to the eastern United States between September 1961 and March 1962. According to the agency's lawyer, "all the women were of a 'high type' and wanted to see the United States even if it meant working as housemaids, although they had worked in shops and offices at home."

> The agency, he continued, taught English to the women, paid their air fares and passport costs, provided life and health insurance and guaranteed return fare after one year. The women, he said, posted $400 performance bonds and signed contracts to work here for $65 to $85 a month to be paid by the agency, which would collect from home owners under separate contracts.

This scheme failed, too. Several employers characterized the arrangement as indentured slavery and refused to pay off their contracts. In addition, some workers complained to the Colombian counsel. The Immigration and Naturalization Service, the Federal Bureau of Investigation, the New York State Labor Department and the Colombian government all investigated the agency and concluded that they were breaking no laws, except for failing to register as a "mass employer of labor to be exported." But Jerome Lefkowitz, New York State's Attorney General, believed that the agency had violated minimum wage laws by paying the workers only $70 monthly instead of $85 a week. On that basis, he succeeded in obtaining an order dissolving the agency.[33]

Ambivalence reigned: customers were ready to take advantage of the chance to hire live-in workers, and they were not overly scrupulous about how they treated their workers. As many as 20,000 women came to New York each year to be maids. Agencies promised them work, but "[o]n some days as many as ten girls [were] left stranded when the jobs fail[ed] to produce the high pay and easy life that had been promised." Indeed, New York State had partly acceded to housewives' desires by allowing agencies to charge a premium for live-in workers and to advance transportation costs to the workers.[34]

The one-year domestic contract system persisted into the 1960s, and by the middle of the decade, employers had found ways to exploit it. In just one example, Mrs. Bernard H. Cole of Newton Center, Massachusetts put in 5 or 6 applications for alien employment certification for domestics "to help the aliens and her friends who needed domestic help." One Jamaican woman, Mrs. Tucker, came to the U.S. in December 1966 on the basis of a June certification, and when she arrived at Mrs. Cole's door to take up her $45 a week job was told "that she had a girl from Haiti and did not have any immediate use for the respondent's services. The respondent declared that Mrs. Cole said she could possibly place the respondent in the home of a friend of hers at a salary of $15 per week." Not surprisingly, Mrs. Tucker looked for another job and found one as a sewing machine operator in Boston for $70 a week. In April of 1967, she was deported because she had not entered the country with the correct certification.[35]

Housewives still wanted household help on their own terms, unwilling to accept that the new relationship with their help must be a two-way street. The women's movement, as discussed in the previous chapter, was pivotal in improving employers' view of their workers. Servants also took action.

CIVIL RIGHTS AND MOVEMENT OUT OF DOMESTIC SERVICE

While housewives were floundering, trying to bring in white workers, African-American women were preparing to leave the occupation. Especially in a city like New York, where in the 1950s the financial sector was booming and office buildings were filling, more and more African-American women became office cleaners, and some were able to fill back-office clerical jobs. These may not have been the biggest steps, but they took black women away from close, one-on-one supervision, and in some cases put them in unions where they had control over their wages, hours and working conditions.

Black women also benefited somewhat from improved education levels and from legislation such as the Manpower Development and Training Act (MDTA), passed in 1962. Three years later, over 300,000 men and women nationally had prepared for new vocations under the MDTA. From 1963 to 1972, over 37,000 young men and women, two-thirds of them non-white, completed programs in New York City's five MDTA-funded Job Skills Centers. Women learned clerical skills or got licensed practical nurse training. In addition to the Job Skills Centers, New York City during the 1960s had a mix of public and private job-training initiatives, including those of Job Opportunity in Neighborhoods, Harlem Youth Opportunities Unlimited— Associated Community Teams (HARYOU-ACT), Mobilization for Youth, the Job Corps, and the Neighborhood Youth Corps. They received federal, state and city funding. Mayor Robert F. Wagner wanted the programs to help eliminate poverty by training participants in skills that would be marketable then and in the future.[36]

While they were helping minorities to learn job skills, New York City's administrations also expressed support for civil rights. The New York City Commission on Human Rights (CCHR) began in 1955 as the Committee on Intergroup Relations; the city renamed it in 1963. That same year, the CCHR established a Business Employment Division to "break down barriers in the employment of Negroes and members of other minorities in industries holding contracts with the city," an area in which the city had great influence, if not control. The CCHR also vigorously supported the Civil Rights Act of 1964.[37]

The city's 1962 minimum wage law was expected to benefit mostly African-Americans. Four years later, more domestics became eligible for unemployment insurance when New York State changed its law to cover full-time domestics who worked alone and earned at least $500 a quarter. Previously, only households that employed four or more domestics had been liable for the tax. The law rewarded stability and good working conditions: families who went through several domestics a year would pay higher taxes than those who kept the same maid for years. The law affected about 21,000 New York State employers, most of them in the New York City metropolitan area.[38]

Praise for the city's efforts was not unanimous. Black labor leader A. Philip Randolph took issue with the minimum wage floor of $1.25 proposed in 1962; he was chairman of the Citizen's Committee for a $1.50 Minimum Wage. It was only after the city added a provision for a raise to $1.50 after one year that the National Association for the Advancement of Colored People (NAACP) supported the bill. Mayor Robert F. Wagner received a verbal thrashing in 1964 from Isiah Brunson, chairman of the Brooklyn Congress on Racial Equality (CORE), for the "lip service" he gave to the needs and rights of blacks in New York City.[39]

That same year, Brunson and CORE were involved in a fight specifically concerning domestics. Representatives of Local 1412 of the American Federation of State, County and Municipal Employes (AFSCME), in cooperation with the NAACP and CORE, forced the Great Neck, NY state employment office to treat job seekers with more respect. As a result, the head of employment division ordered that the office open an hour earlier, that extra seating be provided, and "that it be made clear to [job seekers] that they might remain at the office all day if they wished."[40]

Black women were less and less happy working as domestics. They knew employers were prejudiced against them. Between 1950 and 1963, although only a quarter or fewer employers specified a racial or ethnic preference in their want ads, 95 percent of those who did wanted white workers. Among domestics who placed "situation wanted" ads, black women increasingly refrained from specifying their race. By 1963, only one percent identified themselves as "colored."

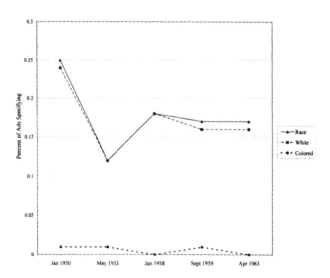

Chart 8. Help Wanted Advertisements, The New York Times, 1950–1963

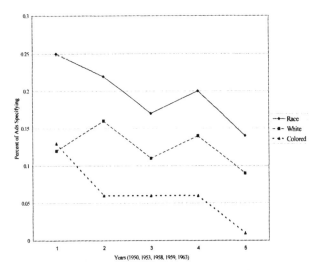

Chart 9. Situations Wanted Advertisements, The New York Times, 1950–1963

Maggie Holmes, a domestic in Chicago, went to one job and asked where the mop was.

> She say she don't have no mop. I said "Don't tell me you mop the floor on your knees. I know you don't." They usually hide these mops in the clothes closet. I go out behind all these clothes and get the mop out. (Laughs.) They don't get on their knees, but they don't think nothin' about askin' a black woman. She says, "All you—you girls . . ." She stop. I say, "All you *niggers,* is that you want to say?" She give me this stupid look. I say, "I'm glad you tellin' me that there's more like me." (Laughs.) I told her, "You better give me my money and let me go, 'cause I'm gettin' angry." So I made her give me my carfare and what I had worked that day.[41]

In 1970, a black teacher's aide in New York City decided to look for summer work as a domestic. She said that her experience was no different than in 1958, when she had been "lured" to New York with the promise of "$50 a week with your own room and TV." In the agency office,

> Well-married white women were walking up and down looking at all of us trying to choose. It was like a slave market, and they said things like, 'She can't speak proper English. I don't want her around my chil-dren,' and 'She's too dirty. I don't want her in my home.'[42]

The seeds were there for change. In seeming accord with the city's training efforts, the economy was expanding. The U.S. Labor Department noted in 1965 that service jobs outside the home "had been growing at three times the pace of total employment in the last 10 years." It expected that the largest growth in the labor force would come from women. As a measure of the change in women's employment, in the 1920s, the ratio of jobs advertised in *The New York Times* for men to women was about 3 or 4 to 1. In the 1960s, it was about 1.5:1. And where household employment was the first part of the classified section in the 1920s, by the 1960s it was at the end of the section. [43]

So although New York City lost 76,000 manufacturing jobs between 1960 and 1965, other sectors of its economy (financial and other services) were growing enough to absorb new workers.[44]

But African American women were still largely trapped in domestic work. That changed as a result of legislation. Through peaceful and violent demonstrations, African Americans forced federal, state and local governments to deal both with ending discrimination in higher-wage fields and with training blacks for jobs in those fields. Two acts—the Civil Rights Act, signed in July 1964 and the Economic Opportunity Act, signed in August 1964—created more opportunities for black women.[45]

The results were impressive and almost immediate. The number of black women working as domestics in the U.S. dropped over one-third from 1964 to 1970, while those in other fields rose by over one-fifth (see Table 22). In absolute numbers, more black women now worked in other fields than had left domestic service. An expanding economy provided room for black women to get better jobs.[46]

For African-American women above a certain age, the change came too late. In pre-civil rights Alabama, Grady Hutchinson, although bright enough to finish high school at age 16, had been unable to attend college. She moved to New York City, where she worked as a maid and housekeeper. Although she was unable to realize her ambitions, Grady had the satisfaction of seeing all her children get an education and jobs in a bank, a hospital and the New York City subway system.[47]

Even more dramatic were the changes when charted to 1974 (Table 23). Between 1962 and 1974, the number of blacks in domestic service plunged 55 percent, while the number of clerical workers rose 177 percent. Non-private household service workers, the one occupation in which African-Americans were already represented, rose 45 percent.[48]

In the years since 1974, the situation changed even more markedly for African-American women. By way of comparison, in 1960, almost 40 percent of employed black women nationwide were domestic workers. That

Table 22. Occupation of Employed Women by Race, 1964, 1970 (as percent of employed women), United States

	1964		1970	
	Black	White	Black	White
White collar workers	23	61	38	64
Professional & technical	8	14	11	15
Teachers, except college	5	6	5	6
Managers & administrative	2	5	3	5
Sales workers	2	8	3	8
Clerical workers	11	34	21	36
Blue collar workers	15	17	19	16
Service workers	56	19	43	19
Private household	33	5	18	3
Farm workers	6	3	2	2

Source: La Frances Rodgers-Rose, "Some Demographic Characteristics of the Black Woman: 1940 to 1975," in *The Black Woman*, La Frances Rodgers-Rose, ed. (Beverly Hills: Sage Publications, 1980): 34. Used with permission.

proportion dropped to 19.5 percent in 1970, 10 percent in 1977, and one percent in 1990. Many of those were there by choice; some may have been counted as business owners. For example, one Manhattan woman, fed up with the treatment she received as a legal secretary, took her severance pay and bought a red wagon, some sturdy clothes, and cleaning supplies and started her own cleaning business. Three years later, she had two people working for her and was planning to expand. An African American, she was performing housework, but her relationship with employers was business-like. She was on equal terms with them.[49]

IMMIGRATION LEGISLATION AND A REPLACEMENT LABOR FORCE

The same liberal spirit that prompted the passage of the Civil Rights Act also fueled the passage of the 1965 Immigration Act. Congress intended

Table 23. Occupational Distribution of Employed Black Persons, 1962 and 1974, United States (numbers in thousands)

Occupational Group	Employed blacks				Blacks as percent of all employed	
	1962	1974	Change 1962–1974		1962	1974
			Number	Percent		
All employed	7,132	9,315	2,183	30.6	10.4	10.8
Professional	382	970	588	153.9	4.7	7.9
Managerial	184	380	196	106.5	2.5	4.2
Sales	115	214	99	86.1	2.6	4.0
Clerical	509	1,414	905	177.8	5.1	9.4
Craft workers	443	874	431	97.3	5.1	7.6
Operatives	1,430	2,041	611	42.7	11.8	14.7
Nonfarm laborers	950	832	-118	-12.4	26.8	19.0
Farmers and farm managers	194	64	-130	-67.0	7.5	3.9
Farm laborers	580	190	-390	-67.2	25.3	13.5
Service workers, except private household	1,284	1,863	579	45.1	19.8	18.4
Private household	1,062	474	-588	-55.4	44.3	38.5

Source: Stuart H. Garfinkle, "Occupations of Women and Black Workers, 1962–74," *Monthly Labor Review* (November, 1975): 27.

at least in part to open immigration to more people of color—or at least non-northern Europeans. The law also increased the number of immigrants overall, creating a labor pool to take the vacated places of African-American women domestics.

The Hart-Celler Immigration Act of 1965 ended the Asia-Pacific Triangle immigration exclusions and established a set of entry preferences based on family ties and occupational skills. It lowered European quotas. Although the quotas it imposed for the first time on the Western Hemisphere worked to the disadvantage of most Latin and South American countries—thereby

Table 24. Visa Preference System (1965 Immigration Law)

Preference	Description	Percent of available visas
First	Unmarried adult sons and daughters of U.S. citizens	20
Second	Spouses and unmarried sons and daughters of permanent resident aliens	26
Third	Members of the professions, scientists, and artists of exceptional ability, and their spouses and children	10
Fourth	Married sons and daughters of U.S. citizens, and their spouses and children	10
Fifth	Brothers and sisters of U.S. citizens, and their spouses and children	24
Sixth	Skilled and unskilled workers in occupations for which labor is in short supply in this country, and their spouses and children	10
Seventh (non-preference)	Open to immigrants not entitled to visas under any of the other six preferences (inactive 1978-1986)	Numbers vary by year

Source: Elizabeth Bogen, *Immigration in New York* (New York: Praeger, 1987): 28.

increasing the number of illegal aliens from them—the newly independent West Indian countries benefited from quotas of their own.[50]

Under the new law's provisions, domestics could enter permanently and apply for citizenship in five years. They could presumably be admitted under the sixth preference (see Table 24).[51]

African-American women played a role in the debate on immigration legislation. Because no one realized the effect the Civil Rights Act would have, legislators and witnesses assumed domestic service still belonged to black women. Legislators debated the wisdom of letting in unskilled foreign domestics. Lawmakers and their constituents worried that immigrants would take household jobs for less money than African Americans and thus cause unemployment.[52]

This was why Myra C. Hacker, the Vice President of the New Jersey Coalition of Patriotic Societies, wanted to make it harder for foreign help to come into the country.

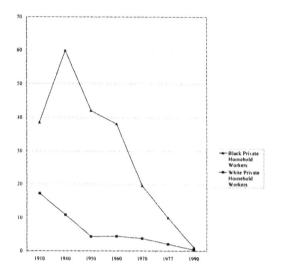

Chart 10. Percentage of Women Employed as Domestics, United States, 1910–1990
Source: Elizabeth Higginbotham, "Laid Bare By the System: Work and Survival for Black and Hispanic Women," in Amy Swerdlow and Hanna Lessinger, ed., *Class, Race and Sex: The Dynamics of Control* (Boston: G.K. Hall, 1983): 207; Decennial Census of the Population, 1990.

> In an ad in the New York Times as of last Sunday there is mentioned specifically the fact that maids may be secured for $25 less a week if gotten from the Latin American countries. My own associates, connected with women's groups, have found quite a little unemployment and suffering among the low-priced help because . . . certain foreign help is preferred. . . . [53]

In a similar vein, Congressman Frank L. Chelf of Kentucky said,

> If we are going to recognize more and more of Jamaica and those areas, if we have got to have more colored folks in the United States, that is all right. That is, if we need them. However, I really and truly think that we have got all the troubles that we can say grace over with our own American native-born colored people in providing them jobs. They should come first with education and employment. [54]

Labor experts allayed these fears with their low estimates of newcomers. Attorney General Nicholas Katzenbach expected only about 7,000 a year from Jamaica, Trinidad and Tobago. He went so far to say, "If . . . we could predict a large increase in the amount of immigration from the

Western Hemisphere, then I think we might be justified in putting a ceiling on such immigration."[55]

Everyone assumed that Western Hemisphere immigrants would be largely unskilled and sixth preference, unable to come because the first through fifth preference categories would use up the immigration quotas. They forgot how popular Western Hemisphere domestics were, even though domestic servants had figured directly in their discussions about entry preferences. At one point during the hearings, Secretary of Labor Willard Wirtz assured the House Subcommittee that he did not foresee the law allowing in "individuals that will work purely as domestics in the United States" or cause unemployment.[56]

At the time, this was not an unrealistic expectation. Despite strenuous efforts by agencies to recruit foreign maids, only about 8,500 had entered the United States in 1964, the year before the Hart-Celler Act passed. Of those, a third were European.

What that figure did not reflect, however, was that many West Indians who wanted to emigrate as servants were unable to do so. For example, newly independent countries Jamaica and Trinidad/Tobago were restricted to a yearly quota of 100 immigrants; they were still bound by the quotas they had had under colonial rule.[57]

The immigration quota for West Indians was lifted on December 1, 1965, and there was no limit on Western Hemisphere migration until 1968, when the new Immigration Act went into full effect. During that three-year period, a quarter of foreign-born female immigrants intended to work in private households. Twenty percent of all West Indian immigrants who arrived in the United States between 1962 and 1971 were private household workers.[58]

The groups who now sought domestic work—Western Hemisphere immigrants—were more likely to immigrate than were Europeans, who shunned domestic work (Table 25). And the 1965 Act helped them come. In 1965, only about 1600 Jamaicans came to the U.S. Three years later, when the law took full effect, ten times that number arrived.

These immigrants were most likely to settle in New York City. Of the 1,500 who came in March 1968 alone, barely one-fifth came to join relatives. The rest, even though they came under the sixth preference category, were domestics. Between 1967 and 1969, the majority of the visas issued in the West Indies were granted to private household workers who were female.[59]

The key to the influx of Western Hemisphere domestics was that while European countries had individual quotas, Western Hemisphere immigrants were governed only by the hemispheric total of 120,000 immigrants per year. Popular opinion held that the 1965 law "virtually closed Europe as a source of domestic help." The wait for an English maid could be as long as

Table 25. Immigrants Admitted by Select Origin 1960, 1979

	1960	1979
Europe	138,426	60,845
Asia	24,956	189,293
Africa	2,319	12,838
Select Latin American and Caribbean origin		
Mexico	32,684	52,096
West Indies	14,047	74,074
Central America	6,661	17,547
South America	13,048	35,344
Subtotal	66,440	179,061
Total	265,398	460,348

Sources: United States Immigration and Naturalization Service, "Tabulation of Immigrants Admitted by Country of Birth" (unpublished, 1981), cited in Saskia Sassen-Koob, "Exporting Capital and Importing Labor: The Role of Women," in *Female Immigrants to the U.S.: Caribbean, Latin American and African Experiences*, Delores M. Mortimer and Roy S. Bryce-Laporte, eds., RIIES Occasional Papers No. 2, Research Institute on Immigration and Ethnic Studies (Washington, D.C.: Smithsonian Institution, 1981): 210.

four years compared to several months for a Caribbean or Latin American maid. In June 1968, *The New York Times* speculated, "[H]alf the 120,000 visas that will be granted to Latin Americans in the year after July 1 will be granted to prospective sleep-in maids."[60]

It was a dream come true for employers, and it helped potential immigrants enter the country. Foreign-born women's proportion of the domestic servant labor force was rising in 1970. After 1965, black immigrant women quickly became a large presence in domestic service. Though they made up only one-twentieth of the female work force, they were almost one-quarter of female domestic household workers. At the same time, the number of private household workers began again to decline, by about 200,000 between 1973 and 1977.[61]

In the early years after the Hart-Celler Act went into effect, it was Afro-Caribbean women who flocked to the United States to fill domestic service openings. Like European immigrants before them, Caribbean

Table 26. Intended Occupation of Immigrants, 1965–70 and 1970 Occupation of Foreign-Born

Occupation	1965–70 Immigrants		1970 Foreign-Born	
	Male	Female	Male	Female
Total Number	566,342	367,695	454,872	309,090
Percent				
Manager	6.6	1.3	5.0	1.4
Professional	25.8	24.4	22.4	15.6
Clerical	5.3	22.1	7.0	22.4
Sales	2.7	2.3	3.0	3.4
Craftsmen	22.8	2.0	17.5	2.2
Operatives	10.1	13.5	21.4	31.3
Private Household Service	0.4	24.0	0.2	7.2
Other Service	7.1	8.1	13.4	14.4
Farm Owner/Manager	2.9	0.5	0.1	0.0
Farm Laborer	4.6	0.5	3.0	1.1
Laborer	11.6	1.3	6.9	1.0

Source: Adapted from S.M. Tomasi and Charles B. Keely, *Whom Have We Welcomed?: The Adequacy and Quality of United States Immigration Data for Policy and Evaluation* (Staten Island, N.Y.: The Center for Migration Studies, 1975): 65.

immigrants saw domestic service as a way to learn American culture. And employers liked them.[62]

New York families' prejudice against African Americans did not extend to Afro-Caribbean servants. Although their skin was dark, these workers did not have the baggage of the American racist heritage. These women came from another country, they spoke with an appealing foreign accent, they tended to be well-educated, and they had a different attitude about themselves than African-American workers.

West Indian blacks were the dominant racial group in their homelands. This, combined with the rigorous British education they received, gave them, according to one author, "a highly secularized Protestant ethic

Table 27. Immigrants Admitted by Selected Origin 1960, 1966, 1970, 1979

Country	1960	1966	1970	1979
West Indies				
Dominican Republic	756	16,503	10,807	17,519
Haiti	931	3,801	9,932	6,433
Jamaica	1,340	2,743	15,033	19,714
Central America				
El Salvador	1,019	1,415	1,698	4,479
Guatemala	627	1,584	2,130	2,583
Honduras	755	1,958	1,263	2,545
Panama	1,722	1,594	1,630	3,472
South America				
Argentina	2,878	4,414	3,443	2,856
Brazil	1,399	2,397	1,919	1,450
Colombia	2,989	9,504	6,724	10,637
Ecuador	1,576	4,111	4,410	4,383
Peru	1,657	1,474	909	4,135

Source: United States Immigration and Naturalization Service, "Tabulation of Immigrants Admitted by Country of Birth" (Unpublished, 1981), cited in Sassen-Koob, "Exporting Capital and Importing Labor," 211.

which finds expression in a strong belief in self, discipline, drive and determination." In addition, American whites gave them preferential treatment because "they served as proof that Blacks in general were also making it in America. And, if their 'foreignness' was stressed, it was with the implied notion that if Afro-Americans were more like West Indians they, too, could make it." And in fact, their social and occupational mobility was more like white European female immigrants than native-born American blacks.[63]

In addition to West Indians, twelve and half percent of black Cuban female immigrants worked in private households in the U.S. Haitian women worked as domestics and as factory workers. Minette Alphonse came from Haiti in 1965 with her husband and four young children. At home, she had her own servants; here, she worked for others. She lived out and worked part-time for two families.[64]

As time went on, more Latin and South American immigrants came (Table 27), although New York had few Mexican arrivals until the 1990s (unlike the Southwestern United States). They took private and public service sector jobs; compared with all women, they are disproportionately represented as cleaning women, domestic workers, childcare workers and cooks.[65]

Despite the fairly liberal provisions of the 1965 Act, illegal immigration became more common. In 1968, two months before the law went into full effect, "One immigration official said there were perhaps 20,000 illegal maids in the metropolitan area alone," although the district director of the INS would say only that the number was "sizable."[66]

Domestic service was a popular occupation for illegal aliens because it was relatively easy to find jobs. Employers wanted live-in workers, and undocumented workers were willing to live in. They were also more vulnerable and therefore more malleable. New arrivals needed work, and as more Spanish-speaking women came, a job like domestic service, which required few language skills, was attractive. This was true for legal immigrants, too, of course, but illegal immigrants were especially popular. In the words of a Roslyn, Long Island, woman, "you hardly have to pay them anything."[67]

Although the government decried lawbreaking, some writers believed that the 1965 Immigration Act, by restricting legal immigration from the Western Hemisphere, made illegal entry "more feasible" than legal entry. One indication that this might be true was the rise in the demand for tourist visas to the U.S. from Caribbean countries.[68]

The late 1960s and early 1970s tension between African-American workers and the white establishment only increased the traffic in illegal importation of domestics from the Western Hemisphere. For example, Adelaida S., a 45-year old Colombian woman who arrived in the United States in August 1971 on a tourist visa, found domestic employment within one week. Despite the difficulties in obtaining visas for her to remain in the country, her boss wanted her to stay. "In the past few years," he said, "many of my friends have become apprehensive about employing American black domestic help."[69]

Dominican women began to move to the United States after their dictatorial leader, Rafael Molino Trujillo ("El Jefe"), was assassinated in 1961; they began to take some domestic service jobs. They were part of an upsurge in undocumented alien migration. Between 1962 and 1964, of 136,195 Dominicans who entered the United States, 108,225 were tourists who remained illegally.[70]

An INS official charged that "immigration lawyers, who set themselves up as hiring agents in Jamaica and the Dominican Republic, among other places, were taking advantage of the chronically short supply of sleep-in maids to get the women in the country." They charged the housewives a fee of more than the $150 a typical employment agency would charge, and immigrants paid 10 to 15 times what visa application fees would be. But this was for *sleep-in* maids, who were in perennially short supply, since live-in situations were rife with abuse.[71]

Sleep-in maids were supposed to be making $66 a week, according to "prevailing wage" laws. But few new immigrants made that much.[72]

In fact, it was the new immigration law that forced the issue of undocumented workers into the open. Shortly after the law went into effect, after a conference on June 12, 1968 among immigration and state officials, INS agents went door to door in the NY metropolitan area and arrested 128 "alien maids and cooks on charges of violation of the immigration laws" in not having proper job certification. "The visits," reported Charles Grutzner in *The New York Times*, "have brought tearful despair to the workers and indignant protests from the housewives suddenly deprived of their services."[73]

And the U.S. Labor Department restricted the entry of live-in servants "to households in which there are working mothers with children of preschool age," and said that "'there will be no certification' for households with nonworking mothers." Their reasoning was that many workers were not actually living in or working as domestics, and that many employers were "substandard." They also wanted to increase wages by decreasing the labor pool. "The department's concern is not so much that the immigrants compete with Americans for low-skill jobs, but that the 'substandard' employers who hire them might have to pay higher wages if they did not have a foreign labor supply to draw on."[74]

Although it is difficult to determine the exact number of undocumented workers, it is worth noting that among Mexican women in 1980, who in the western United States dominated domestic service, "only 21 percent of the women employed as domestics said they would keep their jobs if they acquired legal documents."[75]

Illegal importation of domestic labor continued. In the mid-1990s, there were still abuses.

> The dirty little secrets behind the closed doors of some upper middle class houses in the suburbs from New York to Los Angeles are the immigrant women who work up to 15-hour shifts, six days a week, for wages amounting to $2 an hour. Typically, it is the new immigrants with shaky

legal status and few options who take these positions at wages that start at about $150 a week in the New York area, $100 in California.[76]

Still, the occupation became a stepping-stone for many. Although many Afro-Caribbean female immigrants did become private household workers, they were also able to advance in the United States. "Thus, those who were nurses in Trinidad became nurse administrators, while domestics became nurses' aides in New York." Haitian immigrant Minette Alphonse worked three jobs daily, including one as a housekeeper and one as a babysitter, and saved her money. She eventually owned four houses and sent all her children to college. One is now a senior executive at a Fortune 500 company.[77]

During the 1980s, many West Indian immigrant women moved into other unskilled occupations in the health or service industries which gave them "more flexibility in working hours . . . , greater job security as a result of unionization, health care benefits, and annual vacations with pay." They could do so because they were here legally. By the end of the twentieth century, the higher-status domestic jobs (nanny, housekeeper) were in the hands of legal immigrants; illegal immigrants networked for part-time cleaning jobs.[78]

When they came to the United States, especially to New York, Hispanic women—Puerto Ricans, Colombians, Cubans, Dominicans—preferred factory work. Those who were illegal immigrants and unable to speak English, however, worked in domestic service. They considered it the lowest status job.[79]

Because of that attitude, the numbers of workers shrank. By 1991, there were only 755,000 workers nationwide, or about 1.4 percent of all employed women. Out of 186,000 African-American private household workers in 1983, there were now only 85,000. Hispanic-origin women had replaced them. Of Mexican-origin women, 27 percent worked as domestics, along with 16 percent of Puerto Rican-origin and 16.5 percent of Cuban-origin women.[80]

In New York City in the 1990s, Latin, South American and West Indian immigrants also did housework, and competition was stiff. When a New York City woman advertised for a housekeeper, she received hundreds of telephone calls, beginning at 6:23 a.m. Two complete answering machine tapes ran out. The phone rang so often, she finally had to leave the house. All but one caller were women; all but four were West Indians.[81]

There were also Eastern Europeans doing paid housecleaning—Poles and Bosnians, for example, who did not speak English very well yet. There were few African American women working in the occupation—and they were certainly not waiting on street corners for day work as they had in the 1930s. By the early 21st century, that was left to illegal immigrants—Poles and Latin Americans alike.[82]

Table 28. Visa Preference System (after 1990 Immigration Law)

Preference	Description	Limit
Family-sponsored preferences		226,000
First	Unmarried sons/daughters of U.S. citizens; their children	23,400[a]
Second	Spouses, children, and unmarried sons/daughters of permanent resident aliens	114,200[b]
Third	Married sons/daughters of US citizens; their spouses and children	23,400[b]
Fourth	Brothers and sisters of U.S. citizens (21 years +); their spouses and children	65,000[b]
Employment-based preferences		140,000
First	Priority workers; their spouses and children	40,040[c]
Second	Professionals with advanced degrees or aliens of exceptional ability; their spouses and children	40,040[b]
Third	Skilled workers, professional (without advanced degrees), needed unskilled workers; their spouses and children	40,040[c]
Fourth	Special immigrants; their spouses and children; up to 5,000 certain religious workers	9,940
Fifth	Employment creation ("Investors"), their spouses and children	9,940
Diversity immigrants		55,000

[a]Plus unused family fourth preference visas; [b]Visas not used in higher preferences may be used in these categories; [c]Plus unused employment fourth and fifth preferences.

Source: Nancy Foner, ed., *New Immigrants in New York* (New York: Columbia University Press, 2001): 38. Used with permission.

Things had changed enough that simply because one worked as a domestic, it did not mean that a woman (and the occupation has always been more than 90 percent female) was at the bottom of the American labor market. There was a scale within domestic work. A West Indian housekeeper was at the top of the scale, and an Eastern European woman who could command $90 to clean two stories of a three-story house was also near the top. Day workers without steady employment were at the bottom of it. Those were primarily non-English-speakers, usually Hispanic and often undocumented. Illegal aliens appeared to be the new occupiers of the bottom rung in American society.[83]

The continuing influx of immigrants into New York City was responsible for the persistence of domestic service, at least one observer believed. Others pointed to immigrants, but also noted the presence of an unequal distribution of wealth in New York.[84]

In the 1990s, immigrants dominated domestic service in New York City. Ruth Milkman found that in 1990, 69 percent of New York City's domestic servants were foreign-born and 21 percent were native-born African-Americans. From an African-American ghetto, domestic service had once again become an immigrant's first step. The former had left a changed occupation to their successors. The power relationship had changed so that workers had more leverage. Even undocumented workers had rights and defenders.[85]

Conclusion
Repercussions of an
Altered Occupation

In 1920, the thought that an issue with a household employee could cause problems for a Presidential administration would have been considered absurd. Yet such problems disrupted both Bill Clinton and George W. Bush's terms of office. Household workers were in the spotlight, thrust there by changed attitudes about immigrants and about household help itself.

As the labor force changed from African-American to foreign-born, the occupation became more negotiated and equalized for documented workers. These were able to use the advances won by their predecessors to maintain an equal footing with their employers. For undocumented workers, whose numbers increased over the decades, things were more difficult, although they, too, benefited in general from employers' attitudinal changes. And domestic service was once again a stepping-stone occupation, as it had been for previous generations of immigrants.

Most immigrant servants' children, especially white or light-colored people, progressed beyond their parents' status. Foreignness and/or inability to speak English were the sole barriers to Europeans' acceptance into American society; education and time eradicated those impediments. Second generation Americans (and some of the first generation) moved into other jobs, whether white, pink or blue-collar.

Until the late 1960s, the same could not necessarily be said for African-American domestics. They could not normally move into other jobs, nor could their children. Starting after 1965, African Americans, though they were not immigrants, finally moved into a pattern like ethnic succession, at least as far as domestic service was concerned. They left a low-status occupation behind, moving on to those of higher status.[1]

By the end of the twentieth century, attitudes concerning domestic service had changed greatly. The employer-employee relationship was usually a negotiated one rather than a lop-sided, dictatorial one. Workers had legal rights, including that of participation in social security. And it was still difficult to find workers, keeping negotiation viable.

The occupation became politicized, too, making the relationship between worker and employer subject to public scrutiny. That resulted in Nannygate.

On January 13, 1993, Zoë Baird, President Bill Clinton's nominee for Attorney General, ran afoul of domestic service regulations. She and her husband had hired illegal Peruvian immigrants to work in their household, and they had paid them off the books, not reporting this income to Social Security or the IRS. Because the Attorney General, as the head of what was then the Immigration and Naturalization Service (INS),[2] was responsible for enforcing immigration law, and because Baird had flouted not just the 1986 immigration law that prohibited hiring undocumented workers, but also income tax regulations, the President had to withdraw her nomination.[3]

Baird had hired the undocumented workers because, like many working families, she could not find willing American workers. At the time, an undocumented Jamaican nanny said of nanny jobs, "These days, most Americans see it as some kind of slavery." And indeed, there were employers who preferred illegal aliens because they, like one Queens woman, wanted "someone who cannot leave the country, who doesn't know anyone in New York, who basically does not have a life. . . . who is completely dependent on me and loyal to my family." This was not, apparently the case with Baird, but it was still easier to find illegal help than legal help.[4]

President Clinton's next choice, New York Federal District Judge Kimba M. Wood, also withdrew because she had hired an illegal alien, although because of the timing of her action (i.e., before the passage of the 1986 law that made it illegal to hire undocumented workers), it was a legal act. Wood also had not paid social security, but again, this did not violate any laws because social security did not cover illegal aliens. The sophistry inherent in this interpretation was evident, however, and the country was in an uproar over Nannygate.[5]

The new Clinton administration was in disarray; several other lower-level nominees stepped down for not paying social security taxes. Ron Brown, the Commerce Secretary, admitted that he had failed to pay social security for a housecleaner (although he remained in his job). The New Jersey gubernatorial and California Senate elections were affected by allegations of illegal alien employment and unpaid social security. Members of the House and Senate announced that they were paid up; whether this had been accomplished recently was not discussed. Payments of social security taxes rose 17 percent in less than three months.[6]

In response, Congress decided not to change the immigration law but rather to raise the Social Security earnings threshold for domestics, which had remained at the 1950 level. This meant that any household worker, including teenage babysitters, who earned more than $50 a quarter from any one employer, came under social security coverage. Since almost every domestic or baby sitter met that criterion, the Social Security law's original intent—to limit the number of the covered—was turned on its head. The Social Security Domestic Reform Act of 1994 simplified filing, by allowing employers to report wages paid on their own 1040 tax forms. The earnings threshold was raised to $1,000 a year in cash wages.[7]

Nannygate concerned the hiring of illegal aliens as nannies. Child-care was largely separate from cleaning and cooking, and working families had more need of the former than the latter by the 1990s. The lessons of the incident, however, reverberated for all kinds of domestic help, and for politicians. President George W. Bush's administration suffered from similar problems in 2001 and 2004.

In 2001, Bush's nominee for Treasury Secretary, Paul O'Neill, had to pay $92 in back taxes because the IRS deemed money he had given a housekeeper to be wages, not gifts. Linda Chavez, the Labor nominee, withdrew her name because she had given money and shelter to an illegal immigrant. And in 2004, Bernard Kerik pulled out of consideration to be the Secretary for Homeland Defense because among other reasons, he had hired an undocumented immigrant housekeeper and failed to pay taxes on her wages.[8]

A national debate was sparked about women's role and the need for domestic help. The debate also included issues such as workers' rights. Americans were outraged at Baird's employees' small wages. It was because domestic servants had protection under the law—like other workers—that this became a political issue. For the first time, domestic workers, in being treated like a political football, were at the center of a political debate. Even when they were part of the debate concerning their coverage by social security, it was as part of a larger group. But now they had center stage.[9]

The furor pointed up how attitudes had changed over the years. There was sympathy for the plight of the working woman (the employer), but there was equal concern for the rights of the workers. Indeed, the incident gave even illegal aliens, the most likely to be abused by employers, the courage to fight for their rights. Now, public opinion was on the workers' side. Where in the beginning of the twentieth century, long hours and low pay were the norm, they were now viewed as abusive, and public conscience was against such conditions.[10]

Fear had kept illegal immigrants from availing themselves of legal protections. For them, the reality could still be 15-hour days for little pay. While legal housecleaners and nannies in the New York area could earn from $400 to $600 a week, illegals often made only about $200 a week, at times for 90-hour weeks.[11]

Dina Aguirre, who arrived illegally from Guatemala, worked in Garden City, New York. "I worked for three weeks without getting paid. I worked from 7 in the morning until 7 at night and sometimes till 11. I asked the woman to pay me and she said, 'I don't owe you anything because you ruined my blouse.' She said, 'Give me your address, and I will send you a bill for all that you owe me.'" With the support of an immigrant rights group and a changed public climate, however, Ms. Aguirre found the courage to sue in small claims court; she won $600.

Not every award was paid, however. Despite her victory in court, Yanira Juarez was still waiting months later for her award of $2,000 in back wages. And the small claims court was more efficient than the New York State Department of Labor, where it could take up to 18 months to investigate a claim.[12]

However clumsy it was, it was noteworthy that all workers, regardless of their immigration status, had so much legal recourse available to them. They needed it as leverage because of some employers' condescension. Jennifer Gordon, of the employee-advocate group Workplace Project in Hempstead, Long Island, said, "I find that a lot of employers feel that they're doing employees a favor by giving them a job."[13]

In total, domestic service was more standardized, but it was still low status and difficult, even for middle-class women who choose to do housework. Louise Rafkin, who cleaned houses for a number of years (and eventually wrote a book based on her experiences), said that although she mostly enjoyed her work and made good money,

> the emotional wear and tear of housecleaning can drain me like soap scum down a freshly scoured sink. . . . I have been referred to as 'you people.' . . . I was told by [one] woman that my background made me too similar to her, and therefore somehow threatening. . . . Overall, I have heard way too much whining about how difficult it is to find 'good help,' always from people who haven't a clue about how to treat good help.[14]

Even the highest paid workers struggled with employers' attitudes. Full-time housecleaners were among them. If they did two dwellings a day for $50 or $60 each, which was normal in New York City, they could earn $500 to $600 a week. In the suburbs, it was not unusual for a housecleaner to demand $90 to $100 for a single house, to be done in a day. And considering that a company like The Maids charged $25 a person hour in Maine in 1998, homeowners were likely to pay $100 or more for a housecleaning, whether it was to a company or an individual.[15]

That was still not very much money, however. Low earnings helped persuade workers to evade taxes and coincidentally remove some of their legal protections. At the most generous extreme, one could figure that a housecleaner worked 50 weeks a year and got 2 weeks paid vacation. At $500 a week, that was $26,000 a year. Income and Social Security taxes could reduce that by as much as 40 percent, leaving only $15,600 a year take-home pay. At $1,300 a month, there was not much left to live on (although these wages put workers well above the federal poverty level). This situation made it likely that workers would not declare their income or ask their employers to pay all Federal Insurance Contributions Act (FICA) taxes, leaving them only with income taxes to pay. If they paid no taxes at all, workers had $2,167 a month to live on.

Women who worked for cleaning franchises, which took out withholding and did all the paperwork for the employers, did even worse. They made $6.50 to $7.00 an hour before taxes, which meant $260 to $280 for a 40-hour week. They received no pay for days they did not work. At 20 percent withholding, they made roughly $10,000 to $11,000 a year (less than $1,000 a month, and just above the poverty level for a single person).[16]

* * *

Low pay, abusive situations and lingering social stigma meant that private household domestic service remained an unattractive occupation.

Interestingly, however, low pay brought employer and employee together in collusion to evade taxes. This was one of the more interesting aspects of the new negotiated relationship. Both parties broke the law together. The employee usually asked the employer to avoid paying taxes, even though it was the employer who would face a penalty if caught. So although they were bound together negatively, the relationship was less one-sided than at the beginning of the twentieth century.[17]

By the end of the twentieth century, there were legal protections for workers, and the occupation was once again a stepping-stone for legal immigrants and for many children of undocumented aliens. American citizens and legal immigrants appear to depart from it as soon as possible, leaving the field to illegal immigrants and those who cannot learn other skills, including speaking English.

African-American women were now part of that cycle. A shortage of white servants, mainly immigrants, made it possible for many southern black women to work in New York City. They were thus poised to take advantage of civil rights and job-training activities of the 1960s, and to

Table 29. Ethnic Distribution of U.S. Domestic Workers, 1990

	Number	Percent of Total
Total	494,920	
White	312,888	63%
Black	136,283	28%
Asian	14,044	3%
Native American	3,856	1%
Other	54,083	11%
Hispanic*	119,588	24%

*May include other ethnic categories

Source: U.S. Department of Commerce, Bureau of the Census, *Decennial Census of the Population*, 1990.

leave domestic service behind. A national commitment to overcoming racism, however short-lived or faint-hearted, had a positive effect on the lives of black domestic workers.

The women's movement and related struggle to elevate housework raised America's consciousness about paid domestic labor, something that surfaced in the indignation about low pay expressed during Nannygate. Legislative protections gave teeth to workers' demands for better working conditions and a more equal relationship.

Structural changes and a continued labor shortage increased workers' leverage in their employment relationship. Despite the continued existence of abuses, particularly for illegal immigrants, by the turn of the 21st century a more equal relationship between employer and employee was accepted and any abuses condemned. Although less important as an occupation for women, domestic service became more flexible and useful to its practitioners. Domestic workers had gained a more equal footing with their employers. This was a dramatic change from the 1920s and 1930s, and marked real progress for this field of employment.

Table 30. Occupation by Race, United States, Women 14 years old and over

	1910		1940		1950		1960		1970		1977	
	B	W	B	W	B	W	B	W	B	W	B	W
Professional and Technical Workers	1.5	11.6	4.3	14.7	5.3	13.3	7.7	14.1	10.0	15.5	13.0	16.0
Managers, Owners, Proprietors	.2	1.5	.7	4.3	1.3	4.7	1.1	4.2	1.4	4.7	3.0	6.0
Clerical and Sales Workers	.3	17.5	1.3	32.8	5.4	39.3	9.8	43.2	21.4	43.4	27.0	43.0
Operatives	1.4	21.2	6.2	20.3	15.2	21.5	14.3	17.6	16.8	14.5	16.0	12.0
Private Household Workers	38.5	17.2	59.9	10.9	42.0	4.3	38.1	4.4	19.5	3.7	10.0	2.0
Service-Not Private Household	3.2	9.2	11.1	12.7	19.1	11.6	23.0	13.1	28.5	15.1	27.0	17.0
Farm Workers	48.0	9.0	12.9	1.2	7.7	2.3	3.5	1.0	.3	1.3	1.0	1.0

Source: Elizabeth Higginbotham, "Laid Bare By the System: Work and Survival for Black and Hispanic Women," in Amy Swerdlow and Hanna Lessinger, eds., *Class, Race and Sex: The Dynamics of Control* (Boston: G.K. Hall, 1983): 207.

Notes

NOTES TO THE INTRODUCTION

1. Faye E. Dudden, *Serving Women: Household Service in Nineteenth-Century America* (Middletown: Wesleyan University Press, 1983): 6–8.
2. There is a full discussion of demand in Chapter Four.
3. Between 1900 and 1910, a peak of 9 million immigrants came to the United States. The 4.5 million who arrived between 1970 and 1980 marked the fourth highest decennial number. Elizabeth Bogen, *Immigration in New York* (New York: Praeger, 1987): 12.
4. Joni Hersch, "The Impact of Nonmarket Work on Market Wages," *The American Economic Review* (May 1991): 158.
5. "To Domestics, a Minimum Wage Is a Raise," *The New York Times*, June 6, 1973; "President Signs Rise in Pay Base to $2.30 an Hour," *The New York Times*, April 9, 1974; Joseph A. Hickey, "Unemployment Insurance Covers Additional 9 Million Workers," *Monthly Labor Review* (May 1978).
6. Childcare, while it may sometimes occur within the context of domestic work, is a distinctly different job from housekeeping. It has always existed as a specialized job, primarily for the wealthy prior to World War II, but more recently for the majority of Americans. Indeed, families who may not have help cleaning often have childcare.
7. Jeanne Boydston, *Home and Work: Housework, Wages and the Ideology of Labor in the Early Republic* (New York: Oxford University Press, 1990): xviii.
8. George J. Stigler, *Domestic Service in the United States 1900–1940*, Occasional Paper 24 (New York: National Bureau of Economic Research, April 1946): 6. Stigler was interested in how prices and wages are determined.
9. This became an issue in the late twentieth century vis-à-vis illegal immigrants, despite the improvements to the relationship as a whole.
10. Louise Rafkin, "Dirty Laundry," *The New York Times Magazine*, January 28, 1996; Interview with Norma Silvestri, Leonia, New Jersey, September 13, 1992; Barbara Ehrenreich, *Nickel and Dimed: On (Not) Getting By in America* (New York: Metropolitan Books, 2001): 72; "For Immigrant

Maids, Not a Job but Servitude," *The New York Times,* February 25, 1996; "At Rally for Domestics' Rights, A Nanny Tells of Mistreatment," *The New York Times,* March 8, 2004.

11. Ehrenreich, *Nickel and Dimed,* 115–119. Sometimes there are small groups of workers who organize. See, for example, "At Rally for Domestics' Rights, A Nanny Tells of Mistreatment," *ibid.*

12. If wages are finally reported, it is the employer who is penalized, so some element of leverage does finally remain with the employer—if she realizes it. "The Household Employee and the Benefits Dilemma," *The New York Times,* March 22, 1984; "Tax Report: Many Filers Ignore Nanny Tax, Expecting Not to Get Caught," *The Wall Street Journal,* December 15, 2004.

13. Mary Romero, *Maid in the U.S.A.* (New York: Routledge, 1992): 27.

14. Interview with Virginia Johnson, who worked as a live-in maid in New York during the 1920s and 1930s, New York City, May 29, 1992; interview with German woman #1, New York City, March 26, 1995. This woman worked as a part-time housecleaner for decades beginning in the 1950s. Despite the stigma, author Louise Rafkin chose housecleaning for a number of years. "I enjoy my work, for the most part. . . . I earn as much as a good mechanic or a bad therapist—between $20 and $45 per hour—more than I can make any other way and still control my life." Louise Rafkin, "Dirty Laundry," *The New York Times Magazine,* January 28, 1996.

15. U.S. Department of Commerce, Bureau of the Census, *Decennial Census of the Population,* 1920–1990. Job descriptions in 1920 included cook, housekeeper, parlor maid, chambermaid, waitress, kitchen maid, lady's maid, laundress, cleaner. In 1970, cleaners, nannies, housekeepers, and to some degree cooks held sway, along with couples, a cook/housekeeper and her houseman/butler/chauffeur husband. Men were housemen, butlers, general men, gardeners, caretakers, chauffeurs, and for the very wealthy before WWII, footmen. "Job Categories," Lindquist Group (domestic employment agency) files, Greenwich, CT.

16. In 2000, the United States government viewed domestic service as so statistically insignificant that the Census Bureau did not break out private household service as a separate occupational category. David Katzman, *Seven Days a Week: Domestic Service in Industrializing America* (New York, 1978) 56, 60, 290, 291, 292; *Facts About Working Women,* Bulletin of the Women's Bureau, No. 46 (Washington, G.P.O., 1925): 2, 23; Allyson Sherman Grossman, "Women in Domestic Work, Yesterday and Today," *Monthly Labor Review* 103 (August 1980), 17–21; Janet M. Hooks, "Women's Occupations Through Seven Decades," *Bulletin of the Women's Bureau 218,* U.S. Department of Labor (Washington, D.C.: G.P.O., 1951); U.S. Bureau of the Census, *Census of Population and Housing,* 1920—2000.

17. Elizabeth Bogen, *Immigration in New York* (New York: Praeger, 1987): 50, 55; Frank D. Bean, Allan G. King, Jeffrey S. Passel, "The Number of Illegal Migrants of Mexican Origin in the United States: Sex Ratio-based Estimates for 1980," *Demography* 20:1 (February 1983): 99–109; J. Gregory Robinson, "Estimating the Approximate Size of the Illegal Alien Population in the United States by the Comparative Trend Analysis of Age-Specific

Death Rates," *Demography* 17:2 (May 1980): 159–176; Jeffrey S. Passel and Karen A. Woodrow, "Geographic Distribution of Undocumented Immigrants: Estimates of Undocumented Aliens Counted in the 1980 Census by State," *International Migration Review* 18:3 (Autumn 1984): 642–671; Robert Warren, Jeffrey S. Passel, "A Count of the Uncountable: Estimates of Undocumented Aliens Counted in the 1980 United States Census," *Demography* 24:3 (August 1987): 375–393; Frank D. Bean, Harley L. Browning and W. Parker Frisbie, "The Sociodemographic Characteristics of Mexican Immigrant Status Groups: Implications for Studying Undocumented Mexicans," *International Migration Review* 18:3 (Autumn 1984): 672–691; Barry R. Chiswick, "Illegal Immigration and Immigration Control," *Journal of Economic Perspectives* 2, no. 3 (Summer 1988): 102–105. George E. Johnson, "The Labor Market Effects of Immigration," *Industrial and Labor Relations Review,* 33:3 (April 1980): 331–341, posits a higher number overall. Jeffrey S. Passel, Karen A. Woodrow, "Geographic Distribution of Undocumented Immigrants: Estimates of Undocumented Aliens Counted in the 1980 Census by State," *International Migration Review* 18:3 (Autumn 1984): 651–652.

18.   Because some immigrant groups eschew private household work altogether, these estimates are likely high. Frank D. Bean, Harley L. Browning and W. Parker Frisbie, "The Sociodemographic Characteristics of Mexican Immigrant Status Groups: Implications for Studying Undocumented Mexicans," *International Migration Review* 18:3 (Autumn 1984): 685; Vernon Briggs, Jr., "Methods of Analysis of Illegal Immigration into the United States," *International Migration Review* 18:3 (Autumn 1984): 635; Robert Warren, Jeffrey S. Passel, "A Count of the Uncountable," 380; Barry Edmonston and James P. Smith, *The New Americans: Economic, Demographic, and Fiscal Effects of Immigration* (Washington, D.C.: National Academy Press, 1997): 193; Marcela Cerrutti and Douglas S. Massey, "On the Auspices of Female Migration from Mexico to the United States," *Demography* 38:2 (May 2001): 187–200; Marta Tienda, Leif Jensen, Robert L. Bach, "Immigration, Gender and the Process of Occupational Change in the United States, 1970–1980," *International Migration Review,* 18:4 (Winter 1984): 1029.

19.   See for example Elizabeth Clark-Lewis' article, "'This Work Had a End': African-American Domestic Workers in Washington, D.C., 1910–1940" in Carol Groneman and Mary Beth Norton, eds., *"To Toil the Livelong Day": America's Women at Work, 1780–1980* (Ithaca, NY: Cornell University Press, 1987), in which she discusses how those women refused to live with their employers.

20.   Linda Martin and Kerry Segrave, *The Servant Problem: Domestic Workers in North America* (Jefferson, N.C.: McFarland & Co., Inc., 1985): 100.

NOTES TO CHAPTER ONE

1.   Mrs. A.E. Johnson Agency placement books, 1920–21, held at the Lindquist Group offices, Greenwich, CT; Martin Harris in Jeff Kisseloff, *You Must*

Remember This: An Oral History of Manhattan from the 1890s to World War II (New York: Harcourt Brace Jovanovich, 1989): 108; Olive Huber in Kisseloff, *You Must Remember This,* 397.

2. Cecilia M. Rio, "From Feudal Serfs to Independent Contractors: Class and African American Women's Paid Domestic Labor, 1863–1980" (University of Massachusetts, 2001).

3. Even though perhaps only about 15 percent of households employed servants (see discussion in Chapter Four on demand for servants), Americans expected to be able to achieve middle-class status and hire a servant. Elites provided a model for the rest of society to copy, and their struggles with housework and domestic arrangements reverberated throughout American culture. See, for example, T.J. Jackson Lears' discussion in "From Salvation to Self-Realization: Advertising and the Therapeutic Roots of the Consumer Culture, 1880–1930," in Richard Wightman Fox and T.J. Jackson Lears, eds., *The Culture of Consumption: Critical Essays in American History* (New York: Pantheon Books, 1983): 4–5. See also Maureen E. Montgomery, *Displaying Women: Spectacles of Leisure in Edith Wharton's New York* (New York and London: Routledge, 1998). For discussions of actual social mobility (versus residential mobility) and aspirations toward it, see for a small sample of the available literature: C. Wright Mills, *White Collar* (New York: Oxford University Press, 1953); Stephan Thernstrom, *Poverty and Progress: Social Mobility in a Nineteenth-Century City* (Cambridge: Harvard University Press, 1964); Stephan Thernstrom, *The Other Bostonians: Poverty and Progress in the American Metropolis, 1880–1970* (Cambridge: Harvard University Press, 1973); Howard P. Chudacoff, *Mobile Americans: Residential and Social Mobility in Omaha, 1880–1920* (New York: Oxford University Press, 1972); Harold K. Kerbo, *Social Stratification and Inequality: Class Conflict in Historical and Comparative Perspective* (New York: McGraw-Hill, 1996); Anselm L. Strauss, *The Contexts of Social Mobility: Ideology and Theory* (Chicago: Aldine Publishing Co., 1971); Peter M. Blau and Otis Dudley Duncan (with Andrea Tyree), *The American Occupational Structure* (New York: John Wiley & Sons, 1967); and Richard Parker, *The Myth of the Middle Class* (New York: Liveright, 1972).

4. David Katzman, *Seven Days a Week: Domestic Service in Industrializing America* (Urbana, IL: University of Illinois Press, 1981), 273; Elizabeth Clark-Lewis, *Living In, Living Out: African American Domestics in Washington, D.C., 1910–1940* (Washington: Smithsonian Institution Press, 1994): 104.

5. Interracial Household Employment Committee, Louisville, Kentucky, Minutes, February 28, 1935, Records Files Collection, YWCA of the U.S.A., National Board Archives, New York (hereinafter YWCA Records), Reel 97.3; Mary Romero, *Maid in the U.S.A.* (New York: Routledge, 1992): 4; Lillian W. Betts, "The Principles of Housekeeping," in *The Woman's Book* (New York: Charles Scribner's Sons, 1894): *passim.*

6. "Emancipated," "A Servant's Viewpoint," *The New York Times,* May 6, 1927. "A Maid" echoed this sentiment in 1946: "I can tell you why girls do

not want to do housework. A maid often works from 7 to 10—children's breakfast at 8, the family's dinner at 8:30 in the evening, and all the different work and meals in between. When you are 40 you look like you are 60." Letters, *The New York Times Magazine,* August 25, 1946. See Judith Rollins, *Between Women: Domestics and Their Employers* (Philadelphia: Temple University Press, 1985): 70–72, 99 on 72-hour weeks for live-in maids in the 1960s and 1970s in the Boston, Massachusetts area.

7. Mary V. Robinson, "Domestic Workers and Their Employment Relations," *Bulletin of the Women's Bureau* 39 (Washington, D.C.: U.S.G.P.O., 1924): 24–25.

8. There were also "useful" maids and men, a catchall term that faded away over time. The idea behind it, however, became more current, in that household staffs got smaller and individuals performed a greater variety of tasks. Mrs. A. E. Johnson Agency placement books.

9. B. Eleanor Johnson, "Household Employment in Chicago," *Bulletin of the Women's Bureau* 106 (Washington, D.C.: U.S.G.P.O., 1933): 19. See also the description of tasks in Amey E. Watson, "Household Employment in Philadelphia," *Bulletin of the Women's Bureau* 93 (Washington, D.C.: U.S.G.P.O., 1932): 24–25.

10. For more on the availability of dryers, see advertisements in *The New York Times* and women's magazines in the 1930s and 1940s.

11. *Alice Adams* (RKO, 1935).

12. New York State Employment Service Specifications, in "Community Household Employment Programs," *Bulletin of the Women's Bureau* 221 (Washington, D.C.: U.S.G.P.O., 1948): 43.

13. "Application for Household Position," National Archives, Record Group 86. Women's Bureau, Division of Research, Unpublished Materials, 1919–1972, 1956 (hereinafter "Women's Bureau Unpublished Materials, 1956"): "Domestic Workers. Household Employment" (1912–1956), Box 286.

14. "Outline for Training Course," Women's Bureau Unpublished Materials, 1956, Box 286.

15. Elizabeth Clark-Lewis, *Living In, Living Out,* 149; see the discussion in Rollins, *Between Women,* about employers' desire for a personal relationship with someone upon whom they can rely and with whom they can talk, 117–120.

16. Margaret T. Mettert, "Injuries in Personal Service Occupations in Ohio," *Bulletin of the Women's Bureau* 151 (Washington, D.C.: U.S.G.P.O., 1937): 7.

17. Watson, "Household Employment in Philadelphia," 63. See also Mettert, "Injuries in Personal Service Occupations in Ohio."

18. General Comics postcard, September 1941, author's collection; Rollins, *Between Women,* 182–3.

19. Congressman Isaac Siegel (R, NY) reported in 1920, "The supply of both Irish and colored help in New York, once constituting the main dependence, has been depleted." *The New York Times,* April 25, 1920; Katzman, *Seven Days A Week,* 56, 60, 290, 291, 292.

    Historical Statistics of the U.S., Colonial Times to 1970, Part 1 (U.S. Dept. of Commerce, Bureau of The Census, 1975): Series D182–232, 132;

U.S. Department of Commerce, Bureau of the Census, *Decennial Censuses of the Population,* 1920–1990.

See Chapter Four for a full discussion of employers' prejudice against African-American servants.

20. Martin Harris in Kisseloff, *You Must Remember This,* 108, Elizabeth Bogen, *Immigration in New York* (NY: Praeger, 1987): 12; Doris Weatherford, *Foreign and Female: Immigrant Women in America, 1840–1930* (New York: Schocken Books, 1986): 147.

21. Evelyn Crookhorn in Kisseloff, *You Must Remember This,* 398; A.E. Johnson Agency record books, 1920–21; Hasia Diner, *Erin's Daughters in America: Irish Immigrant Women in the Nineteenth Century* (Baltimore: The Johns Hopkins University Press, 1983): 94; Joanne J. Meyerowitz, *Women Adrift: Independent Wage Earners in Chicago, 1880–1920* (Chicago: University of Chicago Press, 1988): 24.

22. Lars Ljungmark, "On Emigration, Social Mobility, and the Transfer of Capital," *The Swedish-American Historical Quarterly* 41 (July 1990): 159. Europeans were notorious for treating servants "like . . . beast[s]." Weatherford, *Foreign and Female,* 150.

23. Evelyn Crookhorn in Kisseloff, *You Must Remember This,* 400.

24. Diner, *Erin's Daughters,* 50–51, 93.

25. Diner, *Erin's Daughters,* 94; Ljungmark, "On Emigration," 100.

26. Romero, *Maid in the U.S.A.,* 27.

27. "Community Household Employment Programs," 44; *The New York Times,* July 1, 1928. The story about the maid and the color scheme was on the first page of the newspaper's business section. For a discussion of domestics' being their role and not individuals, see Trudier Harris, *From Mammies to Militants: Domestics in Black American Literature* (Philadelphia: Temple University Press, 1982): 12–13.

28. Lillian W. Betts, "The Principles of Housekeeping," in *The Woman's Book* (New York: Charles Scribner's Sons, 1894): 131. The Harris family's servants lived on the top floor of their brownstone but "had to bathe down in washtubs in the basement laundry. There was a toilet there for them, too." Martin Harris in Kisseloff, *You Must Remember This,* 108.

29. Olive Huber, who grew up in a brownstone on Manhattan's East Side, remembered that her family's "in-help . . . lived on the top floor, where there were a lot of little rooms." Olive Huber in Kisseloff, *You Must Remember This,* 397. Barbara Bainbridge McIntosh recalled a "maids' dormitory" at 34 Gramercy Park. B. McIntosh in Kisseloff, *You Must Remember This:* 397–8; "Average Sizes and Typical Layouts of Maids' Rooms and Kitchens," *Buildings and Building Management,* August 26, 1929.

See also, for example, 125–135 East 63rd Street, which put servants in the rear on the first floor, behind the professional offices. *Real Estate Record and Builders Guide,* June 3, 1922: 692.

See Frieda S. Miller, "The Situation in New York," Report of the Symposium on Household Employment, New York, New York, November 28, 1939, YWCA Records, Reel 98.4: 3; interview with German woman #2 re 1955 arrival, March 26, 1995; "Miss Burroughs" in "Proceedings of the Women's Industrial Conference," Women's Bureau, U.S. Department of Labor (Washington: U.S.G.P.O., 1923): 48.

Rollins, *Between Women*, 171–2; Harris, *From Mammies to Militants*, 14–15; Roena Bethune, "My First Job in New York [late 1950s]," in Linda K. Kerber and Jane De Hart-Mathews, eds., *Women's America: Refocusing the Past*, 2d ed. (New York: Oxford University Press, 1987): 397–98.

30. "A Servants' Viewpoint," *The New York Times*, May 6, 1927.

31. Diner, *Erin's Daughters*, 93; A. E. Johnson Agency placement books, employee records, 1917–1963.

32. A. E. Johnson Agency placement books 1917–1921; Lucy Maynard Salmon, *Domestic Service* (New York, 1897). Clerks earned more cash—between $45 and $80 a month—but they had to pay for rent, food and clothing (instead of having a uniform).

33. *Decennial Census of the Population*, 1900, 1920; Katzman, *Seven Days a Week*, 56, 60, 290, 291, 292.

Over 8.5 million American women worked outside the home in 1920, or 21.1 percent of all American women. One quarter of them worked in domestic and personal service. "Facts About Working Women," *Bulletin of the Women's Bureau* 46 (Washington: U.S.G.P.O., 1925): 2, 23.

34. "A Domestic Nine-Hour Day," *The New York Times*, May 4, 1927.

In 1921, Andrew Lazare of the Lazare Employment Bureau reported a 10 percent drop in placements from the previous year, down from 12,000 cooks. "Many housewives are doing their own work and others who have had five and six servants have reduced their staff to two or three," he said. "Home Help Still Short," *The New York Times*, September 11, 1921.

In January 1926, the New York State Employment offices reported 99.1 applicants for domestic and personal service to each 100 requests for such workers, representing a slight shortage in the supply. In January 1927, however, the ratio of applicants to jobs offered was 110.5 to 100.0. The economy was already slowing. "Surveys Domestic Labor," *The New York Times*, July 17, 1927.

35. William E. Leuchtenberg, *The Perils of Prosperity, 1914–1932* (Chicago: University of Chicago Press, 1958): 190; Dorothy M. Brown, *Setting a Course: American Women in the 1920s* (Boston: Twayne Publishers, 1987): 20.

There were no restrictions on immigrants from the Western Hemisphere, but because of political and economic conditions in South and Central America, few people emigrated. European colonies such as Jamaica fell under the parent country's quotas. See Chapter Five for a full discussion of immigration.

36. "Want Million Girls to Work $7 a Week," *The New York Times*, January 6, 1920; "Quotas and Servants," *The New York Times*, July 13, 1927; "Servant Shortage Put Up to Coolidge," *The New York Times*, March 31, 1927. Congressman Isaac Siegel (R, NY) blamed the literacy test portion of the immigration laws, instituted prior to 1920, for the shortage of servants. He suggested that to "meet one of our own pressing needs," there be exemptions for servants, just as there were for Mexican laborers in the Southwest. "Why Not Import Your Servant?" *The New York Times*, April

25, 1920; "Would Admit Illiterate Servants," *The New York Times,* May 20, 1920.

37. "Want Million Girls to Work $7 a Week," *The New York Times,* January 6, 1920.

38. ""Variations in Employment Trends of Women and Men," *Bulletin of the Women's Bureau* 73 (Washington: U.S.G.P.O., 1930): 34, 6–7.

   In 1920, more than a quarter of all working women in the U.S. were in domestic and personal service (a drop from 31.3 percent in 1910), but manufacturing claimed 22.6 percent and clerical had jumped to 16.7 from 7.3 percent. Indeed, only domestic service and agriculture had suffered drops. "Facts About Working Women," *Bulletin of the Women's Bureau* 46 (Washington: U.S.G.P.O., 1925): 9; Janet M. Hooks, "Women's Occupations Throughout Seven Decades [1870–1940]," *Bulletin of the Women's Bureau* 218 (Washington: U.S.G.P.O., 1951): 75–80, 84, 94; *Decennial Census of the Population,* 1930; "Solving the Problem of Servants," *The New York Times,* October 20, 1920; "Tells of Shortage of Alien Laborers," *The New York Times,* April 18, 1920.

39. Brown, *Setting a Course,* 81.

40. "Variations in Employment Trends of Women and Men," *Bulletin of the Women's Bureau* 73 (Washington: U.S.G.P.O., 1930): 42–43; "A Domestic Nine-Hour Day," *The New York Times,* May 4, 1927.

41. "A Domestic Nine-Hour Day." 165 young Irish women arrived in June 1921, and most of them wanted to be stenographers, not servants. "Irish Girls Seek Careers," *The New York Times,* June 21, 1921.

42. "Home vs. Office Work," *The New York Times,* September 21, 1926.

43. "A Domestic Nine-Hour Day." "153,088 Negroes in City," *The New York Times,* February 26, 1921.

44. Geoffrey Perrett, *America in the Twenties: A History* (New York: Simon & Schuster, 1982): 244; "Topics of the Times: Solving the Problem of Servants," *The New York Times,* October 20, 1920.

45. Telephone interview with Virginia Johnson, Brooklyn, New York, May 29, 1992; Calvin B. Holder, "The Causes and Composition of West Indian Immigration to New York City, 1900–1952," *Afro-Americans in New York Life and History* 11:1 (January 1987): 13–14; Marshall, "Black Immigrant Women in *Brown Girl Brownstones,*" 89; "Negroes Flock to North," *The New York Times,* October 25, 1923; "Negroes Lured to North," *The New York Times,* November 6, 1923.

   "[T]he years following World War I . . . witnessed the first major wave of West Indian immigration." Perrett, *America in the Twenties:* 242.

   African-Americans realized that immigrants were a threat to their jobs. See Arnold Shankman, *Ambivalent Friends: Afro-Americans View the Immigrant* (Westport, CT: Greenwood Press, 1982): 156–165.

46. Paule Marshall, "Black Immigrant Women in *Brown Girl Brownstones,*" in *Caribbean Life in New York City: Sociocultural Dimensions,* Constance R. Sutton and Elsa M. Chaney, eds. (NY: Center for Migration Studies of New York, Inc., 1987): 87–89.

47. "Servant Shortage Put Up to Coolidge," *The New York Times*, March 31, 1927.

48. One African-American woman leader noted, "Notwithstanding her culture and training, the average white woman still thinks of the negro woman in terms of domestic service and assigns to her a place of inferiority in society." "Finds Color Bar Growing," *The New York Times*, July 10, 1928.

49. "Facts About Working Women," *Bulletin of the Women's Bureau* 46 (Washington: U.S.G.P.O., 1925): 23, 26, 28–9, 32, 37–9; United States Department of Commerce, Bureau of the Census, *Decennial Census of the United States*, 1940; Daniel O. Price, "Occupational Changes among Whites and Nonwhites, with Projections for 1970," in Norval D. Glenn and Charles M. Bonjean, *Blacks in the United States* (San Francisco: Chandler Publishing Company, 1969: 63.

50. See, for example, the comments in Elaine Bell Kaplan, "'I Don't Do No Windows': Competition Between the Domestic Worker and the Housewife," in Valerie Miner and Helen E. Longino, *Competition: A Feminist Taboo?* (New York: The Feminist Press, 1987).

51. A.E. Johnson Agency placement books 1917–1921. Some of today's equivalents to these wages would be: $50–60 in 1918 equals $611.29–733.55 in 2003; $1.50 equals $18.34 while $2.50 equals $30.56; $75 equals $916.93. "What is its Relative Value in US Dollars?," Economic History Services, http://www.eh.net/hmit/compare. The values are based on the Bureau of Labor Statistics' Commodity Price Index (CPI).

52. "Home Help Still Short," *The New York Times*, September 11, 1921; A.E. Johnson Agency record books 1917–1921; "What is its Relative Value in US Dollars?" $3.10 in 1921 was the equivalent of $31.88 in 2003, compared to $44.01 for $3.60 in 1918. In purchasing power, then, the drop was a whopping 28 percent, not the face value drop of 14 percent.

53. A.E. Johnson Agency placement books 1917–1921; "Turning Tide in the Domestic Servant Market," *The New York Times Book Review and Magazine*, December 5, 1920. The "dear old $35 a month figure" from 1917 was worth approximately $503.31 in 2003 dollars. In 1922, twice that amount ($70) was worth only $770.22, because of inflation. "What is its Relative Value in US Dollars?."

54. A.E. Johnson Agency placement books, 1917–1921.

55. Helen Bullitt Lowry, "Turning Tide in the Domestic Servant Market," *The New York Times Book Review and Magazine*, December 5, 1920.

56. "Home Help Still Short," *The New York Times*, September 11, 1921.

57. "Home vs. Office Work," *The New York Times*, September 21, 1926.

58. "Home Help Still Short."

59. "Why Servant Girls Leave Perfectly Luxurious Homes," *The New York Times*, November 16, 1924.

60. Marshall, "Black Immigrant Women in *Brown Girl Brownstones*," 89; Virginia Johnson interview, New York City, May 29, 1992; Charlotte Wu (Virginia Johnson's daughter) interview, New York City, May 20, 1992.

61. bell hooks, *YEARNING: race, gender, and cultural politics* (Boston: South End Press, 1990): 42.

62. hooks, *YEARNING*, 46.

63. "Mistress of Small Apartment Has Her Own Servant Problem," *The New York Times*, August 17, 1924; Elizabeth Clark-Lewis, "'This Work Had a End'": 204.

64. "Domestic Service Put on Eight-Hour Basis," *The New York Times*, June 14, 1925; Lucy Maynard Salmon, *Domestic Service* (New York, 1897), *passim*. The significant drop in the number of servants (over one-fifth) between 1900 and 1920 demonstrates Salmon's failure to make her case.

65. "Domestic Service Put on Eight-Hour Basis," *The New York Times*, June 14, 1925.

66. "Domestic Service Put on Eight-Hour Basis"; "Household Assistants," *The New York Times*, April 24, 1921.

67. "Home Help Still Short," *The New York Times*, September 11, 1921.

68. "A Servant's Viewpoint," *The New York Times*, May 6, 1927.

69. See for example, "Fanny Christina Hill," in Sherna Berger Gluck, *Rosie the Riveter Revisited: Women, the War and Social Change* (New York: Meridian, 1987):33–34.

70. See the discussion in Maurine Weiner Greenwald, *Women, War, and Work: The Impact of World War I on Women Workers in the United States* (Ithaca, NY: Cornell University Press, 1990): xiv.

71. Leuchtenberg, *The Perils of Prosperity*, 161.

72. See, for example, "Why Housemaids Are Scarce," *The New York Times*, September 24, 1926. This was a female job, and that it was not attractive to men was evident in New York court rulings that held that workers like watchmen or caretakers (typically male jobs) could not be considered domestic servants. "Court Says Gardener is Domestic Servant," *The New York Times*, September 18, 1927.

73. Lillian W. Betts, "The Principles of Housekeeping," 116.

74. Brown, *Setting a Course*, 7.
    Other appliances that made cooking and cleaning easier were electric toasters, percolators, waffle irons, clothes irons and electric grills, electric refrigerators, ironing machines, sewing machines, vacuum cleaners, washing machines, dishwashers and exhaust fans. *Real Estate Record and Builders Guide*, April 30, 1927: 11; April 2, 1927: 13.

75. *Real Estate Record and Builders Guide*, July 3, 1920: 13; William E. Leuchtenberg, *The Perils of Prosperity*, 190. One writer had predicted in 1894, "Electricity is the household servant of the near future." Betts, "The Principles of Housekeeping," 119.

76. *Real Estate Record and Builders Guide*, March 5, 1927: 11; *Real Estate Record and Builders Guide*, May 28, 1927: 15. Electric-powered appliances were not the only innovations. The Lombardy (56th and Park Avenue) extolled its gas-operated refrigerators, showing the man of the house preparing to serve drinks with ice cubes to his wife and their two guests. *Real Estate Record and Builders Guide*, June 11, 1927: 10.

77. *Real Estate Record and Builders Guide*, October 23, 1920: 583–584.

78. "Scottish Lassies Turning to Canada," *The New York Times,* September 28, 1924.
79. *Real Estate Record and Builders Guide,* March 18, 1922: 345. Laundries were a good example. Between 1914 and 1924, commercial laundry use went up 57 percent. New York City's Stancourt Laundry reassured its clients, "Linens and Lingerie NEVER Come in Contact with those of any other Family!" even though 50,000 women used the service. And when it came back home, a maid could put it away. Stancourt also played to the other end of the economic scale with an illustration of a housewife making a bed. *The New York Times,* April 17, 1927.
80. "Servants and Machinery," *The New York Times,* December 21, 1929.
81. *Real Estate Record and Builders Guide,* October 2, 1920: 455.
82. For example, between 1922 and 1923 real estate transfers and conveyances in New York City increased by 19 percent. Real estate activity in the first nine months of 1923 was the "greatest in American history," according to the National Association of Real Estate Boards. 1924 brought even greater, and very diversified, activity. *Real Estate Record and Builders Guide,* April 19, 1924: 7; May 17, 1924: 7; January 29, 1927: 7; January 5, 1929: 5, 9.
83. *Real Estate Record and Builders Guide,* March 16, 1929: 5.
84. "The Servant Problem," *The New York Times,* November 28, 1928. In another, earlier comment, the *Times* noted:

    The 'houseful of servants' common to a past generation is no more. Homes have shrunk from houses to apartments, and from large apartments to tiny ones. Many mansions have been put on the market, as their owners have moved to apartments, and once spacious houses have undergone conversion into dwellings for two, three or four families. New buildings follow the trend toward contracted living quarters. . . . Now there is seldom room for more than one servant. . . .

    "Mistress of Small Apartment Has Her Own Servant Problem," *The New York Times,* August 17, 1924.
85. The wealthy still had live-in help. The cooperative building at 1060 Fifth Avenue (87th Street had maids' rooms, as did 30 Sutton Place and 775 Park Avenue. See advertisements in the Real Estate section, *The New York Times,* February 3, 1929.

    A middle-income building, Buckingham Hall, 789 St. Marks Avenue, Brooklyn, advertised modern housekeeping apartments with full kitchens. Presumably day workers could come in, as could cooks. Real Estate section, *The New York Times,* August 17, 1924.

    120 West 58th Street featured "Real Kitchens" and "Extra Maids' Lavatory in 4 rooms." Jackson Heights, Queens, had apartments with one bathroom off the kitchen, so it would be usable by a live-out maid or cook without inconveniencing the rest of the household. Real Estate section, *The New York Times,* June 20, 1923.

    Tenement-class buildings, like those built by Metropolitan Life in Astoria and Corona, Queens had no service entrances in apartments. The architects assumed that housewives alone would be doing housework and consulted "the housewife herself, who could count better than anyone else the steps saved in performing her housework and the time she economized." *Real Estate Record and Builders Guide,* June 24, 1922: 775–6.

86. *Real Estate Record and Builders Guide,* April 30, 1927: 7.

Edward P. Doyle of the Real Estate Board "pointed out that a strict construction of the Tenement House Law in its present form would convert any high-class apartment hotel into a 'tenement' if a Tenement Department Inspector discovered the occupants using a coffee percolator or a few cups and saucers." Doyle "insisted that a kitchen properly should consist of a room equipped with such conveniences as a cook stove, sink, ice-box and other conveniences and intended altogether for culinary purposes." The Real Estate Board promoted legislation to suspend "the provisions of the Tenement House Law which ban the use of gas plates, electric coffee percolators and similar devices in apartment hotels and studio apartments by classifying such structures as 'tenements' whenever occupants avail themselves of such conveniences." *Real Estate Record and Builders Guide,* February 19, 1927: 11.

87. Real Estate Record and Builders Guide, April 8, 1922: 425.

NOTES TO CHAPTER TWO

1. The first newspaper article on this phenomenon in New York was in *The Harlem Liberator,* a black communist paper, on July 22, 1933.

In 1940, the mayor's office listed 13 Bronx corners, 9 Brooklyn and Richmond markets, and 3 Queens marts, most of which were near subway stations. Undoubtedly, they missed many more. Brenda Clegg Gray, *Black Female Domestics in the Depression* (New York: Garland Publishing Co., 1993): 58.

A contemporary observer noted:

At the bottom of the worker scale is the 'slave market' as it exists in certain cities. New York has 200 slave markets, according to the Domestic Workers' Union. You can bargain for household help in the Bronx on almost any corner above 167th Street. Colored workers, mostly women, stand there in little groups waiting to be hired. Each carries a bundle containing her work clothes and the lunch she will eat hastily on her own time. They work for 35 cents an hour, although 50 cents is the standard rate. Some who are desperate or cold or tired of standing will work for 25. They say that they are sometimes asked to go for 15. Most jobs last three or four hours.

Evelyn Seely, "Our Feudal Housewives,"
The Nation (May 28, 1938): 613.

2003 wage equivalents were: 50 cents equaled $6.51, 35 cents equaled $4.56, 25 cents equaled $3.26, and 15 cents equaled $1.95. "What Is Its Relative Value in US Dollars?," Economic History Services, http://eh.net/hmit/compare/. These conversions are based on the Bureau of Labor Statistics' Commodity Price Index (CPI).

2. Marvel Cooke and Ella Baker, "The Bronx Slave Market," *The Crisis,* November 1935. Cooke considered Baker to be "very good politically, but she was harem-scarem . . . undisciplined," so Cooke took it upon herself to go to the slave market, write the piece and "let her use her name on it." Kathleen Currie interview with Marvel Cooke, Women in Journalism oral history project of the Washington Press Club Foundation, Harlem, NY, November 1, 1989, in the Oral History Collection of Columbia University and other repositories: 107; Marvel Cooke interview with author, Harlem, NY, January 25, 1996.

3. By 1936, the percentage of women just seeking work in domestic work had risen to 51 percent from 30 percent in 1930. Although there was fairly high unemployment in domestic service, there was more in other occupations. This indicates that women had turned to domestic work from those other jobs. Winifred Wandersee, *Women's Work and Family Values, 1920–1940* (Cambridge, MA: Harvard University Press, 1981): 85, 89, 93; Janet M. Hooks, "Women's Occupations Throughout Seven Decades [1870–1940]," *Bulletin of the Women's Bureau* 218 (Washington: U.S.G.P.O., 1951): 75–80, 84, 94.

   "Household Workers," *The New York Times,* January 19, 1932, cited by Donna L. van Raaphorst, *Union Maids Not Wanted: Organizing Domestic Workers, 1870–1940* (NY: Praeger, 1988): 224. Van Raaphorst goes on to say, "so powerful was this stigma that in the early days of the Depression service vacancies went unfilled. Unemployed women were so reluctant to adopt the stigma that went along with domestic work that they sometimes preferred to remain unemployed."

   The Charity Organization Society reported that among the poor families whose cases they handled, "67 per cent of all the women unemployed are the chief wage earners of their families, and that 53 per cent of them come from the domestic service group. . . . The next largest group, 25 per cent from factory work." *The New York Times,* March 24, 1930.

4. U.S. Department of Commerce, Bureau of the Census, *Decennial Census of the Population,* 1900, 1920; Katzman, *Seven Days A Week,* 56, 60, 290, 291, 292.

5. Guichard Parris and Lester Brooks, *Blacks in the City: A History of the National Urban League* (Boston: Little, Brown and Co., 1971): 204.

6. U.S. Department of Commerce, Bureau of the Census, *Decennial Census of the Population,* 1920, 1930; "Facts About Working Women," *Bulletin of the Women's Bureau* 46 (Washington, G.P.O., 1925): 2; "Household Employment: An Outline For Study Groups," United States Department of Labor, Women's Bureau, November 1940: Introduction. National Archives, RG 86, Women's Bureau, Division of Research, Unpublished Materials, 1919–1972. 1956: "Domestic Workers. Household Employment" (1912–1956), Box 286. Domestic Workers—Bibliography; Allyson S. Grossman, "Women in Domestic Work: Yesterday and Today," *Monthly Labor Review* (August 1980): 17–21.

7. Wandersee, *Women's Work and Family Values,* 85, 89, 93.

8. "Negro Household Employees During Current Unemployment Crisis," Records Files Collection, YWCA of the U.S.A., National Board Archives, New York (hereinafter YWCA Records), Reel 98.4: 2; Gray, *Black Female Domestics*, 89, quoting Dorothy Dunbar Bromley, "Are Servants People?," *Scribner's Magazine* 94 (December 1933): 377. Alice Kessler-Harris points out,

> If the market sustained a general level of wages, it did not prevent competition among workers. The depression witnessed a small influx of white women into domestic and public household service. At the upper levels, white women replaced nonwhites, setting off a ripple effect that resulted in real suffering among the poorest workers at the lowest wage levels characteristic of day workers.

Alice Kessler-Harris, *Out to Work: A History of Wage-Earning Women in the United States* (New York: Oxford University Press, 1982): 270–1.

The drop from $60 to $35 was equivalent in 2003 dollars to $851.86 to $496.92. "What Is Its Relative Value in US Dollars?."

A Brooklyn, New York, YWCA secretary reported in 1935, "Whereas before the depression the laundry work was taken care of outside, now this has been added to the work given to the domestic help." This was a nationwide phenomenon. Cited in Mary V. Anderson, "The Plight of the Negro Domestic Laborer," May 1935, YWCA Records Reel 98.4: 4.

9. Lucy Randolph Mason (Gen. Secy of the Nat'l Consumers Union), "The Perfect Treasure," A.J.L.A. (Junior League) News Reel (February 1934) in YWCA records, Reel 97.3. Randolph added, "Studies indicate that wages of $5 a week were common throughout the country and that vast numbers of workers received $1, $2 or $3 a week while a considerable number worked for non-cash wages, but were compensated only by room and board."

Ten dollars in 1933 was the equivalent of $141.98 in 2003, $5 equaled $70.99, $3 equaled $42.59, $2 equaled $28.40, and $1 equaled $14.20. Because of deflation, these amounts actually had more purchasing power in 1933 than they did in 1928, when their respective equivalents were $107.35, $53.67, $32.20, $21.47, and $10.73. "What Is Its Relative Value in US Dollars?."

10. William Leach, *Land of Desire: Merchants, Power, and the Rise of a New American Culture* (New York: Vintage Books, 1993): 266.

11. Judith Rollins, *Between Women: Domestics and Their Employers* (Philadelphia: Temple University Press, 1985): 78–79; Trudier Harris, *From Mammies to Militants: Domestics in Black American Literature* (Philadelphia: Temple University Press, 1982): 18–19.

12. Naomi Waller Washington in Jeff Kisseloff, *You Must Remember This: An Oral History of Manhattan from the 1890s to World War II* (New York: Harcourt Brace Jovanovich, 1989): 327.

13. Frank Byrd, "Harlem House-Rent Parties: (#3) Bernice," October 4, 1938. Library of Congress, MSS Division, WPA Federal Writers' Project Collection, Beliefs and Customs—Folk Stuff, Folklore New York.

14. In 1937, white wage-earning families averaged $1,743 a year; the Labor Department said a single woman needed at least $1,192 in annual income.

But the average white maid brought in a maximum of $1,000 a year. "Cost of Living," *Monthly Labor Review* 44:1 (January 1937): 236; Frieda S. Miller [of the Women's Bureau], "Living Costs of Working Women in New York," *Monthly Labor Review* 45:3 (March 1938): 577; "Recession Lowers Servants' Wages; Agencies Report Scarcity of Scandinavian and British Trained Domestics," *The New York Times*, May 17, 1938. Cooks were the highest paid workers, with wages ranging from $90 to $125 a month.

By 2003 standards, wages were low. The average yearly wage was equivalent to $22,300.67, and a single woman's needs equaled $15,250.95. $1,000 a year was equivalent to $12,724.42. At $12.50 a week (or $159.93 in 2004 dollars), a domestic could make only $650 a year (equivalent to $8,316.37), assuming 52-week employment. "What Is Its Relative Value in US Dollars?."

15. Interracial Household Employment Committee, Louisville, Kentucky, Minutes, February 28, 1935, YWCA Records, Reel 97.3; "Fanny Christina Hill," in Sherna Berger Gluck, *Rosie the Riveter Revisited: Women, the War and Social Change* (New York: Meridian, 1987): 33. The Women's Bureau reported,

> [H]ousehold employees are working an average of 10 to 12 hours a day . . . , and many of them are given no annual vacations and rarely are they paid for over-time work. The most common work-week in industry is 40–44 hours, about 20 hours or nearly three work-days less a week than domestic service commonly requires.

"Household Employment: The Problem of 2,000,000 [Women] Workers," RG 86, Women's Bureau, Division of Research, Unpublished Materials 1919–1972. 1956: "Domestic Workers. Household Employment (1912–1956)." Box 286.

16. "Wages and Hours of Labor," *Monthly Labor Review* 32:5 (May 1931): 137–138; Jacqueline Jones, *Labor of Love, Labor of Sorrow: Black Women, Work and the family, From Slavery to the Present* (New York: Vintage, 1985): 209. See also the discussion in Phyllis Palmer, *Domesticity and Dirt: Housewives and Domestics Servants in the United States, 1920–1945* (Philadelphia: Temple University Press, 1989): 71–81.

"Domestic Help Found Scarce," *The New York Times*, January 24, 1937.

17. "Domestic Help Found Scarce."

18. Steven Ruttenbaum, *Mansions in the Clouds: The Skyscraper Palazzi of Emery Roth* (New York: Balsam Press, Inc., 1986): 170; Richard Plunz, *A History of Housing in New York City: Dwelling Type and Social Change in the American Metropolis* (New York: Columbia University Press: 1990): 195–6, 198; "Study Our Plans for Small Homes," *The New York Times*, September 4, 1938; *The Architectural Forum* (April 1935): 275; *The Architectural Forum* (February 1935): 173–5.

Norge sponsored a large supplement in the March 1935 *Architectural Forum* to display kitchenette and kitchen possibilities using their appliances. Three out of the four designs were for small apartments or houses. Only the last was "for a larger family with possible maid service." *The*

Architectural Forum, advertising supplement (March 1935): 11–24; *The Architectural Forum* (April 1935): 276; *The Architectural Forum,* 1930– 1935 *passim.*

19. National Committee on Household Employment, "Proposals for a Voluntary Agreement in Household Employment," Women's Bureau Unpublished Materials. 1956: "Domestic Workers. Household Employment (1912–1956)." Box 286; Gertrude M. King letter, *The New York Times,* September 15, 1930.

20. *The New York Times,* March 29, 1930.
    W.A.C. of Webster, Massachusetts wrote:
    From time to time, I read of the City of New York spending millions monthly for relief, and of the number of persons desperate and out of work and on the dole, as it were. This situation holds true in practically all of the larger cities, I believe, and at the same time if a person desires to hire a domestic helper who would be well treated and receive about $30 monthly clear, together with a nice home, it is impossible to obtain one. What is the answer?.
    "A Problem," *The New York Times,* April 21, 1935.

21. Gertrude M. King letter, *The New York Times,* September 15, 1930.

22. National Committee on Household Employment, "Proposals for a Voluntary Agreement in Household Employment," Women's Bureau Unpublished Materials. 1956: "Domestic Workers. Household Employment (1912–1956)." Box 286; "Servants Assail 'Slavery' in Homes," *The New York Times,* March 22, 1935.
    In 1937, Marvel Cooke reported,
    Until very recently, a girl on a "sleep-in" job many times worked as much as fourteen to sixteen hours a day. She was on call at all times. Even her day off, she might be asked to do her employers a "special favor" and have to work, with no time off later for consideration.
    Marvel Cooke, "Times Bad? Employment Heads Insist Things Are Picking Up," *New York Amsterdam News,* July 17, 1937.

23. Alice Kessler-Harris notes:
    The change in status of the servant from sleep-in domestic to day worker reflected the change in household structure. Compared to the sleep-in maid, the day worker gained immeasurably in personal freedom, yet she still lacked the advantages of impersonal work. Day workers got no paid holidays or sick leave. They worked an unpredictable schedule. Excluded from social security benefits until 1952 and from Federal minimum wage provisions until 1974, domestic workers labored at the lowest possible pay.
    Alice Kessler-Harris, *Women Have Always Worked: A Historical Overview* (Old Westbury, NY: The Feminist Press, 1981): 83–4; "Houseworker Wanted," *The New York Times,* August 29, 1930.

24. *The New York Times,* January 5, 1930: classified ads, pp. 1–3; "Employed Women Are Younger Now," *The New York Times,* February 7, 1937.

25. For payment patterns, see, for example, "Questionnaire," National Archives, Record Group 86, Women's Bureau, Unpublished Materials 1919–1972,

1956: Domestic Workers, Box 286, Domestic Workers: Forms & Instructions. See also Kathleen Currie, interview with Marvel Cooke, Harlem, NY, November 1, 1989, Washington Press Club Foundation: 110–111.

26. Chicago was similar to New York City in its dependence upon first immigrant and then African-American servants. But employers there were even more racist than New Yorkers. The Women's Bureau did a 1933 survey in Chicago of 250 employers and 250 employees. The author wrote, "From the reports of employers their general preference was for the foreign-born white worker. . . . Apparently those having no choice employed Negro workers." In fact, 42 percent of those queried in Chicago employed foreign-born white workers, 28 percent native-born white, and only 30 percent African-American, which was more skewed than New York, despite comparable intra-U.S. migration patterns and New York's status as the major entry point for immigrants. B. Eleanor Johnson, "Household Employment in Chicago," *Bulletin of the Women's Bureau* 106 (Washington, D.C.: U.S.G.P.O., 1933): 6, 26.

27. By 1938, Dora Jones of the Domestic Workers Union estimated that 70 percent of all black women workers in New York City (native born or West Indian) were servants, the majority of them general houseworkers, the lowest rung of the ladder. Nationally, two-thirds of all non-white women were in private and public housekeeping fields by 1940, while only 17 percent of white women were so engaged. No group did especially well during the Depression, but African-Americans fared the worst. Jones, *Labor of Love*, 200.

In the Chicago survey, "where both native white and Negro workers were employed, the native-white employee was the nursemaid or practical nurse and the Negro the houseworker." Johnson, "Household Employment in Chicago," 27.

The proportion of non-white women in housekeeping jobs went up even as their share of the female labor force went down from 49 to 47 percent. Hooks, "Seven Decades," 142–4.

28. As a matter of course, black women were steered toward domestic work.

Edna W. Unger, director of the Emergency Relief Bureau in the city, told one black woman who had written her for help 'obtaining a position as a nurse's aide' to go to the New York State Employment Agency on East 50th Street. 'This division maintains a free service in placing qualified people in domestic positions and they may be able to help you.'

Gray, *Black Female Domestics*, 39.

29. Marvel Cooke, "Times Bad? Employment Heads Insist Things Are Picking Up," *New York Amsterdam News*, July 17, 1937.

30. Marvel Cooke, "Dixie Girl Exposes Racket of Employment Agencies," *New York Amsterdam News*, April 24, 1937.

31. The Travelers Aid Society brought agency abuses to the attention of the Ashland Place, Brooklyn, YWCA. Josephine Carroll, a social worker at the Y, reported to the 1931 meeting of the Y's National Committee on Employer-Employee Relationships in the Home, that as a result of being brought to

New York by one unscrupulous commercial employment agency, "The girls are held practically as slaves . . . with no time off and no chance to meet other people and learn the true condition of affairs." "Says Servant Girls Are Duped in Homes," *The New York Times*, April 15, 1931; Gray, *Black Female Domestics*, 50–51.

32. One of the frequenters of the Bronx Slave Market played the horses. "'Who we gwine play in the nex' race?' asked Mae Lou. 'I walk way up in de Bronix t'day—didn' git no job. On'y had one nickel. Thought I'd play today and git sup'm. Nickel ain' nuthin.'" [sic] Vivian Morris, "Race Horse Row," March 22, 1939. Library of Congress, MSS Division, WPA Federal Writers' Project Collection, Beliefs and Customs—Folk Stuff, Folklore New York.

33. Arnold Manoff, "Folk-Stuff: Women and Cards," September 27, 1938. Library of Congress, MSS Division, WPA Federal Writers' Project Collection, Beliefs and Customs—Folk Stuff, Folklore New York.

34. Vivian Morris, "Bronx Slave Market," November 30, 1938, Library of Congress, MSS Division, WPA Federal Writers' Project Collection, Beliefs and Customs—Folk Stuff, Folklore New York. Note: Morris transcribed her interview in colloquial spelling, which I have not altered.

35. Vivian Morris, "Bronx Slave Market." Cheating was common. When Marvel Cooke visited the revived slave markets during the 1949–50 recession, her employer attempted to run the clock ahead and cheat Cooke out of an hour's pay. The other women at the corner had warned her to set her watch with the woman's clock, however, so Cooke was able to outwit the employer. Kathleen Currie, interview with Marvel Cooke, Harlem, NY, November 1, 1989, Washington Press Club Foundation: 110–111.

   Sometimes employers attempted to avoid paying anything at all. Tessie Voggensberger, a white domestic, was forced in 1939 to sue Adrian C. Humphreys, a Federal Securities and Exchange Commission trial examiner, for back wages of $126.50. "Official Sued by Maid for Salary," *New York Amsterdam News*, February 11, 1939.

36. Brian Lanker, interview, "Queen Mother Audley Moore" in *I Dream a World: Portraits of Black Women Who Changed America* (New York: Stewart, Tabori, and Chang, 1989): 103; Gray, *Black Female Domestics*: 78–84. See also the discussion in Palmer, *Domesticity and Dirt*, 72.

37. Vivian Morris, "Bronx Slave Market."

38. "Expenditures for Electrical Appliances for Workers in 42 Cities," *Monthly Labor Review* 45:2 (February 1938): 448–451. Black Americans tended to buy smaller appliances, like irons, and only the richest of them bought refrigerators and sewing machines. Unlike whites, few African Americans mentioned buying washing machines.

39. As Ruth Schwartz Cowan points out, it was a "safe assumption that most middle-class homes had switched to new methods of cooking [etc.] by the time the depression began." Ruth Schwartz Cowan, "The 'Industrial Revolution' in the Home: Household Technology and Social Change in the Twentieth Century," in *Women's America: Refocusing the Past*, 2nd. ed., Linda K. Kerber and Jane DeHart-Mathews, eds. (New York, 1987):

332; "Servants Not Displaced," editorial, *The New York Times*, March 23, 1935; *The Architectural Forum* (April 1935): 275–6.

40. Vivian Morris, "Bronx Slave Market."
41. Marvel Cooke, "Modern Slaves," *New York Amsterdam News*, October 16, 1937.
42. Rosalyn Terborg-Penn, "Survival Strategies Among African-American Workers: A Continuing Process," in *Women, Work and Protest*, Ruth Milkman, ed. (Boston: Routledge & Kegan Paul, 1985): 144–146.
43. Vivian Morris, "Domestic Workers Union," February 2, 1939. Library of Congress, MSS Division, WPA Federal Writers' Project Collection, Beliefs and Customs—Folk Stuff, Folklore New York; *The WPA Guide to New York City* (New York: Pantheon Books, 1939, rep. 1982): 260.
44. Marvel Cooke, "Some Ways to Kill the Slave Market," *The Daily Compass*, January 12, 1950.
45. Louise Granger to Committee on Household Employment, June 15, 1937, YWCA records, Reel 97.3. There was also a National Domestic and Migrant Workers Association active in Westchester County, New York in the early 1960s. Maudie Adams, "Looking at White Plains," *Westchester County Press*, May 4, 1963.
46. "Meeting of the Sub-Committee on Household Employment," October 11, 1937, YWCA records, Reel 97.3.
47. Robert Weisbrot, *Father Divine and the Struggle for Racial Equality* (Urbana, IL: University of Illinois Press, 1983): 141.
48. Weisbrot, *Father Divine*: 141.
49. Frank Byrd, "'PEACE IN THE KINGDOM' (Religious Cult of Father Devine) [sic]," September 5, 1938. Library of Congress, MSS Division, WPA Federal Writers' Project Collection, Beliefs and Customs—Folk Stuff, Folklore New York.
50. Weisbrot, *Father Divine*: 141. Some contemporary observers didn't believe that Father Divine demanded higher wages. "He also allows his followers to work on a cheaper wage scale, thereby bringing down the wage scale in the domestic servant field. "Father" gets a percentage of the pittance that they earn." Vivian Morris, "Negro Cults in Harlem," January 9, 1939. Library of Congress, MSS Division, WPA Federal Writers' Project Collection, Beliefs and Customs—Folk Stuff, Folklore New York.
51. Jay Jackson, "Tisha Mingo," *New York Amsterdam News*, August 21, 1937; November 6, 1937; November 27, 1937. Jackson was a well-known cartoonist in the black community and was certainly aware of the irony of his cartoon. Tim Jackson, "Jay Jackson," *Salute to Pioneering Artists of Color* (http://www.clstoons.com/paoc/jjackson.htm).
52. Myrtle Taylor to the editor, *New York Amsterdam-News*, October 23, 1937.
53. New York City had about 161,000 women engaged in domestic service in 1930, and 116,226 domestic servants in 1940. *Decennial Census of the Population*, 1930, 1940. See the tables following the introduction for more detailed information.
  The drop in the proportion of private household workers in the female labor force was much more marked. From 29.6 percent of all employed

women in 1930, the ratio dropped to 20.4 percent in 1940 and then to 8.4 percent in 1950. Allyson S. Grossman, "Women in Domestic Work: Yesterday and Today," *Monthly Labor Review* (August 1980): 17–21.

54. "Katie is Leaving," 10; Robert A. Armstrong and Homer Hoyt, *Decentralization in New York* (Chicago: Urban Land Institute, 1941).

During the summer, there was usually a small surge in supply, but since wealthier families who normally went to Europe and shut their houses needed to stay in the U.S., not even that small relief was afforded maid-hunters. "Servant 'Problem' Is Laid to Defense," *The New York Times*, June 12, 1941.

55. Between 1940 and 1945, the female labor force grew more than 50 percent, the proportion of those employed went from 27.6 percent to 37 percent, and in 1946 women accounted for 36.1 percent of civilian labor force. "Women's employment grew in every occupational field but that of domestic service," and especially in factory defense work, as well as in office work and the service industries. "[O]f greatest importance were the opportunities for women to work in jobs where rates [of pay] were historically higher." Eugenia Kaledin, *Mothers and More: American Women in the 1950s* (Boston: Twayne Publishers, 1984): 21.

The biggest gainers were factory work and clerical work, and defense industry employment rose 460 percent. Susan M. Hartmann, *The Home Front and Beyond: American Women in the 1940s* (Boston: Twayne Publishers, 1982): 21, 78.

56. Vivian Morris, "Domestic Workers' Union," February 2, 1939. Library of Congress, MSS Division, WPA Federal Writers' Project Collection, Beliefs and Customs—Folk Stuff, Folklore New York.

57. "Slave Markets in City Protested," *The New York Times*, May 19, 1938; "Would End Abuse in Job Soliciting," *The New York Times*, March 12, 1939; "'Slave Markets' in Bronx Decried," *The New York Times*, December 1, 1939.

58. "Slave Mart Under Quiz," *New York Amsterdam News*, February 1, 1939; "'Slave Market' Probed," *New York Amsterdam Star-News*, March 8, 1941; "City 'Slave Marts' Studied by Mayor," *The New York Times*, February 27, 1941, March 20, 1941, March 21, 1941, April 27, 1941, May 2, 1941; "Center Opened to End Bronx 'Slave Markets,'" *New York Herald Tribune*, May 2, 1941; "Slave Market Shelter Open," *Amsterdam Star-News*, May 10, 1941; "'Slaves' Like Job Bureau," *The New York Times*, May 3, 1941; "Bronx Job Center Opens" *The New York Times*, July 1, 1941; "6,000 Placed in Jobs," *The New York Times*, September 29, 1941.

59. Marvel Cooke, "Some Ways to Kill the Slave Market," *The Daily Compass*, January 12, 1950; "Center Opened . . . ," *New York Herald Tribune*, May 2, 1941.

60. Street corner markets were not completely eradicated. In the early twenty-first century, immigrant women gathered on Brooklyn sidewalks to wait for work. Wages were higher than the twentieth-century slave markets: $8 an hour compared to an equivalent of $3.20 (for 35 cents in 1937). "Brooklyn Poles and Jews Refashion Old World Ties," *The New York Times*, March

28, 2002; "Invisible to Most, Women Line Up for Day Labor," *The New York Times,* August 15, 2005.

61. Author interview with Marvel Cooke, Harlem, NY, January 25, 1996.
62. Marvel Cooke, "I Was a Part of The Bronx Slave Market," *The Sunday Compass Magazine,* January 8, 1950.
63. In the late 20th century, there was a more task-based system, which in turn worked even better for workers. Pay was based upon the completion of "cleaning the house," for example, and it was up to the worker how long it took to do it. Clearly, the fewer hours needed to accomplish a task, the better for the worker. Task-based work was the logical outcome of the hourly wage, which was itself better for workers in the long run than weekly or monthly wages and indefinite hours.

NOTES TO CHAPTER THREE

1. Catherine McKenzie, "Domestic Help: A National Issue," *The New York Times,* June 5, 1938.
2. Robert H. Wiebe, *The Search for Order: 1877–1920* (New York: Hill and Wang, 1967): 212–13; David J. Saposs, "Voluntarism in the American Labor Movement," in Harry N. Scheiber, ed., *United States Economic History: Selected Readings* (New York: Alfred A. Knopf, 1964): 475.
3. "$7 a Week Servant Coming," *The New York Times,* January 4, 1920.
4. Elizabeth Clark-Lewis, *Living In, Living Out: African American Domestics in Washington, D.C., 1910–1940* (Washington: Smithsonian Institution Press, 1994): 106; "New Rules for Servants," *The New York Times,* January 16, 1921.
5. Phyllis Palmer, *Domesticity and Dirt: Housewives and Domestic Servants in the United States, 1920–1945* (Philadelphia: Temple University Press, 1992): 114, citing Mary T. Waggaman, "Efforts to Standardize the Working Day for Domestic Service," *Monthly Labor Review* 9 (August 1919): 515.
6. Julie A. Matthaei, *An Economic History of Women in America: Women's Work, The Sexual Division of Labor, and the Development of Capitalism* (New York: Schocken Books, 1982): 200–1; Barbara Bergman, *The Economic Emergence of Women* (New York: Basic Books, Inc., 1986): 20–21.
7. Maurine Weiner Greenwald, *Women, War, and Work: The Impact of World War I on Women Workers in the United States* (Ithaca: Cornell University Press, 1990 ed.): 13–32.
8. Sharon Harley, "For the Good of Family and Race: Gender, Work and Domestic Roles in the Black Community, 1880–1930," in Micheline R. Malson, et al., eds., *Black Women in America: Social Science Perspectives* (Chicago: University of Chicago Press, 1990): 167–8; Bonnie Thornton Dill, "'The Means to Put My Children Through': Child-Rearing Goals and Strategies Among Black Female Domestic Servants," in LaFrances Rodgers-Rose, ed., *The Black Woman* (Beverly Hills: Sage Publications, 1980): 108; Soraya Moore Coley, "And Still I Rise: An Exploratory Study of

Contemporary Black Private Household Workers" (The Graduate School of Social Work and Social Research of Bryn Mawr College, 1981): 9–10.

9. Hasia Diner, *Erin's Daughters in America: Irish Immigrant Women in the Nineteenth Century* (Baltimore: The Johns Hopkins University Press, 1983): 77–78; Susanne Sinke with Stephen Cross, "The International Marriage Market and the Sphere of Social Reproduction: A German Case Study," in Donna Gabaccia, ed., *Seeking Common Ground: Multidisciplinary Studies of Immigrant Women in the United States* (Westport, CT: Praeger, 1992): 67–88; Lars Ljungmark, "On Emigration, Social Mobility, and the Transfer of Capital," *The Swedish-American Historical Quarterly* 41 (July 1990): 159; Evelyn Nakano Glenn, *Issei, Nisei, War Bride: Three Generations of Japanese American Women in Domestic Service* (Philadelphia: Temple University Press, 1986): 76–79; Mary Romero, *Maid in the U.S.A.* (New York: Routledge, 1992): 155–157.

10. Henry Crookhorn in Jeff Kisseloff, *You Must Remember This: An Oral History of Manhattan from the 1890s to World War II* (New York: Harcourt Brace Jovanovich, 1989): 401; cited in bell hooks, *YEARNING: race, gender, and cultural politics* (Boston: South End Press, 1990): 43.

11. A. E. Johnson Agency placement books and employee records, 1917–1921, held at the Lindquist Group offices, Greenwich, CT; A. E. Johnson Agency checkbook, November 1926; A. E. Johnson Agency scrapbook; *The WPA Guide to New York City* (New York: Pantheon Books, 1982): 512–513, 529–541; "Bronx," "Olinville," "Elevated railways," "Williamsbridge," in Kenneth T. Jackson, ed., *The Encyclopedia of New York City* (New Haven: Yale University Press, 1995).

12. Greenwald, *Women, War, and Work*, 23; A. E. Johnson Agency placement books, 1917–1921.

13. There were only some 12,000 domestic workers who were members of the YWCA in the early 1930s, or less than six percent out of perhaps 200,000 total members. Palmer, *Domesticity and Dirt:* 118; Susan Lynn, *Progressive Women in Conservative Times: Racial Justice, Peace, and Feminism, 1945 to the 1960s* (New Brunswick, NJ: Rutgers University Press, 1992): *passim;* "Aid Urged for Negro Girls," *The New York Times,* January 14, 1920; "Clubs for Servant Girls," *The New York Times.*

There was a domestic worker union in New York City in 1901. Rosalyn Terborg-Penn, "Survival Strategies Among African-American Workers: A Continuing Process," Ruth Milkman, ed., *Women, Work and Protest* (Boston: Routledge & Kegan Paul, 1985): 144–146. See Chapter Two for more on domestic worker unions.

14. Palmer, *Domesticity and Dirt:* 112–113.

15. Palmer, *Domesticity and Dirt,* 114; Nancy Schrom Dye, *As Equals and As Sisters: Feminism, the Labor Movement and the Women's Trade Union League of New York* (Columbia: University of Missouri Press, 1980): 162–163. For more information on the WTUL, see also Elizabeth Anne Payne, *Reform, Labor and Feminism: Margaret Dreier Robins and the Women's Trade Union League* (Urbana: University of Illinois Press: 1988).

16. Palmer, *Domesticity and Dirt,* 114.

17.   Irish women, although unschooled and often illiterate, recognized that
       what they had to offer was highly sought after by Americans and that
       . . . they could take a role in setting the terms of their labor, quitting a
       job when it did not conform to their needs or their standards.
                                        Diner, *Erin's Daughters*, 86, 93.
18.   "Why Servant Girls Leave Perfectly Luxurious Homes," *The New York
       Times*, November 16, 1924. As far as wages went, the *Times'* editors bit-
       terly remarked in March 1923, "Nobody but the well-to-do can afford to
       employ 'domestic helpers,' 'household assistants,' or by whatever name of
       reverence or magnification they may be called." "Swiss Hired Girls," *The
       New York Times*, March 25, 1923.
19.   "College Girls as Servants Will Study Labor Problems," *The New York
       Times*, July 13, 1924.
20.   The Evening and Continuation Schools of New York City, "the largest
       employment agency for domestic service in the country" made another
       conservative effort when it began to teach newly arrived immigrants how
       to cook in American households. "It has been too easy for immigrant girls
       to pick up fifty-dollar jobs without any training and to learn American
       ways while drawing wages, explained Morris E. Siegel, director." "Teach-
       ing the Foreign-Born to Cook in American Style," *The New York Times*,
       August 3, 1924.
21.   Home economics had begun to be treated as a profession around the turn
       of the century. See Susan Strasser, *Never Done: A History of American
       Housework* (New York: Pantheon, 1982): 205–223.
22.   Mary Coates Hubbard, "Two Worlds: Observations of a Sentinel Set
       Between Them," *The New York Times Magazine*, June 22, 1924.
23.   "A Domestic Nine-Hour Day," *The New York Times*, May 4, 1927.
24.   Phyllis Palmer, "Housewife and Household Worker: Employer-Employee
       Relationships in the Home, 1928–1941," in Carol Groneman and Mary
       Beth Norton, eds., *"To Toil the Livelong Day": America's Women at Work,
       1780–1980* (Ithaca, NY: Cornell University Press, 1987), *passim*. See the
       end of this chapter for an example of a contract. "A Housewives' Union,"
       The New York Times, April 4, 1920.
25.   "Two Nations Linked on Servant Problem," *The New York Times*, Novem-
       ber 27, 1928; "The Servant Problem," *The New York Times*, December 5,
       1928.
26.   Palmer, *Domesticity and Dirt*: 124–5.
27.   Palmer, *Domesticity and Dirt*: 124–5.
28.   "A Plan for Research in Household Employment," 2–3. Mary Anderson,
       director of the Women's Bureau noted in 1938, "Household employ-
       ment came into disrepute particularly during the depression. Standards
       of employment—already none too high in many places—dropped at a
       rapid rate." Mary Anderson, "The Household Worker and Her Job," U.S.
       National Archives, RG 86, Women's Bureau. Division of Research. Unpub-
       lished Materials, 1919–1972, 1956: Domestic Workers. "Domestic Work-
       ers. Household Employment (1912–1956)" (hereinafter "Women's Bureau
       Unpublished Materials 1956"), Box 286.

29. "Meeting of the Sub-Committee on Household Employment," October 11, 1937. YWCA of the U.S.A., National Board Archives, New York, Records File Collection (hereinafter "YWCA Archives"), Reel 97.3.

30. "Housewives Want No Servants' Union," *The New York Times,* January 27, 1938; "Wider State Help to Jobless Backed," *The New York Times,* February 6, 1938; Mrs. Jean Brown letter, "Collective Action by Servants Urged," *The New York Times,* April 25, 1938; Evelyn Seely, "Our Feudal Housewives," *The Nation* (May 28, 1938); "Description of Household Employment Program," Women's Bureau Unpublished Materials 1956.

31. Catherine MacKenzie, "Katie is Leaving—Again," *The New York Times Magazine,* August 31, 1941: 10; "Domestic Servant Shortage Stirs New Welfare Activity," *The New York Times,* November 9, 1941; "Features on Women Workers," August 28, 1946, Women's Bureau Unpublished Materials 1956, Box 299.

32. "Domestics Set Up New Job Demands," *The New York Times,* May 4, 1943.

33. "Domestic Workers' Wages and Hours, New York State, 1948," *Monthly Labor Review* (October 1949). Although the title said 1948, the figures in the article were from 1946.

34. "Legal Comment on Current Issues: The Law of Domestic Servants," *The New York Times,* January 5, 1930.

35. National Committee on Household Employment, "Proposals for a Voluntary Agreement in Household Employment," Women's Bureau Unpublished Materials 1956, Box 286.

36. "Changed Attitude on Servants Urged," *The New York Times,* November 19, 1941; "Housewives Urged to Train as Bosses," *The New York Times,* November 26, 1941; "How to Get a Maid Debated by Women," *The New York Times,* November 29, 1939. Despite their shortcomings, voluntary contracts remained popular. In 2002, a group of workers demonstrated for passage of a New York City law that recommended but did not require such a contract. "Wage Bill Would Protect Housekeepers and in May 2003. "New Protections for Nannies are Approved by Council," *The New York Times,* May 15, 2003.

37. "Meeting of the Consultant Committee on Household Employment Training Courses in Resident Schools and Camps for Unemployed Women, January 10, 1935," Women's Bureau Unpublished Materials 1956; Jon A. Peterson, Notes on a conversation with Helen Hoff Peterson, Columbus, OH, July 6, 1992.

38. Arthur B. Johnson, "Release to the Meriden [CT] Record & Meriden Journal," Women's Bureau Unpublished Materials, 1956: Domestic Workers; "Project for Training Household Workers," Women's Bureau Unpublished Materials 1956; "Application for Household Position," Women's Bureau Unpublished Materials 1956, Box 287, Domestic Workers: Forms & Instructions.

39. Gray, *Black Female Domestics:* 47–48; "Notes of the Local Schools," *The New York Times,* November 21, 1937. The Harlem Trade School was well regarded nationally; the Women's Bureau used it as a model in a

1939 Symposium on Household Employment. Judith Weisenfeld, "'The More Abundant Life': The Harlem Branch of the New York City Young Christian Women's Association, 1905–1945," (Princeton University, 1992): 171.

40. "WPA Ready to Start School for Servants," *The New York Times*, December 27, 1935.
41. "In Classroom and on Campus," *The New York Times*, February 16, 1936; "WPA Model House Opened by Ridder," *The New York Times*, June 6, 1936; "Household Help School to Open in Westchester," *The New York Times*, July 12, 1936; "Will Renew Household Training," *The New York Times*, March 21, 1937; "Domestics Taught Household Crafts," *The New York Times*, March 28, 1937.
42. "Domestic Help: A National Issue," *The New York Times*, June 5, 1938.
43. The WPA was one of the few government training programs to include African-Americans. "In Classroom and on Campus," *The New York Times*, February 16, 1936; "Will Renew Household Training," *The New York Times*, March 21, 1937; "Choice of 74 Jobs Awaits First Graduates of WPA Project," *The New York Times*, April 7, 1936; "WPA Model House Opened by Ridder," *The New York Times*, June 6, 1936; "Domestics Taught Household Crafts," *The New York Times*, March 28, 1937.
44. MacKenzie, "Katie is Leaving," 10; "Domestic Servant Shortage Stirs New Welfare Activity," *The New York Times*, November 9, 1941; "Features on Women Workers," August 28, 1946, Women's Bureau Unpublished Materials 1956, Box 299.
45. Lynn, *Progressive Women in Conservative Times*, 41, 56–59.
46. "Training of Household Workers Urged to Solve Labor Problem," *The New York Times*, May 8, 1938. In 1933, there were 12,000 domestic servant members of the YWCA. Palmer, *Domesticity and Dirt*: 118.
47. "Domestic Servant Shortage Stirs New Welfare Activity," *The New York Times*, November 9, 1941.
48. Women's Bureau, U.S. Department of Labor, *Milestones: The Women's Bureau Celebrates 65 Years of Women's Labor History* (Washington: U.S.G.P.O., 1985): 10–11.
49. Jill Quadagno, *The Transformation of Old Age Security: Class and Politics in the American Welfare State* (Chicago: The University of Chicago Press, 1988): chapter 5, *passim*.
50. For a discussion of the pros and cons of including domestics (and agricultural workers), see, for example, Quadagno, *Transformation of Old Age Security*, chapter 5 and Robert C. Lieberman, *Shifting the Color Line: Raced and the American Welfare State* (Cambridge, MA: Harvard University Press, 1998), chapters 2 and 3.
51. "Wages of Domestic Workers," Women's Bureau Unpublished Materials 1956, Box 286.
52. "Description of Household Employment Program," Women's Bureau Unpublished Materials 1956; "Household Employment: The Problem of 2,000,000 Workers." Women's Bureau Unpublished Materials 1956, Box 286.

53. "Household Employment: An Outline For Study Groups," United States Department of Labor, Women's Bureau, November 1940: Introduction. Women's Bureau Unpublished Materials 1956, Box 286, Domestic Workers—Bibliography.

54. Mary Anderson, "The Household Worker and Her Job." Women's Bureau Unpublished Materials 1956, Box 286.

55. "Housewives Want No Servants' Union," *The New York Times*, January 27, 1938; "Wider State Help to Jobless Backed," *The New York Times*, February 6, 1938; Mrs. Jean Brown letter, "Collective Action by Servants Urged," *The New York Times*, April 25, 1938; "Sponsors Face Fight on 60-Hour Week for Household Workers," *The New York Times*, January 2, 1938; "Bill Gives to City Fuller Home Rule," *The New York Times*, January 7, 1938; "Changes Favored in Home Rule Act," *The New York Times*, February 27, 1938; "60-Hour Week for Household Workers Again Asked in Bill at Albany This Week," *The New York Times*, January 8, 1939; "Lehman Nominates His Whole Cabinet," *The New York Times*, January 10, 1939.

56. Jones, *Labor of Love*, 210.

57. See, for example, Lieberman, *Shifting the Color Line*, 43, 56.

58. Civil service and professional workers were not covered by wage and hour standards, either, but de facto regulation protected the former, and their high status and earnings guarded the latter.

59. "Wages are Soaring for Domestic Help—But Scarcity is Growing Here Due to Better Jobs in the War Factories," *The New York Times*, December 17, 1942.

60. "Maid Supply Scant Despite Higher Pay," *The New York Times*, January 24, 1944; D'Ann Campbell, *Women at War with America: Private Lives in a Patriotic Era* (Cambridge, MA: Harvard University Press, 1984): 104. The 2003 equivalent to $20–25 a week was about $210–$262. "What is its Relative Value in US Dollars?," Economic History Services, http://www.eh.net/hmit/compare.

61. Susan M. Hartmann, *The Home Front and Beyond: American Women in the 1940s* (Boston: Twayne Publishers, 1982): 89, 92.

62. "Servant Problem Looks Less Grim," *The New York Times*, February 26, 1944.

63. "Domestic Service Beckons to Many," *The New York Times*, April 20, 1945.

64. "Wartime Shifts," 3.

65. "Courses Planned for Domestic Help," *The New York Times*, June 9, 1945.

66. MacKenzie, "Katie is Leaving," 21.

67. "Women Get Ready for Legislature," *The New York Times*, January 3, 1945; "Rift Grows on Bill for Domestics' Aid," *The New York Times*, March 30, 1946; "Dewey Approves Insuring Servants," *The New York Times*, April 2, 1946; "$535,429 Awarded Injured Servants," *The New York Times*, April 18, 1949.

68. "Insure Domestics, Employer Advised," *The New York Times*, April 6, 1946; "Servant's Injury Can Cost $56,000," *The New York Times*, June

29, 1958. Insurance companies today offer special household insurance policies for domestic help. "Personal Finance—Family Finance: Protecting Against Nanny Lawsuits; Insurance Policies Arise As Domestic Workers Grow, Along With Those Suing," *The Wall Street Journal,* July 30, 2003.

69. "The Social Security Program: Its Purpose—Its Methods—Its Progress" 1936, National Archives. RG 47. Records of the Social Security Administration, Records of the Social Security Board, Central File, Master File, 1935–47, Box 3, PI 183, Entry 20, 011 Jan–June 1936: 1; Mary Anderson, "The Household Worker and Her Job," Women's Bureau Unpublished Materials 1956, Box 286. Some domestic workers (those in households that employed four or more full-time workers) were covered under unemployment insurance in New York State in 1935, but the federal government did not cover any domestics until 1976. "Unemployment Insurance," *The New York Times,* March 15, 1936; Joseph A. Hickey, "Unemployment Insurance Covers Additional 9 Million Workers," *Monthly Labor Review* (May 1978).

70. Whether domestics could afford to contribute any money to an OASI scheme was not addressed until the 1940s. Quadagno, *Transformation of Old Age Security,* chapter 5; Hugh Downs, "Must We Age?," *Parade Magazine,* August 21, 1994.

71. Social secretaries were not considered domestics, and neither were librarians, carpenters, etc. employed in private homes. "Social Secretaries Taxable," *The New York Times,* December 29, 1937.

    Southern Congresspeople were against inclusion the most, since there were huge numbers of farm workers, as well as domestics, in their states.

    "The Social Security Program: Its Purpose—Its Methods—Its Progress" 1936: 1; Lieberman, *Shifting the Color Line,* 99–100.

72. Sheryl R. Tynes, *Turning Points in Social Security: From "Cruel Hoax" to "Sacred Entitlement"* (Stanford: Stanford University Press, 1996): 107; Quadagno, *Transformation of Old Age Security:* 117, chapter 6, "The Politics of Old Age Assistance"; Lieberman, *Shifting the Color Line:* 43, 56.

73. Health insurance was the third part, and it received little attention during the 30s. Quadagno, *Transformation of Old Age Security:* 130–137.

74. Wandersee, *Women's Work and Family Values:* 85, 89, 93; Jones, *Labor of Love:* 200.

    For a history of the legislation, see Lieberman, *Shifting the Color Line,* chapters 2 and 3, and Quadagno, *Transformation of Social Security,* chapter 5. Other histories of the Social Security Act and its origins include Roy Lubove, *The Struggle for Social Security, 1900–1935* (Cambridge, MA: Harvard University Press, 1968); Jerry R. Cates, *Insuring Inequality: Administrative Leadership in Social Security, 1935–1954* (Ann Arbor: University of Michigan Press, 1983); Raymond Richards, *Closing the Door to Destitution: The Shaping of the Social Security Acts of the United States and New Zealand* (University Park, PA: The Pennsylvania State University Press, 1994); Edward D. Berkowitz, *Mr. Social Security: The Life of Wilbur J. Cohen* (Lawrence, KS: The University Press of Kansas, 1995). A historiographical essay through 1980 can be found in Clarke A. Chambers, "Social

Reform, Social Work, and Social Security: A Subject Revisited," in John N. Schacht, ed., *The Quest for Security: Papers on the Origins and the Future of the American Social Insurance System* (Ames, IA: The Center for the Study of the Recent History of the United States, 1982).

75. Mary Anderson, "An Occupational Analysis of Household Employment," 1938. Women's Bureau Unpublished Materials 1956, Box 286; "Suggested Standards for Household Employment," n.d. Women's Bureau Unpublished Materials 1956, Box 286; Anderson, "Social Security for Household Employees," May 13, 1939, Women's Bureau Unpublished Materials 1956, Box 286: 3.

76. "Household Employment: The Problem of 2,000,000 Workers." Women's Bureau Unpublished Materials 1956, Box 286.

77. Anderson, "Social Security for Household Employees," May 13, 1939, 1.

78. "Household Employment: An Outline For Study Groups," United States Department of Labor, Women's Bureau, November 1940: 2. Women's Bureau Unpublished Materials 1956, Box 286. Domestic Workers—Bibliography; "Extracts from letters . . . ," Women's Bureau Unpublished Materials 1956, Box 291. Domestic Workers 1937; e.g., Gloria Langford to Eleanor Roosevelt, June 30, 1936, New York City Municipal Archives, LaGuardia Administration, Department of Hospitals File, Box 3166.

79. "From 7 to 10," Letters, *The New York Times Magazine*, August 25, 1946.

80. "Domestic Workers and Legislation," April 1940, p. 1. Women's Bureau Unpublished Materials 1956, Box 286. Domestic Folder—Mrs. Daniel's Folder.

81. "Move to Enlarge Security Program," *The New York Times*, January 12, 1941; "Summary of the Social Security Board's Proposals Regarding Changes in the Social Security Act," April 16, 1940: 2. National Archives. RG 47. Records of the Social Security Administration, Records of the Social Security Board, Central File, Master File, 1935–47 (hereinafter SSB Records, 1935–47), Box 3, PI 183, Entry 20, 011.1, Jan.–June 1940.

The SSB estimated in 1940 that there were roughly 10 million self-employed workers, 5 million agricultural workers, 6 million public employees, and 2 million domestic workers, none of whom were covered under the Social Security Act. Wilbur J. Cohen memo to A. J. Altmeyer, October 13, 1943. National Archives. RG 47. Records of the Social Security Administration, Office of the Commissioner, Executive Director files 1948-1941. General Correspondence. Box 111—720 (hereinafter SSA Executive Director files).

"Memorandum to the Administrator," May 17, 1940 re: Summary of Report to the Committee relative to S. 33565, "A Bill to amend the Social Security Act and the Internal Revenue Code, to establish adequate standards of unemployment compensation, and for other purposes.": 2. SSB Records 1935–47. Box 4, 011.1 Amendments; "The Federal Social Security Programs," *Monthly Labor Review* 70:1 (January 1950): 2.

82. I.S. Falk, Director, S.S.A., to Mr. David S. Roswell, September 19, 1946, National Archives, RG 47 Records of the Social Security Administration, Division of Research and Statistics. General Correspondence, 1946-1950

(NN3–47–86–6) (hereinafter SSA Research Division Correspondence). Box 24 055.01 1947–1946 (folder 21): 1; Tynes, *Turning Points*, 107; Lieberman, *Shifting the Color Line*, 93.

83. "Defense Put First in A.F.L. Program," *The New York Times*, January 13, 1941.

84. "Ways and Means Lists Tax Bills," *The New York Times*, September 19, 1941; W.G. Curtis, chairman of the executive committee of the Insurance Economic Society of America. "War Seen a Screen for Socialist Ideas," *The New York Times*, October 17, 1942.

85. "Widened Security Covers Women Help," *The New York Times*, January 22, 1944; "Dewey Demands Old-Age Pensions for All Classes," *The New York Times*, September 23, 1944; "Text of the Prepared Statement of Henry A. Wallace," *The New York Times*, January 26, 1945; *Congressional Record—House*, 79th Congress: 991[8].

86. Mr. Lynch of New York, *Congressional Record—House*, July 19, 1946: 9926; "Summary of Hearings on Social Security, Committee on Ways and Means, House of Representatives," April 6, 1946, SSA Research Division Correspondence, Box 7, (36) 032.1 Ways and Means 1946; "Report of House Ways and Means Committee Hearings on Extension of Social Security," March 6, 1946, SSA Research Division Correspondence, Box 7, (36) 032.1 Ways and Means 1946: 3–4; Reps. Carlson and Robertson worried about small businesses and cost. Commerce Secretary Henry A. Wallace, who was in favor of extension, said that OASI would make farmers competitive. "Summary of Hearings on Social Security, Committee on Ways and Means, House of Representatives, April 4, 1946" 4/5/46, SSA Research Division Correspondence, Box 7, (36) 032.1 Ways and Means 1946: 1–2; Lieberman, *Shifting the Color Line*, 103–105

87. "Social Security and Consumer Spending," 11/20/47, SSA Research Division Correspondence. Box 24, 056, 1949–1946 (35): 1–2.

88. "Summary of Hearings on Social Security, Committee on Ways and Means, House of Representatives, March 13, 1946" 3/13/46, SSA Research Division Correspondence, Box 7, (36) 032.1 Ways and Means 1946: 1.

89. "Summary of Hearings on Social Security, Committee on Ways and Means, House of Representatives, March 13, 1946," 2.

90. "Summary of Hearings on Social Security, Committee on Ways and Means, House of Representatives, March 13, 1946," 2.

91. . . . [F]rom the inception of the Social Security Act, the insurance provisions were never too meaningful to the bulk of the Black labor force. It was and still is the non-contributory aspects of the Act (Old-Age Assistance and now Supplemental Security Insurance) and aid to dependent children, etc., which was most applicable to a generally low wage and highly unemployed labor group.

Frank G. Davis, *The Black Community's Social Security* (Washington, D.C.: University Press of America, 1978): 66.

Robert C. Lieberman disagrees with this at least partially, stating that because OASI had a minimum benefit level, low-wage workers were often "bumped up" to that level. Lieberman, *Shifting the Color Line*: 89.

92. Frieda S. Miller memorandum to Miss Spring, March 17, 1949, "Old Age and Survivors Insurance testimony." Women's Bureau Unpublished Materials 1956, Box 299, "Domestic Workers—1949; *Congressional Record—House,* October 5, 1949: 13914.

93. I.S. Falk Memorandum, October 18, 1946 re: Material on Social Security for Council of Economic Advisers, "Recommended Discussion on Social Security for Council of Economic Advisors." SSA Research Division Correspondence, Box 24, 056, 1949–1946 (35): 3. The SSA's position was:

> If, over a long period, we are to maintain a prosperous market and its concomitant a high level of employment, we must strengthen consumer purchases and assure a level of investment that is sufficiently high to match the savings flow from a high employment and income level. Social security takes a prominent place among programs designed to maintain a high level of employment. . . . The economic impact of social security measures is felt both in the total level of consumer spending and in the income- and employment-creating force of private investment.

"Social Security and Consumer Spending," November 20, 1947. SSA Research Division Correspondence. Box 24, 056, 1949–1946 (35): 1–2; "The Extension of Old-Age and Survivors Insurance to Agricultural and Domestic Service Workers and to the Self-Employed," Division of Tax Research, Treasury Department, November 1947. Women's Bureau Unpublished Materials 1956, Box 299, Domestic Workers—1947; Memo to Household Employment Folder from Adelia B. Kloak, November 8, 1948. Women's Bureau Unpublished Materials, 1956: Domestic Workers, Box 299, "Domestic Workers—1948"; Oscar R. Ewing, Administrator, to Hon. Eugene D. Milliken, Chairman, Committee on Finance, United States Senate, March 12, 1948. SSA Research Division Correspondence, Box 3 (45) 011.1 S. 1679 1949–1947: 2.

94. *Congressional Record—House,* October 3, 1949: 13841.

95. When Florence DuBoise Mooers of the National Executive Housekeepers Association testified in 1949 before the House Ways and Means Committee advocating extension of Social Security benefits to domestic workers, the Committee members asked no questions, unlike their interactions with other witnesses. Federal Security Agency, Social Security Administration, "Hearings before House Ways and Means Committee on OASDI Legislation," April 21, 1949. SSA Research Division Correspondence, Box 7, (35) 032.1 Ways and Means 1950–1947; FSA, SSA, "Hearings before House Ways and Means Committee on OASDI Legislation," April 22, 1949. SSA Research Division Correspondence, Box 7, (35) 032.1 Ways and Means 1950–1947; FSA, SSA, "Hearings Before House Ways and Means Committee on OASDI Legislation," March 24, 25, 28, 29, 30, 31, 1949. SSA Research Division Correspondence. Box 7, (35) 032.1 Ways and Means 1950–1947: 1.

96. *Congressional Record—House,* October 5, 1949: 13952; Tynes, *Turning Points,* 107–112.

97. *Congressional Record—House,* October 3, 1949: 13813.

98. "Security Status of 350,000 Shifted," *The New York Times,* July 21, 1950.

99. The total covered under OASI went up by 9,700,000 people (44,700,000 up from 35,000,000). Broken down, the figures were:

Nonfarm self-employed (with annual incomes of at least $400)—4,700,000;

Agricultural workers—850,000;

Domestic workers—1,000,000;

Nonprofit employees (voluntary coverage; employer's choice)—600,000;

State and local government employees (also voluntary, except for some compulsorily-covered transit workers)—1,450,000;

Federal employees not already covered—200,000;

Employees outside the U.S. and territories—150,000;

Employees in Puerto Rico and the Virgin Islands—400,000;

Simultaneous employer-employees—350,000.

"Digest of Major Changes in New Social Security Bill," *The New York Times,* August 18, 1950.

100. "Forms Ready Soon for Servants' Tax," *The New York Times,* November 16, 1950; "Maids' Deduction Form Ready; Housewives: 'Will Nellie Hate Me?'" *The New York Times,* November 29, 1950; "U.S. Instructs Women in Accounts as Social Security Goes to Maids," *The New York Times,* November 30, 1950; "Detailed Booklet on Maid Tax Issued," *The New York Times,* December 6, 1950; "Housewives Speed Tax Applications," *The New York Times,* January 7, 1951.

101. "Coverage to Rise in Social Security," *The New York Times,* January 1, 1951; "Housewives Speed Tax Applications"; "Housewives Excel as Tax Collectors" *The New York Times,* April 17, 1951; "Filing of Maid Tax Slowed by Mix-Up," *The New York Times,* April 28, 1951; "Maid-Tax Payers Rush Collectors," *The New York Times,* May 1, 1951.

102. "Tax Problem for Maids," *The New York Times,* November 28, 1950; "Security for Houseworkers," Josephine Condon to the Editor, *The New York Times,* June 2, 1953; "Maids' Deduction Form Ready; Housewives: 'Will Nellie Hate Me?'"; "Domestic Workers Urged to Register," *The New York Times,* December 25, 1950; "Bars Social Security," *The New York Times,* January 7, 1951; "Housewives Speed Tax Applications,"; "Housewives Excel as Tax Collectors."

103. "Texas Housewives Rebel at Paying Tax for Maids," *The New York Times,* April 30, 1951.

104. "Women Tax Rebels Face Action By U.S.," *The New York Times,* July 29, 1951; "'Tax-Rebelling' Wives Empty Bank Accounts Ahead of Treasury Agents, Who Get $36.03," *The New York Times,* August 7, 1951; "Treasury Still Duns Housewives for Tax," August 8, 1951; "Housewives Hire Martin Dies," *The New York Times,* August 17, 1951; "10 Housewives Dun U.S.," *The New York Times,* August 22, 1951; "Dies Leads Tax Fight for Wives in Texas," *The New York Times,* November 26, 1951; "11 Housewives Fight U.S.," *The New York Times,* February 15, 1952; "Housewife Loses Fight on Social Security Plan," *The New York Times,*

July 1, 1952; "Housewives See Slavery in Servants' Security Tax," *The New York Times*, May 27, 1953; "U.S. Taps 4 Bank Accounts," *The New York Times*, June 24, 1953; "Tax 'Rebel' Loses Plea," *The New York Times*, August 19, 1953; "Housewife Loses Long Tax 'Revolt,'" *The New York Times*, January 5, 1954.

105. "Eisenhower Wins Pensions Victory," *The New York Times*, August 21, 1954; "More Domestics to Get Security," *The New York Times*, February 19, 1955. Most agricultural workers were also included, along with the self-employed. The 1954 amendments were by far the most inclusive changes to the program. Lieberman, *Shifting the Color Line*, 92, 113; Quadagno, *Transformation of Old Age Security*, 148.

106. "Tax is Paid on Servants, But Just Try to Hire One," *The New York Times*, May 3, 1955.

NOTES TO CHAPTER FOUR

1. Reproduced in Frieda S. Miller [Director, Women's Bureau], "Can We Lure Martha Back to the Kitchen?" *The New York Times Magazine*, August 11, 1946.

2. Author interview with Sarah Henry Lederman, New York City, October 1993.

3. Phyllis Palmer, *Domesticity and Dirt: Housewives and Domestic Servants in the United States, 1920–1945* (Philadelphia: Temple University Press, 1989): 8.

4. George J. Stigler, "Domestic Servants in the United States, 1900–1940," *Occasional Paper 24*: April 1946 (New York: National Bureau of Economic Research): 21.

5. Urban families spent an aggregate of $522 million on household help over the 1935–36 year, or $30.79 a family, compared to $116 million or $20.42 per family for rural nonfarm households and $61 million or $9.01 for rural farm households. *Family Expenditures in the United States* (Washington, DC: National Planning Board, 1941): 30, cited in Stigler, *Domestic Servants*, 22.

   In New York City during 1935–36, a 3–4 person family earning $2,500—$2,999 a year spent an average of $41 on household help, compared with $703 for those earning $7,500—$9,999. "Family Expenditure in New York City," Bureau of Labor Statistics *Bulletin 643*, Vol. II, pp. 133 ff., cited in Stigler, *Domestic Servants*, 23. "Family Expenditures in Selected Cities," Bureau of Labor Statistics *Bulletin 648*, 303 ff., cited in Stigler, *Domestic Servants*, 23. Stigler did not care to extrapolate beyond this careful statement because "[o]n the whole the data behave so erratically as to defy generalization." Stigler, *Domestic Servants*, 23 n. 35.

6. See, for example, J. C. Furnas and the staff of the *Ladies' Home Journal*, *How America Lives* (New York: Henry Holt & Co., 1941): 36–37, 149, 288; Catherine MacKenzie, "Katie is Leaving—Again," *The New York Times Magazine*, August 31, 1941: 10; Campbell, *Women at War With America*, 173.

7. U.S. Department of Commerce, Bureau of the Census, *Decennial Census of the Population*, 1940.

8. "Regular Jobs for Household Help," *Monthly Labor Review* (October 1965): 1288.

9. "If Spring Comes, Can Mops Be Far Behind?," *The New York Times*, April 3, 1997.

10. A. E. Johnson Agency, New York City, order and employee books, 1917–1922, 1958–1964, held at The Lundquist Group, Greenwich, CT; "Regular Jobs for Household Help," 1288.

11. "Regular Household Jobs," 1229; "I: Labor Force Employment and Unemployment," *Monthly Labor Review 1964–65 Statistical Supplement:* Table I-4.

12. U.S. Bureau of the Census, 15th and 16th Censuses, 1930 and 1940; Allyson S. Grossman, "Women in Domestic Work: Yesterday and Today," *Monthly Labor Review* (August 1980): 17–21; D'Ann Campbell, *Women at War with America: Private Lives in a Patriotic Era* (Cambridge, MA: Harvard University Press, 1984): 239, Table 1; Mary Elizabeth Pidgeon, "Changes in Women's Employment During the War," Women's Bureau, U.S. Department of Labor, *Special Bulletin* 20 (June 1944): vi; "Fewer Servants by the Year," editorial, *The New York Times*, May 29, 1946.

13. Harold Goldstein, "The Changing Occupational Structure," *Monthly Labor Review* (December 1947): 655; "Changes in Women's Employment," 27; Harold Wool and Lester M. Pearlman, "Recent Occupational Trends," *Monthly Labor Review* (December 1947): 142, 144; Eugenia Kaledin, *Mothers and More: American Women in the 1950s* (Boston: Twayne Publishers 1984): 21; Susan M. Hartmann, *The Home Front and Beyond: American Women in the 1940s* (Boston: Twayne Publishers, 1982): 21, 78.

14. "I: Labor Force Employment and Unemployment," *Monthly Labor Review 1964–1965 Statistical Supplement:* Table I-4; Chaplin, *Blue Collar World*, 529. In 1960, three percent of New York City's private household workers listed themselves as babysitters. *Decennial Census of the United States*, 1960.

15. Rosalind Rosenberg, *Divided Lives: American Women in the Twentieth Century* (New York: Hill & Wang, 1992): 3–4; Susan Ware, *Modern American Women: A Documentary History* (Belmont, CA: Wadsworth Publishing Company, 1989): 1–4; Matthaei, *An Economic History of Women in America*, chapter 8; *The New York Times*, March 21, 1930; Gwendolyn Hughes Berry, "Mothers in Industry," *Annals of the American Academy of Political and Social Science* (May, 1929): 316–317, quoted in Pidgeon, "Women in Industry," 19.

16. Barbara Ehrenreich and Deidre English, *For Her Own Good: 150 Years of the Experts' Advice to Women* (New York: Doubleday, 1978): 145.

17. Annegret S. Ogren, *The Great American Housewife: From Helpmate to Wage Earner, 1776–1986* (Westport, CT: Greenwood Press, 1986): 139. See also Matthaei, *An Economic History of Women in America*, chapter 8.

18. Ehrenreich and English, *For Her Own Good:* 163.

19. Steven Mintz and Susan Kellogg, *Domestic Revolutions: A Social History of American Family Life*, (New York: The Free Press, 1988): 160.
20. *The Best Years of Our Lives* (Samuel Goldwyn, 1946).
21. Josephine Ripley, "To Change the Subject: Too Many Cooks . . . No, Indeed," *Christian Science Monitor*, September 11, 1941, in Women's Bureau, Division of Research, Unpublished Materials 1919–1972, 1956, Domestic Workers, Household Employment (1941), Box 294, Domestic Workers—1941.
22. "Community Services for Women War Workers," *Women's Bureau Special Bulletin* 15 (1944), *passim*; Frieda S. Miller, Director, Women's Bureau, "Who Works, Where, and Why?" in *The American Woman: Her Changing Role—Worker, Homemaker, Citizen*, Women's Bureau Conference, February 17–19, 1948 (U.S. Dept. of Labor, 1948): 25.
23. The proportion of American families owning vacuums, refrigerators and washing machines dropped an average of 6 percent between 1941 and 1945. *Women at War with America*, 82–3, 85, 173, 224.
24. "Seven Decades," 144, 146. Campbell, *Women at War with America*, 174.
25. Frieda S. Miller, "Who Works, Where, and Why?," 5–26; Hartmann, *Home Front and Beyond*, 62.
26. Lucy G. Allen, *Table Service* (Boston: Little, Brown & Co., 1943): Jacket, 10.
27. "Wages are Soaring for Domestic Help—But Scarcity is Growing Here Due to Better Jobs in the War Factories," *The New York Times*, December 17, 1942.
28. See, for example, "Houseworker Wanted," *The New York Times*, August 29, 1930.
29. William H. Whyte, Jr., *The Organization Man* (Garden City, NY: Doubleday, 1957): 333, 334.
30. Richard M. Nixon, cited in Elaine Tyler May, *Homeward Bound: American Families in the Cold War Era* (New York: Basic Books, 1988): 17.
31. Mary Roche, "The New 'Servants': Machines and Husbands," *The New York Times*, June 5, 1955.
32. *The Architectural Forum* (April 1935).
33. (Mrs.) Edith M. Stern, "Hours, Ergs, Servants," Letters to the Editor, *The New York Times Magazine*, July 3, 1955.
34. Ruth Schwartz Cowan, *More Work For Mother: The Ironies of Household Technology from the Open Hearth to the Microwave* (New York: Basic Books, Inc., 1983): 178.
35. "Housewife's Duties Heavier than in Past," *The New York Times*, October 10, 1953.
36. Nash-Kelvinator advertisement, *The New York Times*, December 29, 1949; Gimbels advertisement, *The New York Times*, June 8, 1947; Gimbels advertisement, *The New York Times*, July 27, 1947.
37. Hazel Kyrk, *Economic Problems of the Family* (New York: Harper & Brothers, 1933): 99, cited in Matthaei, *An Economic History of Women in America*, 167.
38. Cowan, *More Work For Mother*: 178.
39. "How to Write Finis to Compromise Living," *The New York Times*, April 15, 1951, VIII, advertisements, advertisement p. 9.; "With Love . . . From

Lawrence Brook," advertisement, *The New York Times,* September 23, 1956, VIII, 5.

40. Ehrenreich and English, *For Her Own Good:* 167.
41. Annegret S. Ogren, *The Great American Housewife: From Helpmate to Wage Earner, 1776–1986* (Westport, CT: Greenwood Press, 1986): 185.
42. Ogren, *Great American Housewife,* 154.
43. Angela Davis, *Women, Race and Class* (New York: Vintage Books, 1981): 12.
44. Mintz and Kellogg, *Domestic Revolutions,* 181–182; Helena Z. Lopata, *Occupation: Housewife* (New York: Oxford University Press, 1971): 139–140.
45. See Philip Wylie, *Generation of Vipers* (1942, reissued 1955). Also see William Chafe, *The American Woman: Her Changing Social, Economic, and Political Roles, 1920–1970* (New York: Oxford University Press, 1972): 201–202; Gimbels advertisement, *The New York Times,* November 17, 1946.
46. An informal survey of "30-odd women," "The 'Housewife' vs. the 'Homemaker'? Dim View Is Taken of British Report," *The New York Times,* August 18, 1955. See also, "Dancing Housework," editorial, *The New York Times,* June 21, 1963.
47. Joann Vanek, "Time Spent in Housework," *Scientific American* (November 1974): 117–118; Cynthia Kellogg, "Housework is the Road to Boredom," *The New York Times,* July 1, 1955.
48. Whyte, *Organization Man,* 401.
49. "Housework Is the Road To Boredom."
50. Hartmann, *Home Front and Beyond,* 169–170.
51. "No 'Easiest' Way to Do Housework," *The New York Times,* March 26, 1953.
52. Chafe, *The American Woman,* 200.
53. Mirra Komarovksy, *Blue Collar Marriage* (New York: Vintage Books, 1967): 35, 52, 55–58, citing Dorothy Greey Van Bortel and Irma H. Gross, 1954, 34–35.
54. Komarovsky, *Blue Collar Marriage,* 58–60.
55. Edward P. Lazear and Robert T. Michael, *Allocation of Income within the Household* (Chicago: University of Chicago Press, 1988): 37. Based on the 1960–61 and 1972–73 Consumer Expenditure Survey.
56. Mary Roche, "The New 'Servants': Machines and Husbands," *The New York Times,* June 5, 1955; Edith Beal, "Domestics and Jobs," Letter to the Editor, *The New York Times Magazine,* July 3, 1955; Johnson Agency records.
57. Rosenberg, *Divided Lives,* 156–157. See also Brett Harvey, *The Fifties: A Women's Oral History* (New York: HarperCollins Publishers, Inc., 1993), especially Anna Hellman's story: 172; Chafe, *The American Woman,* 226, 230.
58. Daniel Horowitz, "Rethinking Betty Friedan and *The Feminine Mystique:* Labor Union Radicalism and Feminism in Cold War America," *American Quarterly* (March 1996): 15. See also Kaledin, *Mothers and More,* 214.

59. "Meeting of the Sub-Committee on Household Employment," October 11, 1937. YWCA Records, Reel 97.3.
60. Marylin Bender, "Woman's View of Her Position Is Under Study," *The New York Times,* September 2, 1963.
61. Bender, "Woman's View."
62. Peter Bart, "Every Woman's Village: Challenge for the Bored Housewife," *The New York Times,* December 3, 1965.
63. Harvey, *The Fifties,* 210–211.
64. E.g., the "Wife saver" workshop held June 25—July 16, 1954 sponsored U. Conn—Storr's School of Home Economics, inspired by Dr. Lillian M. Gilbreth, industrial consultant, research scientist and mother of 12. At the age of 75, Dr. Gilbreth still had plenty to say on the topic she had been propounding for at least 50 years. "21 End 'Workshop' for Ease in Home," *The New York Times,* July 17, 1954.
65. "Mechanized Society is Isolating American Women, Scientist Says," *The New York Times,* December 16, 1966.
66. Vanek, "Time Spent in Housework," 120; Arlie Hochschild, *The Second Shift: Working Parents and the Revolution at Home* (New York: Viking, 1989): 2; Chafe, *The American Woman,* 191–2.
67. "Housewives' Jobs Found Much Alike," *The New York Times,* October 27, 1953. See also Rosenberg, *Divided Lives,* Chapter 7, "The Family Claim Revisited," 220–244.
68. "For Divorced Wives, Alimony or Severance Pay?" *The New York Times,* March 22, 1967; U.S. Census Bureau, "Income Limits for Each Fifth and Top 5 Percent of Households (All Races): 1967 to 2000" (Table H-1), published in March 2000 Current Population Survey; http://www.census.gov/income/ftp/histinc/CPI-U-RS/household/h01.lst.
69. David Chaplin, "Domestic Service and the Negro," in Arthur B. Shostak and William Gomberg, eds., *Blue-Collar World: Studies of the American Worker* (Englewood Cliffs, NJ: Prentice-Hall, Inc., 1964): 535.
70. Christiane Collange, *The Well-Organized Woman* (New York: Avon Books, 1971): 132–133. First published in France, 1969.
71. Patricia Hill Collins, "The Social Construction of Black Feminist Thought," in Micheline R. Malson, et al., eds., *Black Women in America: Social Science Perspectives* (Chicago: The University of Chicago Press, 1990): 300.
72. See, for example, Rosalind Rosenberg, *Divided Lives: American Women in the Twentieth Century* (New York: Hill & Wang, 1992): 195.
73. Jane Davison and Lesley Davison, *To Make a House a Home: Four Generations of American Women and the Houses They Lived In* (New York: Random House, 1994): 219.
74. Pat Mainardi, "The Politics of Housework," Nona Glazer-Malbin and Helen Y. Waehrer ed., *Woman in a Man-made World* (Chicago: Rand-McNally College Publishing Co., 1972): 289–92.
75. Davison, *To Make a House a Home,* 215.
76. Harvey, *The Fifties,* 151.
77. Hochschild, *The Second Shift,* 261.

78. Vanek, "Time Spent in Housework," 118–120.
79. Dummkopf is German for "dummy." Amy Vanderbilt, *Amy Vanderbilt's New Complete Book of Etiquette: The Guide to Gracious Living* (Garden City, NY: Doubleday & Co., Inc., 1962): 374, 381.
80. Carolyn Reed in Robert Hamburger, *A Stranger in the House* (New York: Macmillan Publishing Co., Inc., 1978): 163–4.
81. New York State Employment Service Specifications, in "Community Household Employment Programs," *Bulletin of the Women's Bureau*, No. 221 (Washington, D.C.: U.S.G.P.O., 1948): 43; A.E. Johnson Company placement books, 1958–1959.
82. A.E. Johnson Agency job description and wage sheets, 1993; Interview with Gleason Frye, President of Lindquist Group, parent of the A.E. Johnson Agency, Greenwich, CT, June 2, 1995.
83. Julia Wrigley, "Feminists and Domestic Workers," *Feminist Studies* (Summer 1991): 320.
84. Davison, *To Make a House a Home*, 262.
85. Mary Romero, *Maid in the U.S.A.* (New York: Routledge, 1992): 147.
86. Romero, *Maid in the U.S.A.*, 160–161; Barbara R. Bergmann, *The Economic Emergence of Women* (New York: Basic Books, Inc., 1986): 281. Author's observations, George Washington Bridge Port Authority Bus Station, New York City, 8:30 a.m., July 9, 1996; interviews with Beverly McDonald [child care worker], East Orange, NJ, summer 2001. She commuted by train to Maplewood, NJ and Summit, NJ.
87. Bergmann, *Economic Emergence*, 281.
88. Hamburger, *A Stranger in the House*, xiii.

NOTES TO CHAPTER FIVE

1. Foner, Nancy, ed., *New Immigrants in New York* (New York: Columbia University Press, 2001): 48, 50; United States Department of Commerce, Bureau of the Census, 1960, 1970.
2. Aaron Levenstein, *Why People Work* (New York: Crowell-Collier Publishing Co., 1962): 38; cited in Chaplin, "Domestic Service and the Negro": 535.
3. David M. Katzman, *Seven Days a Week: Women and Domestic Work in Industrializing America* (New York: Oxford University Press, 1978): 49; Elizabeth Bogen, *Immigration in New York* (NY: Praeger, 1987): 18–19; Monica Gordon, "Caribbean migration: A Perspective on Women," in Delores M. Mortimer and Roy S. Bryce-Laporte, eds., *Female Immigrants to the U.S.: Caribbean, Latin American and African Experiences*, RIIES Occaisional Papers No. 2, Research Institute on Immigration and Ethnic Studies (Washington, D.C.: Smithsonian Institution, 1981): 30.
4. Katzman, *Seven Days*, 70–72.
5. "The Domestic Worker, '62, Is a Part-Time Helper, a Full-Time Headache," *The New York Times* (November 22, 1962); Trudier Harris, *From Mammies to Militants: Domestics in Black American Literature* (Philadelphia: Temple University Press, 1982), *e.g.*, p. 4; interview with Virginia

Johnson, New York City, May 29, 1992. She came from the South about 1930 and worked as a maid—mostly in Brooklyn—until the late 1960s, living in until World War II and living out thereafter.

6. "Would Admit Cooks," *The New York Times,* December 12, 1925; "Commendable, But Is It Practicable?" *The New York Times,* December 14, 1925; the *Times* ran a long article on the issue two days later: "Let In Servants Is Plea of Bill," *The New York Times,* December 20, 1925; "Quotas and Servants," *The New York Times,* July 13, 1927.

7. Josephine Pinyon Holmes, "Two Minute Reports," Conference on Employer-Employee Relationships in the Home, October 16, 1928, YWCA, Reel 97.4; Brenda Faye Clegg noted that "[i]ntegrated employment agencies sent [black domestics] out on the lowest paying jobs. The more affluent employers preferred to have European servants." "Black Female Domestics During the Great Depression in New York City, 1930–1940" (University of Michigan, 1983): abstract.

8. *Decennial Census of the Population*; Winifred Wandersee, *Women's Work and Family Values,* 89; Marvel Cooke and Ella Baker, "The Bronx Slave Market," *The Crisis* (November 1935): 330.

9. "Negro Household Employees During Current Employment Crisis," June 11, 1931, Records Files Collection, YWCA of the U.S.A., National Board Archives, New York, Reel 98.4

10. Although there were more African-American servants toward the end of the war—1,024,765 in 1944, up from 943,920 in 1940—a much smaller percentage of employed black women were working as servants: 43.7 percent compared to 57 percent. D'Ann Campbell, *Women at War with America: Private Lives in a Patriotic Era* (Cambridge, MA: Harvard University Press, 1984): 75, 76; Table 2, p 240. Discussion Group on Household Employees, Fifth Metropolitan Conference on Employment and Guidance, November 19, 1937, YWCA Records, Reel 97.3; "Negroes in New York City: Occupational Distribution, 1940–47," *Monthly Labor Review* 68:1 (January 1949): 57.

11. "Fanny Christina Hill," in Sherna Berger Gluck, *Rosie the Riveter Revisited: Women, the War and Social Change* (New York: Meridian, 1987): 42.

12. Guichard Parris and Lester Brooks, *Blacks in the City: A History of the National Urban League* (Boston: Little, Brown and Co., 1971): 313; Susan M. Hartmann, *The Home Front and Beyond: American Women in the 1940s* (Boston: Twayne Publishers, 1982): 60, 80.

13. "Negroes in New York City," 57. Nationwide, there had been about one million white domestics in 1940, but during the war that number declined to 670,000. Campbell, *Women at War with America,* 74, 75, 76; Table 2, p. xxx; "Fewer Servants by the Year" editorial, *The New York Times,* May 29, 1946; Hartmann, *Home Front and Beyond,* 90.

14. "Domestic Workers' Wages and Hours, New York State, 1948," *Monthly Labor Review* 69 (October 1949); "Women Workers—Employment Trends, 1900–1950," *Monthly Labor Review* 72 (January 1951); "The Last of Frankfurt-on-the-Hudson," *The New York Times* (August 27, 1992); New York City Department of Planning Bulletin, *Puerto Rican*

Migration to New York City, February 1957, Municipal Archives of the City of New York, Mayoral Papers, Wagner, Robert F., Subject Files 1954–1965 (hereinafter "Wagner Papers"), Box 282, "Puerto Rican Problem in New York City," folder 1957(3); Gluck, *Rosie the Riveter Revisited:* 33–34, 41.

15. U.S. Department of Commerce, Bureau of the Census, *Decennial Census of Population,* 1940, 1950.

16. *Decennial Census of Population,* 1950, 1960; Chaplin, "Domestic Service and the Negro," 527; Mary Romero, *Maid in the U.S.A.,* 87–93; E. Marvin Goodwin, *Black Migration in American from 1915 to 1960: An Uneasy Exodus* (Lewiston, NY: The Edwin Mellin Press, 1990): 20–22.

17. *Decennial Census of Population,* 1970, 1980.

18. Phyllis Palmer, "Housework and Domestic Labor: Racial and Technological Change," in Karen Brodkin Sacks and Dorothy Remy, eds., *My Troubles Are Going to Have Trouble With Me: Everyday Trials and Triumphs of Women Workers* (New Brunswick, N.J.: Rutgers University Press, 1984): 82.

19. *Historical Statistics of the U.S., Colonial Times to 1970, Part 1* (U.S. Dept. of Commerce, Bureau of The Census, 1975): Series D182–232: 132; Leonard Broom and Norval D. Glenn, "The Occupation and Income of Black Americans," in Norval D. Glenn and Charles M. Bonjean eds., *Blacks in the United States* (San Francisco: Chandler Publishing Company, 1969): 25; "Women Workers—Employment Trends, 1900–1950," *Monthly Labor Review* 72 (January 1951); "The Last of Frankfurt-on-the-Hudson," *The New York Times,* August 27, 1992; New York City Department of Planning Bulletin, *Puerto Rican Migration to New York City,* February 1957, Wagner Papers, Box 282, "Puerto Rican Problem in New York City," folder 1957(3).

20. "Nanny-nappers in Park Vie for Women Clad in White," *The New York Times,* September 11, 1964; Linda Martin and Kerry Segrave, *The Servant Problem: Domestic Workers in North America* (Jefferson, N.C.: McFarland & Co., Inc., 1985): 98–100, 110–113; "L.I. Maids Grumbling," *The New York Times,* March 30, 1965.

21. "Servant Shortage Put Up to Coolidge," *The New York Times,* March 31, 1927.

22. "What One Home-maker Thinks," *Women's Press* 22 (February 1928): 83, quoted in Palmer, *Domesticity and Dirt,* 115. See also the discussion in Chapter Three about voluntary contracts and housewives' view that their own needs were paramount. "Women Workers—Employment Trends, 1900–1950," *Monthly Labor Review* 72 (January 1951); Gluck, *Rosie the Riveter Revisited:* 41.

23. Dan Lacey, *The Essential Immigrant* (NY: Hippocrene Books, 1990): 71–78; Bernard A. Weisberger, "A Nation of Immigrants," *American Heritage* (February/March 1994): 75–91; *Congressional Digest* v. 75 (May 1996): 143+.

24. "Women Workers—Employment Trends, 1900–1950," *Monthly Labor Review* 72 (January 1951); Gluck, *Rosie the Riveter Revisited:* 41–42;

"Agency for Maids Barred by State," *The New York Times,* May 23, 1962.

25. "Puerto Rican Girls to Get Jobs Here," *The New York Times,* January 30, 1948; "21 Puerto Ricans Here as Domestics," *The New York Times,* February 28, 1948; "Puerto Rican Girls Like Transition After Week on Jobs in Scarsdale," *The New York Times,* March 5, 1948; "Housemaids Flown to U.S.," *The New York Times,* April 24, 1948.

26. Manuel Cabranes, Consultant to the Commission, NYC Department of Welfare, to Mrs. Shirley Warren, May 23, 1957, in Box 282, 1957 (3) Puerto Rican Problems in New York City, Wagner Papers; *Puerto Rican Migration to New York City,* February 1957, Wagner Papers.

27. "La Guardia Speeds Wind-Up of UNRRA," *The New York Times,* September 14, 1946.

28. "Ruggles of Dollar Gap," *The New York Times,* November 23, 1952; "U.S. Limits Entry of Domestic Help," *The New York Times,* September 19, 1968; Randy Pearl Albelda, "Black and White Women Workers in the Post World War II Period," (University of Massachusetts, 1983): abstract.

29. "Mexican Domestics Problem in El Paso," *The New York Times,* August 30, 1953.

30. "Judge Denounces L.I. Job Agencies for Luring Young Girls From the South," *The New York Times,* September 25, 1957.

31. "Abuses Charged in Maid Agencies," *The New York Times,* March 3, 1962.

32. "U.S. Will Scrutinize Visas of Servants," *The New York Times* (August 9, 1960); "Briton to Visit U.S. to Check on Maids Sent to Americans," *The New York Times,* February 16, 1960; "Alien Contracts Studied on Coast: Some Job Agencies Accused Over Bringing of Girls to U.S. as Servants," *The New York Times,* June 26, 1960.

33. "Importing Maids is Called Legal," *The New York Times,* March 30, 1962; "Bill to Protect Maids Is Killed," *The New York Times,* March 31, 1962; "Agency for Maids Barred by State," *The New York Times,* May 23, 1962.

34. "Importing Maids is Called Legal"; "Bill to Protect Maids Is Killed"; "Parley Hits Abuses in Recruiting Maids," *The New York Times,* May 10, 1962.

35. *Matter of Tucker, In Deportation Proceedings,* A-17455405, July 25, 1967, in Benjamin Gim, "Seminar in Immigration and Naturalization Law," Fall, 1977, Installment II (Columbia University School of Law, privately printed).

36. John M. Leslie to John V. Lindsay, transmitting *New York State Skills Center Performance Report,* April 1973, Municipal Archives of the City of New York, Office of the Mayor, Lindsay, John V., (hereinafter "Lindsay Papers" Departmental Correspondence 1973, NYS and U.S. Government, New York State, Location 110046–50; "Jobless Training Pressed by Wirtz," *The New York Times,* February 5, 1965; "Statement by Mayor Robert F. Wagner," July 31, 1964, Wagner Papers, Box 71, #132 Discrimination 1964;

"Wagner Outlines Drive on Poverty," *The New York Times*, March 12, 1965; News Release, November 10, 1966, Lindsay Papers, Departmental Correspondence 1966—U.S. Government, Box 6858;"Suggested Objectives and Criteria for Program Selection," Anti-Poverty Operations Board, January 7, 1965, discussion draft, Wagner Papers, Box 10, folder 1 "Anti-Poverty."

37. Press Release, February 19, 1963, Wagner Papers, Box 71, Discrimination—COIR Releases 1961–63; "Remarks by Mayor Robert F. Wagner at Rally in Support of the Administration's Civil Rights Bill Sponsored by New York City Central Labor Council," April 8, 1964, Wagner Papers, Box 71, #132 Discrimination 1964; *Congressional Record* May 3, 1965, p. 8916, photocopy in Wagner Papers, Box 71, Discrimination 1965.

38. Minimum wage laws were controversial. The state voided this law in 1963, only to have the city pass another in 1964. New York State finally covered domestics statewide in 1972. The national minimum wage law covered domestics in 1974. The original New York State unemployment insurance law dated back to 1935. "Unemployment Insurance," *The New York Times*, March 15, 1936; "Wagner Signs Bill on Minimum Pay," *The New York Times*, October 23, 1962; "New York City Wage Floor Voided; State Law Sought," *The Wall Street Journal*, March 5, 1963; "New Rights Issue: Housewife's Role," *The New York Times*, August 24, 1963; National Archives, RG 86, Women's Bureau, Division of Research, Unpublished Materials, 1919–1972, Box 362. Private Household Worker Fact Sheet (August 1964); Local Law No. 45, Women's Bureau Unpublished Materials, 1919–1972, Box 362; "Form for New Tax Sent to Housewives; Many Are Annoyed," *The New York Times*, April 7, 1966; "Jobless Payrolls Now Cover Maids," *The New York Times*, July 23, 1966; "Minimum Wage in State Now Due Household Help," *The New York Times*, January 15, 1972; "President Signs Rise in Pay Base to $2.30 an Hour," *The New York Times*, April 9, 1974.

39. Julius C.C. Edelstein to A. Philip Randolph, April 14, 1963, Wagner Papers, Box 217, Folder #59, 1962–65 Minimum Wage; Edward B. Muse, Chairman Legislation & Political Action, NAACP Greenwich Village/Chelsea Branch, to Robert F. Wagner, August 30, 1962, Wagner Papers, Box 217, Minimum Wage Wagner; Isiah Brunson to Robert F. Wagner, April 9, 1964, Wagner Papers, Box 71, #132 Discrimination 1964.

40. "State Job Agency Weighs Bias Charge," *The New York Times*, August 4, 1962. See also Trudier Harris, *From Mammies to Militants: Domestics in Black American Literature* (Philadelphia: Temple University Press, 1982) for a discussion of African-American domestics' anger during the 1960s, pp. 17–33 *passim*.

41. Studs Terkel, *Working: People Talk About What They Do All Day and How They Feel About What They Do* (NY: Pantheon, 1972, 1974): 114.

42. "Domestics Called 'Most Exploited,'" *The New York Times*, September 24, 1970.

43. "Rise of 24 Million in U.S. Labor Force Is Forecast by 1980," *The New York Times* (February 22, 1965); *The New York Times* classified advertisements, 1920–1970 *passim*.

44. "Nonprofit Group Proposed Here To Keep Business and Spur Jobs," *The New York Times*, February 9, 1965.

45. Harvard Sitkoff, *The Struggle for Black Equality, 1954–1980* (New York: Hill and Wang, 1981): 165–66; "Civil Rights—Another Long, Hot Summer?" *The New York Times*, June 13, 1965. See also Bonnie Thornton Dill, "'The Means to Put My Children Through': Child-Rearing Goals and Strategies Among Black Female Domestic Servants," in La Frances Rodgers-Rose, ed., *The Black Woman* (Beverly Hills: Sage Publications, 1980): 110–112.

46. U.S. Department of Commerce, Bureau of the Census, *Census of Population and Housing*, 1970, "Detailed Characteristics: New York"; Eileen Appelbaum and Peter Albin, "Shifts in Employment, Occupational Structure, and Education Attainment" in Thierry Noyelle, ed. *Skills, Wages and Productivity in the Service Sector* (Boulder, CO: Westview Press, 1990), *passim*; Allen, "Family Roles . . .," 675–7; Natalie Sokoloff, *Black Women and White Women in the Professions* (New York: Routledge, 1992), cited in Sheryl McCarthy, "White Men Have Nothing to Fear," *New York Newsday* (December 14, 1992).

47. Howell Raines, "Grady's Gift," *The New York Times Magazine*, December 1, 1991.

48. Stuart H. Garfinkle, "Occupations of Women and Black Workers, 1962–74," *Monthly Labor Review* (November, 1975): 27; La Frances Rodgers-Rose, "Some Demographic Characteristics of the Black Woman: 1940 to 1975," in La Frances Rodgers-Rose, ed., *The Black Woman* (Beverly Hills: Sage Publications, 1980): 34.

49. Elizabeth Higginbotham, "Laid Bare By the System: Work and Survival for Black and Hispanic Women," in Amy Swerdlow and Hanna Lessinger, eds., *Class, Race and Sex: The Dynamics of Control,* (Boston: G.K. Hall, 1983): 207; *Decennial Census of the Population*, 1990; interview with Debbie Cox of Debbie's Cleaning Service, New York City, May 16, 1993.

50. Bogen, *Immigration in New York*, p. 84; Martin and Segrave, *The Servant Problem*, 105; Saskia Sassen-Koob, "Exporting Capital and Importing Labor: The Role of Women," in Delores M. Mortimer and Roy S. Bryce-Laporte, eds., *Female Immigrants to the U.S.: Caribbean, Latin American and African Experiences*, RIIES Occasional Papers No. 2, Research Institute on Immigration and Ethnic Studies (Washington, D.C.: Smithsonian Institution, 1981): 211.

51. "U.S. Limits Entry of Domestic Help," *The New York Times*, September 19, 1968.

52. Martin and Segrave, *The Servant Problem*, 98–100, 110–113; "L.I. Maids Grumbling," *The New York Times*, March 30, 1965; "Ervin Challenges Immigration Bill," *The New York Times*, February 26, 1965.

53. Myra C. Hacker, Testimony, Hearings before Subcommittee No. 1 of the Committee on the Judiciary, House of Representatives, 89th Congress, 1st

Session, on H.R. 2580, to Amend the Immigration and Nationality Act, and for Other Purposes (hereinafter "Immigration and Nationality Act Hearings"), March–June 1965, Document 69, Serial No. 7, May 18, 1965 (Washington: U.S.G.P.O., 1965): 258.

54. Testimony of Attorney General Nicholas deB. Katzenbach, Immigration and Nationality Act Hearings, March—June 1965, Document 69, Serial No. 7 (Washington, D.C.: GPO 1965): 30, 33.

55. Katzenbach Testimony: 15, 23.

56. Katzenbach Testimony: 45; W. Willard Wirtz, Secretary of Labor, Testimony, Immigration and Nationality Act Hearings: 126–30.

57. Martin and Segrave, *The Servant Problem*: 110; "L.I. Maids Grumbling," *The New York Times*, March 30, 1965: 49; Immigration and Nationality Act Hearings," March 5 and 11, 1965 (Washington, D.C.: U.S.G.P.O., 1965): 19–20, 127; Visa Applications 1963, "Immigration," "Hearings Before Subcommittee No. 1 of the Committee on the Judiciary, House of Representatives, Eighty-Eighth Congress, Second Session, on H.R. 7700 and 55 Identical Bills, to Amend the Immigration and Nationality Act," (Washington, D.C.: U.S.G.P.O., 1964).

58. S.M. Tomasi and Charles B. Keely, *Whom Have We Welcomed?: The Adequacy and Quality of United States Immigration Data for Policy and Evaluation* (Staten Island, N.Y.: The Center for Migration Studies, 1975): 5–9.

59. Monica Gordon, "Caribbean Migration: A Perspective on Women" in Delores M. Mortimer and Roy S. Bryce-Laporte, eds., *Female Immigrants to the U.S.: Caribbean, Latin American and African Experiences*, RIIES Occasional Papers No. 2, Research Institute on Immigration and Ethnic Studies, Smithsonian Institution, Washington, D.C., 1981: 30–31; Bogen, *Immigration in New York*, p. 84; Martin and Segrave, *The Servant* Problem, 105; Saskia Sassen-Koob, "Exporting Capital and Importing Labor: The Role of Women," in *Female Immigrants to the U.S.*, 211.

60. "Immigration Brings a Shift in Maids," *The New York Times*, June 23, 1968

61. U.S. Department of Labor, Office of the Secretary, Women's Bureau, *Women Private Household Workers: A Statistical and Legislative Profile* (Washington, D.C., 1978): 2; Gordon, "Caribbean Migration: A Perspective on Women": 30–31; Tomasi and Keely, *Whom Have We Welcomed?*, 65; *Decennial Census of Population*, 1970.

62. Hasia Diner, *Erin's Daughters in America: Irish Immigrant Women in the Nineteenth Century* (Baltimore: The Johns Hopkins University Press, 1983): 94; Lars Ljungmark, "On Emigration, Social Mobility, and the Transfer of Capital," *The Swedish-American Historical Quarterly* 41 (July 1990): 100; Susan Huelsebuch Buchanan, "Profile of Haitian Migrant Woman" in *Female Immigrants to the U.S.*, 122.

63. Dennis Forsythe, "Black Immigrants and the American Ethos: Theories and Observations," in Roy S. Bryce-Laporte and Delores M. Mortimer, eds., *Caribbean Immigration to the United States*, RIIES Occasional Papers No. 1 (Washington, DC: Smithsonian Institution, 1976).

64. Lourdes Casal with assistance of Yolanda Prieto, "Black Cubans in the United States: Basic Demographic Information" in *Female Immigrants to the U.S.,* 318; Susan Huelsebuch Buchanan, "Profile of Haitian Migrant Woman" in *Female Immigrants to the U.S.,* 116–118; Interview with Minette Alphonse (pseudonym), Maplewood, NJ, August 3, 2005.

    Paule Marshall, whose mother was a Barbadian immigrant in the 1920s, writes:

    > Looking back on it now it seems to me that those Barbadian women accepted these ill-paying, low status jobs with an astonishing lack of visible resentment. For them they were simply a means to an end: the end being the down payment on a brownstone house, a college education for their children, and the much coveted middle-class status these achievements represented.

    Paule Marshall, "Black Immigrant Women in *Brown Girl Brownstones,*" in Constance R. Sutton and Elsa M. Chaney, eds., *Caribbean Life in New York City: Sociocultural Dimensions* (NY: Center for Migration Studies of New York, Inc., 1987): 87–89.
65. "La Mujer de Origen Hispano en la Fuerza Laboral," Women's Bureau *Facts on Working Women* 89–1S (August 1989); City of New York, Department of City Planning, *The Newest New Yorkers, 1990–1994* (New York: December 1996): 14; City of New York, Department of City Planning, *The Newest New Yorkers, 1995–1996* (New York: September 1999): 6.
66. "Immigration Brings a Shift in Maids," *The New York Times,* June 23, 1968.
67. "Immigration Brings a Shift in Maids."
68. Susan Huelsebuch Buchanan, "Profile of Haitian Migrant Woman" in *Female Immigrants to the U.S.,* 114.
69. "Illegal Aliens Post Ever-Deepening Crisis," *The New York Times,* October 17, 1971.
70. Rosario, Juan, Anneris Goris, Francisco Angeles, *Movimientos Poblacionales en la Republica Dominicana* (NY: The Dominican Research Center, Inc., n.d.): 84; Tomasi and Keely, *Whom Have We Welcomed?,* 5–9.
71. "Alien 'Maid' Influx Aided by Lawyers, Spurs Inquiry Here," *The New York Times,* November 28, 1967.
72. "Immigration Brings a Shift in Maids," *The New York Times,* June 23, 1968, "U.S. Limits Entry of Domestic Help," *The New York Times,* September 19, 1968.
73. "Alien Domestics Arrested in Area," *The New York Times,* June 29, 1968.
74. "U.S. Limits Entry of Domestic Help," *The New York Times,* September 19, 1968.
75. Reynaldo Baca and Dexter Bryan, "Mexican Undocumented Women Workers in Los Angeles: A Research Note," in *Female Immigrants to the U.S.,* 302.
76. "For Immigrant Maids, Not a Job but Servitude," *The New York Times,* February 26, 1996.
77. Judith Burgess and Meryl James-Gray, "Migration and Sex Roles: A Comparison of Black and Indian Trinidadians in New York City," based on

a 1977 study, in *Female Immigrants to the U.S.*, 100; Minette Alphonse interview.

78. Gordon, "Caribbean Migration . . .," p. 40.
79. Helen I. Safa, "The Differential Incorporation of Hispanic Women Migrants into the United States Labor Force," in *Female Immigrants to the U.S.*, 238–255. See also, Juan Rosario, Anneris Goris, Francisco Angeles, *Movimientos Poblacionales en la Republica Dominicana* (NY: The Dominican Research Center, Inc., n.d.)
80. U.S. Department of Labor, Women's Bureau, *1993 Handbook on Women Workers: Trends and Issues* (Washington, D.C., 1994): 19–20, 50, 53.
81. Interview with Jean Ulitz Mensch, New York City, July 13, 1992.
82. "Invisible to Most, Immigrant Women Line Up for Day Labor," *The New York Times*, August 15, 2005.
83. Interview with Norma Silvestri, Leonia, NJ, September 13, 1992.
84. Adriana Marshall, "Immigration, Labor Demand and the Working Class," *Politics & Society* 1984 13(4): 425–453; George J. Stigler, *Domestic Servants in the United States, 1900–1940* (New York: National Bureau of Economic Research, Occasional Paper 24, 1946): 6, cited in Ruth Milkman, Ellen Reese and Benita Roth, "The Macrosociology of (Paid) Domestic Labor," unpublished paper, January 1996: 6; Milkman, et al., 7. For example, Sweden has almost no domestic servants, "because it is very expensive to pay them a fair salary . . . [and] you as an employer have to pay their tax and social insurance too." Perhaps fairness will lead to domestic work's demise. Milkman, et al., 16, n. 4.
85. Milkman, et al., "The Macrosociology of (Paid) Domestic Labor," 12. Los Angeles is similar to New York, in both its income inequality and population. In 1990, 81 percent of L.A. domestics were foreign-born, and 8 percent were African-American. Minneapolis-St. Paul, on the other hand, with relative income equality and a predominantly white population, had few domestic servants, and 96 percent of them were white.

NOTES TO THE CONCLUSION

1. Whether those jobs were "better" was debatable, especially to a home health care worker who was paid $7.20 an hour and whose hours were halved because of Medicaid cutbacks. The key development is that African American women now had more options than domestic service work. "Just Hanging On," *New York Newsday*, May 17, 1992.
2. Enforcement of immigration laws in 2005 was the responsibility of Immigration and Customs Enforcement, part of the Department of Homeland Security.
3. "Clinton's Choice for Justice Dept. Hired Illegal Aliens for Household," *The New York Times*, January 14, 1993; "Illegal Nanny Hiring is Called Common," *New York Newsday*, January 15, 1993; "Clinton Cancels Baird Nomination for Justice Department," *The New York Times*, January 22, 1993.
4. "Increasingly, 2-Career Family Means Illegal Immigrant Help," *The New York Times*, January 24, 1993; "Despite the Zoë Baird Flap, Legal Nannies

Are a Hard Sell," *The New York Times,* February 7, 1993; "Parents Struggle to Find Nannies," *New York Newsday,* February 10, 1993.

5. "Babysitter Problems Sink Second Clinton Prospect," *The Washington Post,* February 6, 1993; "After Wood and Baird, Illegal-Nanny Anxiety Creeps Across Many Homes," *The New York Times,* February 15, 1993.

6. "G.O.P. Candidates Say They Hired Illegal Aliens," *The New York Times,* January 23, 1993; "Increasingly, 2-Career Family Means Illegal Immigrant Help," *The New York Times,* January 24, 1993; "Anger at Illegal Help Threatens 2 in G.O.P." *The New York Times,* January 25, 1993; "Challenger to Florio [Christine Todd Whitman of N.J.] Will Pay Back Taxes for Illegal Aliens, *The New York Times,* January 26, 1993; "Campaign Refrain: 'My Opponent's a Hypocrite,'" *The New York Times,* November 6, 1994; "Senator's Employee Lacked Work Papers, Agency Says," *The New York Times,* November 5, 1994; "Trouble at Home: Brown Admits He Owed Tax For Cleaner," *New York Newsday,* February 8, 1993; "The Baird Effect," *Newsweek* (October 11, 1993): 6; "Stat Patrol," *Working Woman* (October 1993).

7. Diana Runner, "Changes in Unemployment Insurance Legislation in 1994," *Monthly Labor Review* (January 1995); Cindy Seipel, "Payroll Tax and Immigration Laws for Domestic Service Employ," *The CPA Journal* (April 1995).

8. "Kerik Withdraws as Bush's Nominee for Security Post," *The New York Times,* December 11, 2004; "Bush Choice for Labor Post Withdraws and Cites Furor of Illegal Immigrant Issue," *The New York Times,* January 10, 2001; "New Treasury Secretary Is Snarled in Tax Matter," *The Wall Street Journal,* January 22, 2001.

9. "A Nation of Decent, Law-Breaking Citizens," *The New York Times,* February 14, 1993; "Baird Stands in Part for All Working Mothers," *The New York Times,* January 27, 1993; "Usually, the Illegality in Domestic Work is Benefits Denied," *The New York Times,* January 31, 1993; "If Domestic Work Paid Well . . . ," *The New York Times,* January 31, 1993; "Exploiting Domestic Workers," *New York Newsday,* February 28, 1993; "No Good Nannies? Find a Good Family," *The New York Times,* September 16, 1993.

10. See for example, "At Rally for Domestics' Rights, A Nanny Tells of Mistreatment," *The New York Times,* March 8, 2004; "Domestic Workers Face Blatant Discrimination, Investigations Reveals," *The New York Times,* June 1, 2005.

11. "For Immigrant Maids, Not a Job but Servitude," *The New York Times,* February 25, 1996; "Nanny Get Your Gun," *New York Newsday,* September 25, 1994; "Need a Nanny? Show Her the Money," *The New York Times,* July 26, 1999.

12. "For Immigrant Maids, Not a Job but Servitude."

13. "For Immigrant Maids, Not a Job but Servitude."

14. Louise Rafkin, "Dirty Laundry," *The New York Times Magazine,* January 28, 1996.

15. Interview with Norma Silvestri, Leonia, New Jersey, September 13, 1992; Barbara Ehrenreich, *Nickel and Dimed: On (Not) Getting By in America* (New York: Metropolitan Books, 2001): 72.

16. Ehrenreich, *Nickel and Dime(d)*, 72.

17. Most people assumed penalties would be "mild," however, as no criminal charges had ever been brought as of late 2004. "Tax Report: Many Filers Ignore Nanny Tax, Expecting Not to Get Caught," *The Wall Street Journal*, December 15, 2004.

Bibliography

MONOGRAPHS

Abramovitz, Mimi, *Regulating the Lives of Women: Social Welfare Policy from Colonial Times to the Present* (Boston, MA: South End Press, 1988).

Adams, Charlotte, Housekeeping After Office Hours: A Homemaking Guide for the Working Woman (1953).

Albrecht, Karl and Ron Zemke, *Service America: Doing Business in the New Economy* (Homewood, IL: Dow Jones-Irwin, 1985).

Allen, Frederick Lewis, *Since Yesterday: The 1930s in America: September 3, 1929—September 3, 1939* (New York: Perennial Library, Harper & Row, Publishers, 1939, 1986).

Allen, Lucy G., *Table Service* (Boston: Little, Brown & Co., 1943).

Allen, Robert, *Reluctant Reformers: Racism and Social Reform Movements in the United States* (Washington, DC: Howard University Press, 1983).

Allen, Theodore W., *The Invention of the White Race: The Origin of Racial Oppression in Anglo-America* (London: Verso, 1997).

Altmeyer, Arthur J., *The Formative Years of Social Security* (Madison: The University of Wisconsin Press, 1966).

Armstrong, Robert A. and Homer Hoyt, *Decentralization in New York* (Chicago: Urban Land Institute, 1941).

Asch, Sidney H., *Social Security and Related Welfare Programs*, Legal Almanac Series No. 25 (New York: Oceana Publications, 1952).

Baxter, Freddie Mae, *The Seventh Child: A Lucky Life* (New York: Alfred A. Knopf, 1999).

Bell, Daniel, *The Coming of the Postindustrial Society: A Venture in Social Forecasting* (New York: Basic Books, 1973).

Berch, Bettina, *The Endless Day: The Political Economy of Women and Work* (New York: Harcourt Brace Jovanovich, Inc., 1982).

Bergmann, Barbara, *The Economic Emergence of Women* (New York: Basic Books, Inc., 1986).

Berkowitz, Edward D., *America's Welfare State: From Roosevelt to Reagan* (Baltimore: The Johns Hopkins University Press, 1991).

223

Blau, Peter M. and Otis Dudley Duncan (with Andrea Tyree), *The American Occupational Structure* (New York: John Wiley & Sons, 1967).

Bluestone, Barry, William M. Murphy, and Mary Stevenson, *Low Wages and the Working Poor*, Policy Papers in Human Resources and Industrial Relations 22 (Ann Arbor, MI: The Institute of Labor and Industrial Relations, July 1973).

Blum, John Morton, *V Was for Victory: Politics and American Culture During World War II* (New York: Harcourt Brace Jovanovich, Publishers: 1976).

Bogen, Elizabeth, *Immigration in New York* (NY: Praeger, 1987).

Boris, Eileen and Cynthia R. Daniels, eds., *Homework: Historical and Contemporary Perspectives on Paid Labor at Home* (Urbana, IL: University of Illinois Press, 1989).

Breines, Wini, *Young, White and Miserable: Growing Up Female in the Fifties* (Boston: Beacon Press, 1992).

Boydston, Jeanne, *Home and Work: Housework, Wages and the Ideology of Labor in the Early Republic* (New York: Oxford University Press, 1990).

Brinker, Paul A., and Joseph J. Klos, *Poverty, Manpower, and Social Security* (Austin, TX: Austin Press, 1976).

Brown, Dorothy M., *Setting a Course: American Women in the 1920s* (Boston: Twayne Publishers, 1987).

Browne, Jim, *Management and Analysis of Service Operations* (New York: North-Holland, 1984).

Bryce-Laporte, Roy S. and Delores M. Mortimer, eds., *Caribbean Immigration to the United States*, RIIES Occasional Papers No. 1 (Washington, DC: Smithsonian Institution, 1976).

Burns, Arthur E. and Edward A. Williams, *Federal Work, Security, and Relief Programs*, Works Progress Administration, Division of Social Research, Research Monograph XXIV (New York: Da Capo Press, 1971).

Campbell, D'Ann, *Women at War with America: Private Lives in a Patriotic Era* (Cambridge, MA: Harvard University Press, 1984).

Carpenter, Niles, *Nationality, Color, and Economic Opportunity in the City of Buffalo* (Westport, CT: Negro Universities Press, 1927, 1970).

Cates, Jerry R., *Insuring Inequality: Administrative Leadership in Social Security, 1935–54* (Ann Arbor: The University of Michigan Press, 1983).

Chafe, William, *The American Woman: Her Changing Social, Economic, and Political Roles, 1920–1970* (New York: Oxford University Press, 1972).

Chudacoff, Howard P., *Mobile Americans: Residential and Social Mobility in Omaha, 1880–1920* (New York: Oxford University Press, 1972).

Clark-Lewis, Elizabeth, *Living In, Living Out: African American Domestics in Washington, D.C., 1910–1940* (Washington, D.C.: Smithsonian Institution Press, 1994).

Collange, Christiane, *The Well-Organized Woman* (New York: Avon Books, 1971).

Cowan, Ruth Schwartz, *More Work For Mother: The Ironies of Household Technology from the Open Hearth to the Microwave* (New York: Basic Books, Inc., 1983).

Davis, Angela, *Women, Race and Class* (New York: Vintage Books, 1981).

Davis, Frank G., *The Black Community's Social Security* (Washington, D.C.: University Press of America, 1978).

Davison, Jane and Lesley Davison, *To Make a House a Home: Four Generations of American Women and the Houses They Lived In* (New York: Random House, 1994).

Diner, Hasia, *Erin's Daughters in America: Irish Immigrant Women in the Nineteenth Century* (Baltimore: The Johns Hopkins University Press, 1983).

Dubofsky, Melvyn and Stephen Burwood, eds., *The Depression and the New Deal: The American Economy During the Great Depression* (New York: Garland Publishing, Inc., 1990).

Dye, Nancy Schrom, *As Equals and As Sisters: Feminism, the Labor Movement and the Women's Trade Union League of New York* (Columbia: University of Missouri Press, 1980).

Edmonston, Barry and James P. Smith, *The New Americans: Economic, Demographic and Fiscal Effects of Immigration* (Washington, D.C.: National Academy Press, 1997).

Ehrenreich, Barbara, *Nickel and Dimed: On (Not) Getting By in America* (New York: Metropolitan Books, 2001).

——and Deidre English, *For Her Own Good: 150 Years of the Experts' Advice to Women* (New York: Doubleday, 1978).

Ellison, Mary, *The Black Experience: American Blacks Since 1865* (New York: Barnes and Noble Books, 1974).

England, Paula and George Farkas, *Households, Employment and Gender: A Social, Economic, and Demographic View* (New York: Aldine Publishing Company, 1986).

Evans, Sara M. and Barbara J. Nelson, *Wage Justice: Comparable Worth and the Paradox of Technocratic Reform* (Chicago: The University of Chicago Press, 1989).

Faulhaber, Gerald, Eli Noam, and Roberta Tasley, eds., *Services in Transition: The Impact of Information Technology on the Service Sector* (Cambridge, MA: Ballinger, 1986).

Ferber, Marianne A. and Julie A. Nelson, *Beyond Economic Man: Feminist Theory and Economics* (Chicago: The University of Chicago Press, 1993).

Flowers, Marilyn R., *Women and Social Security: An Institutional Dilemma* (Washington, D.C.: American Enterprise Institute for Public Policy Research, 1977).

Foner, Nancy, ed., *New Immigrants in New York* (New York: Columbia University Press, 2001).

Fox, Bonnie, ed., *Hidden in the Household: Women's Domestic Labour Under Capitalism* (Toronto: The Women's Press, 1980).

Fox, Richard Wightman and T.J. Jackson Lears, eds., *The Culture of Consumption: Critical Essays in American History* (New York: Pantheon Books, 1983).

Frankenberg, Ruth, *White Women, Race Matters: The Social Construction of Whiteness* (Minneapolis: University of Minnesota Press, 1993).

Friedan, Betty, *The Feminine Mystique* (New York: Laurel, 1963, 1983).

Furnas, J. C. and the staff of the *Ladies' Home Journal, How America Lives* (New York: Henry Holt & Co., 1941).

Gelb, Joyce and Marian Lief Pally, *Women and Public Policies* (Princeton, NJ: Princeton University Press, 1982).

Giarini, Orio, ed., *The Emerging Service Economy* (Oxford: Pergamon Press, 1987).

Giddings, Paula, *When and Where I Enter: The Impact of Black Women on Race and Sex in America* (New York: Bantam Books, 1984).

Ginzberg, Eli, *The Negro Potential* (New York: Columbia University Press, 1956).

Glazer, Nathan and Daniel P. Moynihan, *Beyond the Melting Pot: The Negroes, Puerto Ricans, Jews, Italians, and Irish of New York City* (Cambridge, MA: The MIT Press, 1963, 1970).

Glenn, Evelyn Nakano, *Issei, Nisei, War Bride: Three Generations of Japanese American Women in Domestic Service* (Philadelphia: Temple University Press, 1986).

Gluck, Sherna Berger, *Rosie the Riveter Revisited: Women, The War and Social Change* (New York: Meridian, 1987).

Goldman, Eric F., *The Crucial Decade—And After: America, 1945–1960* (New York: Vintage, 1961).

Goodwin, E. Marvin, *Black Migration in America From 1915 to 1960: An Uneasy Exodus* (Lewiston, NY: The Edwin Mellen Press, 1990).

Gordon, David M., Richard Edwards, and Michael Reich, *Segmented Work, Divided Workers: The Historical Transformation of Labor in the United States* (Cambridge: Cambridge University Press, 1982).

Gramsci, Antonio, *Letters from Prison*, Lynne Lawner, ed. (New York: The Noonday Press, 1973).

Gray, Brenda Clegg, *Black Female Domestics in the Depression* (New York: Garland Publishing Co., 1993).

Greenwald, Maurine Weiner, *Women, War, and Work: The Impact of World War I on Women Workers in the United States* (Ithaca: Cornell University Press, 1990).

Griffin, John I. and Jean Namias, *Fact Book: New York Metropolitan Region* (New York: New York City Council on Economic Education, 1965).

Groneman, Carol and Mary Beth Norton, eds., *"To Toil the Livelong Day": America's Women at Work, 1780–1980* (Ithaca, NY: Cornell University Press, 1987).

Hamburger, Martin and Ralph LoCascio, *A Study of Manpower Development and Training Act Programs in New York State* (New York: The Center for Field Research and School Services, School of Education, New York University, 1969).

Hamburger, Robert, *A Stranger in the House* (New York: Macmillan Publishing Co., Inc., 1978).

Hansen, Karen Tranberg, *Distant Companions: Servants and Employers in Zambia, 1900–1985* (Ithaca, NY: Cornell University Press, 1989).

Harris, Diane, *The Woman's Day Guide to Organizing Your Life* (New York: Holt, Rinehart and Winston, 1985).

Harris, Trudier, *From Mammies to Militants: Domestics in Black American Literature* (Philadelphia: Temple University Press, 1982).

Harrison, Bennett, *Education, Training, and the Urban Ghetto* (Baltimore: The Johns Hopkins University Press, 1972).

Harrison, Cynthia, *On Account of Sex: The Politics of Women's Issues, 1945–1968* (Berkeley: University of California Press, 1988).

Hartmann, Susan M., *The Home Front and Beyond: American Women in the 1940s* (Boston: Twayne Publishers, 1982).

Harvey, Brett, *The Fifties: A Women's Oral History* (New York: HarperCollins Publishers, Inc., 1993).

Harzig, Christiane, et al., *Peasant Maids-City Women: From the European Countryside to Urban America* (Ithaca: Cornell University Press, 1997).

Hernandez, Ramona and Francisco Rivera-Batiz, *Dominican New Yorkers: A Socioeconomic Profile, 1997* (New York: The CUNY Dominican Studies Institute, 1997).

Heskett, James L., *Managing in the Service Economy* (Cambridge, MA: Harvard Business School Press, 1986).

Hochschild, Arlie, *The Second Shift: Working Parents and the Revolution at Home* (New York: Viking, 1989).

hooks, bell, *YEARNING: race, gender, and cultural politics* (Boston: South End Press, 1990).

Hoyt, Homer, *The Changing Principles of Land Economics,* Technical Bulletin 60 (Washington, D.C.: Urban Land Institute, 1968).

Hunter, Tera, *To 'Joy My Freedom: Southern Black Women's Lives and Labors After the Civil War* (Cambridge, MA: Harvard University Press, 1997).

Jackson, Kenneth T., *Crabgrass Frontier: The Suburbanization of the United States* (New York: Oxford University Press, 1985).

————ed., *The Encyclopedia of New York City* (New Haven: Yale University Press, 1995).

Jones, Jacqueline, *Labor of Love, Labor of Sorrow: Black Women, Work and the family, From Slavery to the Present* (New York: Vintage, 1985).

Kaledin, Eugenia, *Mothers and More: American Women in the 1950s* (Boston: Twayne Publishers, 1984).

Katzman, David, *Seven Days a Week: Domestic Service in Industrializing America* (Urbana, IL: University of Illinois Press, 1981).

Kerber, Linda K. and Jane DeHart-Matthews, eds., *Women's America: Refocusing the Past* (New York: Oxford University Press, 1987).

Kerbo, Harold K., *Social Stratification and Inequality: Class Conflict in Historical and Comparative Perspective* (New York: McGraw-Hill, 1996).

————, *Out to Work: A History of Wage-Earning Women in the United States* (New York: Oxford University Press, 1982).

Kessler-Harris, Alice, *Women Have Always Worked: A Historical Overview* (Old Westbury, NY: The Feminist Press, 1981).

Kisseloff, Jeff, *You Must Remember This: An Oral History of Manhattan from the 1890s to World War II* (New York: Harcourt Brace Jovanovich, 1989).

Komarovksy, Mirra, *Blue Collar Marriage* (New York: Vintage Books, 1967).

Kuznets, Simon Smith, *Growth, Population, and Income Distribution* (New York: W. W. Norton & Company, Inc., 1979).

Kyrk, Hazel, *Economic Problems of the Family* (New York: Harper & Brothers, 1933).

Lacey, Dan, *The Essential Immigrant* (NY: Hippocrene Books, 1990).

Lanker, Brian, *I Dream a World: Portraits of Black Women Who Changed America* (New York: Stewart, Tabor, & Chang, 1989).

Lazear, Edward P. and Robert T. Michael, *Allocation of Income within the Household* (Chicago: University of Chicago Press, 1988).

Leach, William, *Land of Desire: Merchants, Power, and the Rise of a New American Culture* (New York: Vintage Books, 1993).

Lerner, Gerda, ed., *Black Women in White America: A Documentary History* (New York: Vintage, 1972).

———, ed., *The Female Experience: An American Documentary* (New York: Oxford University Press, 1977).

Leuchtenberg, William E., *The Perils of Prosperity, 1914–1932* (Chicago: University of Chicago Press, 1958).

Levenstein, Aaron, *Why People Work* (New York: Crowell-Collier Publishing Co., 1962).

Levitan, Sar A. and Garth L. Mangum, eds., *The T in CETA: Local and National Perspectives* (Kalamazoo, MI: W.E. Upjohn Institute for Employment Research, 1981).

Lieberman, Robert C., *Shifting the Color Line: Race and the American Welfare State* (Cambridge, MA: Harvard University Press, 1998).

Ljungmark, Lars, *Swedish Exodus* (Carbondale, IL: Southern Illinois University Press, 1979).

Lopata, Helena Z., *Occupation: Housewife* (New York: Oxford University Press, 1971).

———, Cheryl Allyn Miller, and Debra Barnewolt, *City Women: Work, Jobs, Occupation, Careers: Volume 1: America* (New York: Praeger, 1984).

Lubove, Roy, *The Struggle for Social Security* (Cambridge, MA: Harvard University Press, 1968).

Lynn, Susan, *Progressive Women in Conservative Times: Racial Justice, Peace, and Feminism, 1945 to the 1960s* (New Brunswick, NJ: Rutgers University Press, 1992).

Malson, Micheline R., et al., eds., *Black Women in America: Social Science Perspectives* (Chicago: The University of Chicago Press, 1990).

Mangum, Garth L. and John Walsh, *A Decade of Manpower Development and Training* (Salt Lake City: Olympus Publishing Company, 1973).

Mann, Evelyn S. and Joseph J. Salvo, *Characteristics of New Hispanic Immigrants to New York City: A Comparison of Puerto Rican and Non-Puerto Rican Hispanics* (New York, 1984).

Martin, Linda and Kerry Segrave, *The Servant Problem: Domestic Workers in North America* (Jefferson, N.C.: McFarland & Co., Inc., 1985).

Matthaei, Julie A., *An Economic History of Women in America: Women's Work, The Sexual Division of Labor, and the Development of Capitalism* (New York: Schocken Books, 1982).

May, Elaine Tyler, *Homeward Bound: American Families in the Cold War Era* (New York: Basic Books, 1988).

McElvaine, Robert S., *The Great Depression: America, 1929–1941* (New York: Times Books, 1984).

Meehan, Elizabeth M., *Women's Rights at Work: Campaigns and Policy in Britain and the United States* (New York: St. Martin's Press, 1985).

Meyerowitz, Joanne J., *Women Adrift: Independent Wage Earners in Chicago, 1880–1920* (Chicago: University of Chicago Press, 1988).

Milkman, Ruth, *Gender at Work: The Dynamics of Job Segregation by Sex during World War II* (Urbana, IL: University of Illinois Press, 1987).

Mills, C. Wright, *White Collar* (New York: Oxford University Press, 1953).

Mintz, Steven and Susan Kellogg, *Domestic Revolutions: A Social History of American Family Life*, (New York: The Free Press, 1988): 160.

Montgomery, Maureen E., *Displaying Women: Spectacles of Leisure in Edith Wharton's New York* (New York and London: Routledge, 1998).

Muntz, Earl E., *Social Security: An Analysis of the Wagner-Murray Bill* (New York: American Enterprise Association, 1944).

National Commission for Employment Policy, *Sixth Annual Report* (Washington, D.C.: The National Commission for Employment Policy, 1980).

Nelson, Garrison and Clark H. Bensen, *Committees in the U.S. Congress, 1947–1992, Volume 1: Committee Jurisdictions and Member Rosters* (Washington, D.C.: Congressional Quarterly, 1993).

Noyelle, Thierry, ed., *Skills, Wages and Productivity in the Service Sector* (Boulder, CO: Westview Press, 1990).

Ogren, Annegret S., *The Great American Housewife: From Helpmate to Wage Earner, 1776–1986* (Westport, CT: Greenwood Press, 1986).

Oppenheimer, Valerie Kincade, *The Female Labor Force in the United States* (Westport, CT: Greenwood Press, 1976).

Ottley, Roi, *New World A-Coming* (New York: Arno Press, 1968 [reprint of 1943 edition]).

Palmer, Phyllis, *Domesticity and Dirt: Housewives and Domestic Servants in the United States, 1920–1945* (Philadelphia: Temple University Press, 1992).

Parker, Richard, *The Myth of the Middle Class* (New York: Liveright, 1972).

Parris, Guichard and Lester Brooks, *Blacks in the City: A History of the National Urban League* (Boston: Little, Brown and Co., 1971).

Patten, Thomas H., Jr., *Manpower Planning and the Development of Human Resources* (New York: Wiley-Interscience, 1971).

Payne, Elizabeth Anne, *Reform, Labor and Feminism: Margaret Dreier Robins and the Women's Trade Union League* (Urbana: University of Illinois Press: 1988).

Perrett, Geoffrey, *America in the Twenties: A History* (New York: Simon & Schuster, 1982).

Plunz, Richard, *A History of Housing in New York City: Dwelling Type and Social Change in the American Metropolis* (New York: Columbia University Press: 1990).

Quadagno, Jill, *The Transformation of Old Age Security: Class and Politics in the American Welfare State* (Chicago: The University of Chicago Press, 1988).

Rafkin, Louise, *Other People's Dirt: A Housecleaner's Curious Adventures* (Chapel Hill, NC: Algonquin Books of Chapel Hill, 1998).

Riis, Jacob, *How the Other Half Lives*, (New York, Charles Scribner's Sons, 1890).

Roediger, David R., *The Wages of Whiteness: Race and the Making of the American Working Class* (London: Verso, 1991).

Rollins, Judith, *Between Women: Domestics and Their Employers* (Philadelphia: Temple University Press, 1985).

Romero, Mary, *Maid in the U.S.A.* (New York: Routledge, 1992).

Rosario, Juan, Anneris Goris, Francisco Angeles, *Movimientos Poblacionales en la Republica Dominicana* (NY: The Dominican Research Center, Inc., n.d.).

Rosenberg, Rosalind, *Divided Lives: American Women in the Twentieth Century* (New York: Hill & Wang, 1992).

Ruttenbaum, Steven, *Mansions in the Clouds: The Skyscraper Palazzi of Emery Roth* (New York: Balsam Press, Inc., 1986).

Sassoon, Anne Showstack, *Women and the State: The Shifting Boundaries of Public and Private* (London: Unwin Hyman, 1987).

Sealander, Judith, *As Minority Becomes Majority: Federal Reaction to the Phenomenon of Women in the Work Force, 1920–1963* (Westport, CT: Greenwood Press, 1983).

Scheiner, Seth, *Negro Mecca: A History of the Negro in New York City, 1865–1920* (New York: New York University Press, 1965).

Shankman, Arnold, *Ambivalent Friends: Afro-Americans View the Immigrant* (Westport, CT: Greenwood Press, 1982).

Shea, John R., et al., *Years for Decision: A Longitudinal Study of the Educational and Labor Market Experience of Young Women,* Volume One (Columbus, OH: Center for Human Resource Research, The Ohio State University, 1971).

Sheets, Robert G., et al., *The Impact of Service Industries on Underemployment in Metropolitan Economies* (Lexington, MA: Lexington Books, 1987).

Sigelman, Lee and Susan Welch, *Black Americans' Views of Racial Inequality: The Dream Deferred* (New York: Cambridge University Press, 1991).

Sitkoff, Harvard, *A New Deal for Blacks: The Emergence of Civil Rights as a National Issue: The Depression Decade* (New York: Oxford University Press, 1978).

———, *The Struggle for Black Equality, 1954–1980* (New York: Hill and Wang, 1981).

Smuts, Robert W., *Women and Work in America* (New York: Schocken Books, 1959, 1971).

Sokoloff, Natalie, *Black Women and White Women in the Professions* (New York: Routledge, 1992).

Stewart, Alva W., "Social Security: Its Development from Roosevelt to Reagan," *Public Administration Series: Bibliography P-964,* May 1982 (Monticello, IL: Vance Bibiographies, 1982).

Stigler, George J., "Domestic Servants in the United States, 1900–1940," *Occasional Paper 24:* April 1946 (New York: National Bureau of Economic Research).

Strasser, Susan, *Never Done: A History of American Housework* (New York: Pantheon, 1982).

Strauss, Anselm L., *The Contexts of Social Mobility: Ideology and Theory* (Chicago: Aldine Publishing Co., 1971).

Terkel, Studs, *Working: People Talk About What They Do All Day and How They Feel About What They Do* (NY: Pantheon, 1972, 1974).

Thernstrom, Stephan, *The Other Bostonians: Poverty and Progress in the American Metropolis, 1880–1970* (Cambridge: Harvard University Press, 1973).

———, *Poverty and Progress: Social Mobility in a Nineteenth-Century City* (Cambridge: Harvard University Press, 1964).

Tomasi, S.M. and Charles B. Keely, *Whom Have We Welcomed?: The Adequacy and Quality of United States Immigration Data for Policy and Evaluation* (Staten Island, N.Y.: The Center for Migration Studies, 1975).

van Raaphorst, Donna L., *Union Maids Not Wanted: Organizing Domestic Workers, 1870–1940* (NY: Praeger, 1988).

Vanderbilt, Amy, *Amy Vanderbilt's New Complete Book of Etiquette: The Guide to Gracious Living* (Garden City, NY: Doubleday & Co., Inc., 1962).

Wandersee, Winifred, *Women's Work and Family Values, 1920–1940* (Cambridge, MA: Harvard University Press, 1981).

Ware, Susan, *Holding Their Own: American Women in the 1930s* (Boston: Twayne Publishers, 1982).

———, *Modern American Women: A Documentary History* (Belmont, CA: Wadsworth Publishing Company, 1989).

Watts, Jill, *God, Harlem U.S.A.: The Father Divine Story* (Berkeley: University of California Press, 1992).

Weatherford, Doris, *Foreign and Female: Immigrant Women in America, 1840–1930* (New York: Schocken Books, 1986).

Weisbrot, Robert, *Father Divine and the Struggle for Racial Equality* (Urbana, IL: University of Illinois Press, 1983).

Whyte, William H., Jr., *The Organization Man* (Garden City, NY: Doubleday, 1957).

Wiebe, Robert H., *The Search for Order: 1877–1920* (New York: Hill and Wang, 1967).

Willhelm, Sidney M., *Who Needs the Negro?* (Cambridge, MA: Schenkman Publishing Company, Inc., 1970).

The Woman's Book (New York: Charles Scribner's Sons, 1894).

The WPA Guide to New York City (New York: Pantheon Books, 1982).

Wright, Gwendolyn, *Building the Dream: A Social History of Housing in America* (Cambridge, MA: The MIT Press, 1981).

———, *Moralism and the Model Home: Domestic Architecture and Cultural Conflict in Chicago, 1873–1913* (Chicago: The University of Chicago Press, 1980).

Wylie, Philip, *Generation of Vipers* (New York: Pocket Books, 1942, 1955).

Zempel, Solveig, ed., transl., *In Their Own Words: Letters from Norwegian Immigrants* (Minneapolis, MN: University of Minnesota Press, 1991).

ARTICLES AND PAPERS

Allen, Walter R., "Family Roles, Occupational Statuses, and Achievement Orientations Among Black Women in the United States," *Signs* 4:4 (Summer 1979).

Appelbaum, Eileen and Peter Albin, "Shifts in Employment, Occupational Structure, and Education Attainment" in Thierry Noyelle, ed., *Skills, Wages and Productivity in the Service Sector* (Boulder, CO: Westview Press, 1990).

Arnesen, Eric, "Following the Color Line of Labor: Black Workers and the Labor Movement Before 1930," *Radical History Review* 55 (1993).

Baca, Reynaldo and Dexter Bryan, "Mexican Undocumented Women Workers in Los Angeles: A Research Note," in Delores M. Mortimer and Roy S. Bryce-Laporte, eds., *Female Immigrants to the U.S.: Caribbean, Latin American and African Experiences*, RIIES Occasional Papers No. 2, Research Institute on Immigration and Ethnic Studies (Washington, D.C.: Smithsonian Institution, 1981).

Bean, Frank D., Allan G. King, Jeffrey S. Passel, "The Number of Illegal Migrants of Mexican Origin in the United States: Sex Ratio-based Estimates for 1980," *Demography* 20:1 (February 1983).

Bean, Frank D., Harley L. Browning and W. Parker Frisbie, "The Sociodemographic Characteristics of Mexican Immigrant Status Groups: Implications for Studying Undocumented Mexicans," *International Migration Review* 18:3 (Autumn 1984).

Berkowitz, Edward D., "How to Think About the Welfare State," *Labor History* (Fall 1991).

Berry, Gwendolyn Hughes, "Mothers in Industry," *Annals of the American Academy of Political and Social Science* (May 1929).

Bethune, Roena, "My First Job in New York [late 1950s]," in Linda K. Kerber and Jane De Hart-Mathews, eds., *Women's America: Refocusing the Past*, 2d ed., (New York: Oxford University Press, 1987).

Betts, Lillian W., "The Principles of Housekeeping," in *The Woman's Book* (New York: Charles Scribner's Sons, 1894).

Blau, Francine D. and Andrea H. Beller, "Trends in Earnings Differentials by Gender, 1971–1981," *Industrial and Labor Relations Review* 41:4 (July 1988).

Boyd, Robert L., "A Contextual Analysis of Black Self-Employment in Large Metropolitan Areas, 1970–1980," *Social Forces* 70:2 (December 1991).

Briggs, Vernon, Jr., "Methods of Analysis of Illegal Immigration into the United States," *International Migration Review* 18:3 (Autumn 1984).

Broom, Leonard and Norval D. Glenn, "The Occupation and Income of Black Americans," in Norval D. Glenn and Charles M. Bonjean eds., *Blacks in the United States* (San Francisco: Chandler Publishing Company, 1969).

Brown, Charles, "Minimum Wage Laws: Are They Overrated?," *Journal of Economic Perspectives* 2:3 (Summer 1988).

Brown, Elsa Barkley, "'What Has Happened Here': The Politics of Difference in Women's History and Feminist Politics," *Feminist Studies* 18:2 (Summer 1992).

Buchanan, Susan Huelsebuch, "Profile of Haitian Migrant Woman" in Delores M. Mortimer and Roy S. Bryce-Laporte, eds., *Female Immigrants to the U.S.: Caribbean, Latin American and African Experiences* RIIES Occasional Papers No. 2, Research Institute on Immigration and Ethnic Studies (Washington, D.C.: Smithsonian Institution, 1981).

Burgess, Judith and Meryl James-Gray, "Migration and Sex Roles: A Comparison of Black and Indian Trinidadians in New York City," in Delores M. Mortimer and Roy S. Bryce-Laporte, eds., *Female Immigrants to the U.S.: Caribbean, Latin American and African Experiences*, RIIES Occasional Papers No. 2, Research Institute on Immigration and Ethnic Studies, (Washington, D.C.: Smithsonian Institution, 1981).

Burawoy, Michael, "The Functions and Reproduction of Migrant Labor: Comparative Material from Southern Africa and the United States," *American Journal of Sociology* 81:5 (March 1976).

Butcher, Kristin F., "Black Immigrants in the United States: A Comparison with Native Blacks and Other Immigrants," *Industrial and Labor Relations Review* 47:2 (January 1994).

Carlson, Leonard A. and Caroline Swartz, "The Earnings of Women and Ethnic Minorities," *Industrial and Labor Relations Review* 41:4 (July 1988).

Casal, Lourdes with assistance of Yolanda Prieto, "Black Cubans in the United States: Basic Demographic Information" in Delores M. Mortimer and Roy S. Bryce-Laporte, eds., *Female Immigrants to the U.S.: Caribbean, Latin American and African Experiences* RIIES Occasional Papers No. 2, Research Institute on Immigration and Ethnic Studies (Washington, D.C.: Smithsonian Institution, 1981).

Cerrutti, Marcela and Douglas S. Massey, "On the Auspices of Female Migration from Mexico to the United States," *Demography* 38:2 (May 2001).

Chambers, Clarke A., "Social Reform, Social Work, and Social Security: A Subject Revisited," in John N. Schacht, ed., *The Quest for Security: Papers on the Origins and the Future of the American Social Insurance System* (Ames, IA: The Center for the Study of the Recent History of the United States, 1982).

Chaplin, David, "Domestic Service and the Negro," in Arthur B. Shostak and William Gomberg, eds., *Blue-Collar World: Studies of the American Worker* (Englewood Cliffs, NJ: Prentice-Hall, Inc., 1964).

Chiswick, Barry R., "Illegal Aliens in the United States Labor Market: Analysis of Occupational Attainment and Earnings," *International Migration Review* 18:3 (Autumn 1984).

———, "Illegal Immigration and Immigration Control," *Journal of Economic Perspectives* 2:3 (Summer 1988).

Clark-Lewis, Elizabeth, "'This Work Had a End': African-American Domestic Workers in Washington, D.C., 1910–1940," in Carol Groneman and Mary Beth Norton, eds., *"To Toil the Livelong Day": America's Women at Work, 1780–1980* (Ithaca, NY: Cornell University Press: 1987).

Cobble, Dorothy Sue, "Organizing the Postindustrial Work Force: Lessons from the History of Waitress Unionism," *Industrial and Labor Relations Review* 44 (April 1991).

Collins, Patricia Hill, "The Social Construction of Black Feminist Thought," in Micheline R. Malson, et al., eds., *Black Women in America: Social Science Perspectives* (Chicago: University of Chicago Press, 1990).

Cotton, Jeremiah, "Opening the Gap: The Decline in Black Economic Indicators in the 1980s," *Social Science Quarterly* 70:4 (December 1989).

Dill, Bonnie Thornton, "'The Means to Put My Children Through': Child-Rearing Goals and Strategies Among Black Female Domestic Servants," in LaFrances Rodgers-Rose, ed., *The Black Woman* (Beverly Hills: Sage Publications, 1980).

Domhoff, G. William, "Corporate-Liberal Theory and the Social Security Act: A Chapter in the Sociology of Knowledge," *Politics & Society* 15:3 (1986–87).

Espenshade, Thomas J., "Unauthorized Immigration to the United States," *Annual Review of Sociology* (Palo Alto, 1995).

Fainstein, Norman, "The Underclass/Mismatch Hypothesis as an Explanation for Black Economic Deprivation," *Politics & Society* 15:4 (1986–87).

Forsythe, Dennis, "Black Immigrants and the American Ethos: Theories and Observations," in Roy S. Bryce-Laporte and Delores M. Mortimer, eds., *Caribbean Immigration to the United States*, RIIES Occasional Papers No. 1 (Washington, DC: Smithsonian Institution, 1976).

Fuchs, Lawrence H., "Cultural Pluralism and the Future of American Unity: The Impact of Illegal Aliens," *International Migration Review* 18:3 (Autumn 1984).

Funkhouser, Edward and Stephen J. Trejo, "The Labor Market Skills of Recent Male Immigrants: Evidence from the Current Population Survey," *Industrial and Labor Relations Review* 48:4 (July 1995).

Gill, Andrew and Stewart Long, "Is There An Immigration Status Wage Differential Between Legal and Undocumented Workers?: Evidence from the Los Angeles Garment Industry," *Social Science Quarterly* 70:1 (March 1989).

Glenn, Evelyn Nakano, "From Servitude to Service Work: Historical Continuities in the Racial Division of Paid Reproductive Labor," *Signs* 18:1 (Autumn 1992).

Glick, Jennifer E., Frank D. Bean, Jennifer V. W. Van Hook, "Immigration and Changing Patterns of Extended Family Household Structure in the United States: 1970–1990," *Journal of Marriage and the Family* 59:1 (February 1997).

Gordon, Linda, "Black and White Visions of Welfare: Women's Welfare Activism, 1890–1945," *Journal of American History* (September 1991).

Gordon, Monica, "Caribbean migration: A Perspective on Women," in Delores M. Mortimer and Roy S. Bryce-Laporte, eds., *Female Immigrants to the U.S.: Caribbean, Latin American and African Experiences*, RIIES Occasional Papers No. 2, Research Institute on Immigration and Ethnic Studies (Washington, D.C.: Smithsonian Institution, 1981).

Goris, Anneris and Juan E. Rosario, "Dominican Immigrants in New York City," (New York: The Dominican Research Center, Inc., 1991).

Grasmuck, Sherri, "Immigration, Ethnic Stratification, and Native Working Class Discipline: Comparisons of Documented and Undocumented Dominicans," *International Migration Review* 18:3 (Autumn 1984).

Grossman, Jean Baldwin, "Illegal Immigrants and Domestic Employment," *Industrial and Labor Relations Review* 37:2 (January 1984).

Hareven, Tamara K., "The Home and the Family in Historical Perspective," *Social Research* 58:1 (Spring 1991).

Harley, Sharon, "For the Good of Family and Race: Gender, Work and Domestic Roles in the Black Community, 1880–1930," in Micheline R. Malson, et al., eds., *Black Women in America: Social Science Perspectives* (Chicago: University of Chicago Press, 1990).

Harrington, J.W., Jr. and J. R. Lombard, "Producer-service Firms in a Declining Manufacturing Region," *Environment and Planning* 21 (1989).

Hayden, Dolores, "The Grand Domestic Revolution: The Feminist Paradise Palace" in Linda K. Kerber and Jane De Hart-Matthews, eds., *Women's America: Refocusing the Past* (New York: Oxford University Press, 1987).

Heimbold, Lois Rita, "Downward Occupational Mobility During the Great Depression: Urban Black and White Working Class Women," *Labor History* 29 (Spring 1988).

Hersch, Joni, "The Impact of Nonmarket Work on Market Wages," *The American Economic Review: Papers and Proceedings of the 103rd Annual Meeting of the American Economic Association* (May 1991).

Higginbotham, Elizabeth, "Laid Bare By the System: Work and Survival for Black and Hispanic Women," in Amy Swerdlow and Hanna Lessinger, eds., *Class, Race and Sex: The Dynamics of Control* (Boston: G.K. Hall, 1983).

Hill-Scott, Jill, "Child Care in the Black Community," *Journal of Black Studies* 10:1 (September 1979).

Holder, Calvin B., "The Causes and Composition of West Immigration to New York City, 1900–1952," *Afro-Americans in New York Life and History* 11:1 (January 1987).

Johnson, George E., in "The Labor Market Effects of Immigration," *Industrial and Labor Relations Review* 33:3 (April 1980).

Kaplan, Elaine Bell, "'I Don't Do No Windows': Competition Between the Domestic Worker and the Housewife," in Valerie Miner and Helen E. Longino, eds., *Competition: A Feminist Taboo?* (New York: The Feminist Press, 1987).

Klaczynska, Barbara, "Why Women Work," *Labor History* 17 (Winter 1976).

Koussoudji, Sherrie A., "Playing Cat and Mouse at the U.S.-Mexican Border," *Demography* 29:2 (May 1992).

Lasser, Carol, "The Domestic Balance of Power: Relations Between Mistress and Maid in Nineteenth-Century New England," *Labor History* 28 (Winter 1987).

Lazear, Edward P., "Symposium on Women in the Labor Market," *Journal of Economic Perspectives* 3:1 (Winter 1989).

Ljungmark, Lars, "On Emigration, Social Mobility, and the Transfer of Capital," *The Swedish-American Historical Quarterly* XLI (July 1990).

Lyson, Thomas A., "Industrial Change and the Sexual Division of Labor in New York and Georgia: 1910–1930," *Social Science Quarterly* 70:2 (June 1989).

Mackintosh, Maureen M., "Domestic Labour and the Household," in Sandra Burman, ed., *Fit Work for Women* (New York: St. Martin's Press, 1979).

Mink, Gwendolyn, "Welfare Reform in Historical Perspective," *Connecticut Law Review* 26:3 (Spring 1994).

Model, Suzanne, David Ladipo, "Context and Opportunity: Minorities in London and New York," *Social Forces* 75:2 (December 1996).

Moss, Philip and Chris Tilly, "A Turn for the Worse: Why Black Men's Labour Market Fortunes Have Declined in the United States," in Louis Kushnick, ed., *Sage Race Relations Abstracts* 18 (1993).

Palladino, Grace, "When Militancy Isn't Enough: The Impact of Automation on New York City Building Service Workers, 1934–1970," *Labor History* 28 (Spring 1987).

Palmer, Phyllis, "Housework and Domestic Labor: Racial and Technological Change," in Karen Brodkin Sacks and Dorothy Remy, eds., *My Troubles Are Going to Have Trouble With Me: Everyday Trials and Triumphs of Women Workers* (New Brunswick, NJ: Rutgers University Press, 1984).

Papademetriou, Demetrios G. and Nicholas DiMarzio, "A Preliminary Profile of Unapprehended Undocumented Aliens in Northern New Jersey: A Research Note," *International Migration Review* 19:4 (Winter 1985).

Passel, Jeffrey S. and Karen A. Woodrow, "Geographic Distribution of Undocumented Immigrants: Estimates of Undocumented Aliens Counted in the 1980 Census by State," *International Migration Review* 18:3 (Autumn 1984).

Payne, Charles, "Ella Baker and Models of Social Change," *Signs* 14:4 (Summer 1989).

Portes, Alejandro and Saskia Sassen-Koob, "Making It Underground: Comparative Material on the Informal Sector in Western Market Economics," *American Journal of Sociology* 93:1 (July 1987).

"Proposed Legislation on American Immigration Policy," *International Migration Digest* (Spring 1965).

"Queen Mother Audley Moore," in Brian Lanker, *I Dream a World: Portraits of Black Women Who Changed America* (New York: Stewart, Tabori, and Chang, 1989).

Reynolds, Clark W. and Robert K. McCleery, "The Political Economy of Immigration Law: Impact of Simpson-Rodino on the United States and Mexico," *Journal of Economic Perspectives* 2:3 (Summer 1988).

Robertson, Nancy Marie, "Shall We Walk a Little More Slowly?: The Threat of Coeducation to the Racial Policies of the YWCA in the 1920s," unpublished paper given at the American Historical Association Annual Meeting, 1995.

Robinson, J. Gregory, "Estimating the Approximate Size of the Illegal Alien Population in the United States by the Comparative Trend Analysis of Age-Specific Death Rates," *Demography* 17:2 (May 1980).

Rodgers-Rose, LaFrances, "Some Demographic Characteristics of the Black Woman: 1940 to 1975," in LaFrances Rodgers-Rose, ed., *The Black Woman* (Beverly Hills: Sage Publications, 1980).

Rosario, Juan E. and Anneris Goris, "Political Participation of Dominicans in New York City: The Case of Dominicans in Washington Heights/Inwood," (New York: The Dominican Research Center, Inc., 1990).

Safa, Helen I., "The Differential Incorporation of Hispanic Women Migrants into the United States Labor Force," in Delores M. Mortimer and Roy S. Bryce-Laporte, eds., *Female Immigrants to the U.S.: Caribbean, Latin American and African Experiences*, RIIES Occasional Papers No. 2, Research Institute on Immigration and Ethnic Studies, (Washington, D.C.: Smithsonian Institution, 1981).

Saposs, David J., "Voluntarism in the American Labor Movement," in Harry N. Scheiber, ed., *United States Economic History: Selected Readings* (New York: Alfred A. Knopf, 1964).

Sassen-Koob, Saskia, "Exporting Capital and Importing Labor: The Role of Women," in Delores M. Mortimer and Roy S. Bryce-Laporte, eds., *Female Immigrants to the U.S.: Caribbean, Latin American and African Experiences*, RIIES Occasional Papers No. 2, Research Institute on Immigration and Ethnic Studies (Washington, D.C.: Smithsonian Institution, 1981).

Simon, Rita J. and Margo DeLey, "The Work Experience of Undocumented Mexican Women Migrants in Los Angeles," *International Migration Review* 18:3 (Autumn 1984).

Sinke, Susanne with Stephen Cross, "The International Marriage Market and the Sphere of Social Reproduction: A German Case Study," in Donna Gabaccia, ed., *Seeking Common Ground: Multidisciplinary Studies of Immigrant Women in the United States* (Westport, CT: Praeger, 1992).

Smith, Elsie J., "Regional Origin and Migration: Impact on Black Workers," *Journal of Black Studies* 8:3 (March 1978).

Smith, Joan, "The Paradox of Women's Poverty: Wage-earning Women and Economic Transformation," *Signs* 10:2 (Winter 1984).

Stack, Carol B., "Sex Roles and Survival Strategies in an Urban Black Community," in Filomina Chioma Steady, ed., *The Black Woman Cross-Culturally* (Cambridge, MA: Schenkman Publishing Company, Inc., 1981).

Terborg-Penn, Rosalyn, "Survival Strategies Among African-American Workers: A Continuing Process," in Ruth Milkman, ed., *Women, Work and Protest* (Boston: Routledge & Kegan Paul, 1985).

The Dominican Research Center, Inc., "Dominican Studies: The Inclusion of New Immigrant Groups" (New York: The Dominican Research Center, Inc., 1990).

————, "Proposal for a Dominican Councilmatic District: The Redistricting of Washington Heights/Inwood: A Dominican Perspective" (New York: The Dominican Research Center, Inc., March 20, 1991).

Tienda, Marta, Leif Jensen, Robert L. Bach, "Immigration, Gender and the Process of Occupational Change in teh United States, 1970–1980," *International Migration Review* 18:4 (Winter 1984).

Uttal, Lynet, "Custodial Care, Surrogate Care, and Coordinated Care: Employed Mothers and the Meaning of Child Care," *Gender and Society* 10:3 (June 1996).

Vanek, Joann, "Time Spent in Housework," *Scientific American* 231:5 (November 1974).

Wachter, Michael L., "The Labor Market and Illegal Immigration: The Outlook for the 1980s," *Industrial and Labor Relations Review* 33:3 (April 1980).

Waldinger, Roger, "Changing Ladders and Musical Chairs: Ethnicity and Opportunity in Post-industrial New York," *Politics & Society* 15:4 (1986–87).

Warren, Robert, Jeffrey S. Passel, "A Count of the Uncountable: Estimates of Undocumented Aliens Counted in the 1980 United States Census," *Demography* 24:3 (August 1987).

Weisberger, Bernard A., "A Nation of Immigrants," *American Heritage* (February/March 1994).

Wrigley, Julia, "Feminists and Domestic Workers," *Feminist Studies*, 17:2 (Summer 1991).

DISSERTATIONS

Albelda, Randy Pearl, "Black and White Women Workers in the Post World War II Period" (University of Massachusetts, 1983).

Christiansen, Lars David, "The Making of a Civil Rights Union: The National Domestic Workers Union of America" (The Florida State University, 1999).

Clegg, Brenda Faye, "Black Female Domestics During the Great Depression in New York City, 1930–1940" (University of Michigan, 1983).

Coley, Soraya Moore, "And Still I Rise: An Exploratory Study of Contemporary Black Private Household Workers" (The Graduate School of Social Work and Social Research of Bryn Mawr College, 1981).

Hunter, Tera W., "Household Workers in the Making: Afro-American Women in Atlanta and the New South, 1861 to 1920" (Yale University, 1990).

Kim, Lahn Sung, "Maid in Color: The Figure of the Racialized Domestic in American Television" (University of California Los Angeles, 1997).

Lasser, Carol S., "Mistress, Maid and Market: The Transformation of Domestic Service in New England, 1790–1870" (Harvard University, 1982).

Rio, Cecilia M., "From Feudal Serfs to Independent Contractors: Class and African American Women's Paid Domestic Labor, 1863–1980" (University of Massachusetts, Amherst, 2001).

Weisenfeld, Judith, "'The More Abundant Life': The Harlem Branch of the New York City Young Women's Christian Association, 1905–1945" (Princeton University, 1992).

GOVERNMENT PUBLICATIONS

"1948 Handbook of Facts on Women Workers," *Bulletin of the Women's Bureau* 225 (Washington, D.C.: U.S.G.P.O., 1948).

"1950 Handbook of Facts on Women Workers," *Bulletin of the Women's Bureau* 237 (Washington, D.C.: U.S.G.P.O., 1950).

"1952 Handbook of Facts on Women Workers," *Bulletin of the Women's Bureau* 242 (Washington, D.C.: U.S.G.P.O., 1952).

"1954 Handbook of Facts on Women Workers," *Bulletin of the Women's Bureau* 255 (Washington, D.C.: U.S.G.P.O., 1954).

"1956 Handbook of Facts on Women Workers," *Bulletin of the Women's Bureau* 261 (Washington, D.C.: U.S.G.P.O., 1956).

A Bigger Piece of the Pie: The Emerging Role of Women in the New York Economy (New York State Division for Women, December 1988).

Best, Ethel L., "A Study of Change from 8 to 6 Hours of Work," *Bulletin of the Women's Bureau* 105 (Washington, D.C.: U.S.G.P.O. 1933).

———and Ethel Erickson, "A Survey of Laundries and Their Women Workers in 23 Cities," *Bulletin of the Women's Bureau* 78 (Washington, D.C.: U.S.G.P.O., 1930).

Biographical Directory of the United States Congress, 1774—1989 (Washington, D.C.: U.S.G.P.O. 1989).

Biographical Directory of the United States Congress, 1774—Present (Washington, D.C.: http:/bioguide.congress.gov).

Byrne, Harriet A., "Employment in Hotels and Restaurants," *Bulletin of the Women's Bureau* 123 (Washington, D.C.: U.S.G.P.O. 1936).

"Community Household Employment Programs," *Bulletin of the Women's Bureau* 221 (Washington, D.C.: U.S.G.P.O., 1948).

"Changes in Women's Occupations, 1940–1950," *Bulletin of the Women's Bureau* 253 (Washington, D.C.: U.S.G.P.O., 1954).

City of New York, Department of City Planning, *Asians in New York City: A Demographic Summary* (New York, November 1988).

————, *Caribbean Immigrants in New York City: A Demographic Summary* (New York, November 1988).

————, *The Newest New Yorkers: An Analysis of Immigration into New York City During the 1980s* (New York, June 1992).

————, *The Newest New Yorkers: A Statistical Portrait* (New York, August 1992).

————, *The Newest New Yorkers, 1990–1994* (New York, December 1996).

————, *The Newest New Yorkers, 1995–1996* (New York, September 1999).

————, *Puerto Rican New Yorkers in 1990* (New York, 1992).

"Community Services for Women War Workers," *Special Bulletin of the Women's Bureau* 15 (Washington, D.C.: U.S.G.P.O., 1944).

Congressional Digest v. 75 (May 1996).

Congressional Record—House, 1946, 1949–50, 1964–5.

Congressional Record—Senate, 1946, 1949–50, 1964–5.

Correll, Marie, "Standards of Placement Agencies for Household Employees," *Bulletin of the Women's Bureau* 112 (Washington, D.C.: U.S.G.P.O., 1933).

"Cost of Budget in 34 Large Cities," *Monthly Labor Review* (February 1948).

"Cost of Living," *Monthly Labor Review* (January 1937).

Dempsey, Mary V., "The Occupational Progress of Women, 1910 to 1930," *Bulletin of the Women's Bureau* 104 (Washington, D.C.: U.S.G.P.O., 1933).

"Domestic Workers' Wages and Hours, New York State, 1948," *Monthly Labor Review* (October 1949).

Elder, Peyton, "The 1974 Amendments to the Federal Minimum Wage Law," *Monthly Labor Review* (July 1974).

"Employed Mothers and Child Care," *Bulletin of the Women's Bureau* 246 (Washington, D.C.: U.S.G.P.O., 1953).

"Employment of Women in the Early Postwar Period, With Background of Prewar and War Data," *Bulletin of the Women's Bureau* 211 (Washington, D.C.: U.S.G.P.O., 1946).

"Employment of Women in an Emergency Period," *Bulletin of the Women's Bureau* 241(Washington, D.C.: U.S.G.P.O., 1952).

"Expenditures for Electrical Appliances for Workers in 42 Cities," *Monthly Labor Review* (February 1938).

"Facts About Working Women," *Bulletin of the Women's Bureau* 46 (Washington, D.C.: U.S.G.P.O., 1925).

Fain, T. Scott, "Self-Employed Americans: Their Number Has Increased," *Monthly Labor Review* (November, 1980).

"Family Expenditure in New York City," Bureau of Labor Statistics *Bulletin 643,* Vol. II.

"Family Expenditures in Selected Cities," Bureau of Labor Statistics *Bulletin 648.*

Family Expenditures in the United States (Washington, DC: National Planning Board, 1941).

"Federal Social Security Act Amendments of 1950," *Monthly Labor Review* (October 1950).

Fox, Grace, "Woman Domestic Workers in Washington, D.C., 1940," *Monthly Labor Review* (February 1942).

Garfinkle, Stuart H., "Occupations of Women and Black Workers, 1962–74," *Monthly Labor Review* (November, 1975).

Goldstein, Harold, "The Changing Occupational Structure," *Monthly Labor Review* (December 1947).

Gray, Lois S., "The Jobs Puerto Ricans Hold in New York City," *Monthly Labor Review* (October 1975).

Grossman, Allyson Sherman, "Women in Domestic Work, Yesterday and Today," *Monthly Labor Review* (August 1980).

Hearings before Subcommittee No. 1 of the Committee on the Judiciary, House of Representatives, 89th Congress, 1st Session, on H.R. 2580, to Amend the Immigration and Nationality Act, and for Other Purposes, March–June 1965, Document 69, Serial No. 7 (Washington, D.C.: U.S.G.P.O., 1965)

Hickey, Joseph A., "Unemployment Insurance Covers Additional 9 Million Workers," *Monthly Labor Review* (May 1978).

Hill, Joseph A., "Recent Northward Migration of the Negro," *Monthly Labor Review* (March 1924).

Historical Statistics of the U.S., Colonial Times to 1970, Part 1 (U.S. Dept. of Commerce, Bureau of The Census, 1975): Series D182–232.

"History of the Provisions of Old-Age, Survivors, Disability, and Health Insurance, 1935–1977," U.S. Dept of Health, Education and Welfare, Social Security Administration, Office of the Actuary (Washington, D.C.: U.S.G.P.O., March 1978).

Hooks, Janet M., "Women's Occupations Through Seven Decades," *Bulletin of the Women's Bureau* 218, U.S. Department of Labor (Washington, D.C.: G.P.O., 1951).

Howe, Wayne J., "The Business Services Industry Sets Pace in Employment Growth," *Monthly Labor Review* (April 1986).

"Household Employment in New York State, 1938–39," *Monthly Labor Review* (October 1940).

"Household Workers and Their Employers Under Old-Age, Survivors, Disability, and Health Insurance," *Social Security Household Worker Statistics 1964* (Washington, D.C.: U.S.G.P.O., 1968).

Howe, Wayne J., "The Business Services Industry Sets Pace in Employment Growth," *Monthly Labor Review* (April 1986).

"I: Labor Force Employment and Unemployment," *Monthly Labor Review 1964–65 Statistical Supplement:* Table I-4.

"Immigration Restriction and the 'Scarcity' of Domestic Servants," *Monthly Labor Review* (July 1927).

Jackson, Tim, "Jay Jackson," *Salute to Pioneering Cartoonists of Color* (http://www.clstoons.com/paoc/jjackson.htm).

Johnson, B. Eleanor, "Household Employment in Chicago," *Bulletin of the Women's Bureau* 106 (Washington, D.C.: U.S.G.P.O., 1933).

Kutscher, Ronald E. and Jerome A. Mark, "The Service-Producing Sector: Some Common Perceptions Reviewed," *Monthly Labor Review* (April 1983).

———and Valerie A. Personick, "Deindustrialization and the Shift to Services," *Monthly Labor Review* (June 1986).

"La Mujer de Origen Hispano en la Fuerza Laboral," Women's Bureau *Facts on Working Women* 89–1S (August 1989).

"Labor Force and Employment: V. Labor Force, Employment, and Unemployment," *Monthly Labor Review* (February 1949).

Labor Force Statistics Derived from the Current Population Survey: A Databook, Volume I (Washington, D.C.: U.S.G.P.O., September 1992).

Levitan, Sar A. and Frank Gallo, "Work and Family: The Impact of Legislation," *Monthly Labor Review* (March 1990).

Lowell, Ruth Fabricant, *Report: The Labor Market in New York City: A Study of Jobs and Low-Income Area Workers in 1970* (New York: The City of New York Department of Social Services, Office of Public Affairs, 1975).

Mettert, Margaret T., "Injuries in Personal Service Occupations in Ohio," *Bulletin of the Women's Bureau* 151 (Washington, D.C.: U.S.G.P.O., 1937).

Miller, Frieda S., "Living Costs of Working Women in New York," *Monthly Labor Review* (March 1938).

"Negro Women in Industry in 15 States," *Bulletin of the Women's Bureau* 70 (Washington, D.C.: U.S.G.P.O., 1929).

"Negroes in New York City: Occupational Distribution, 1940–47," *Monthly Labor Review* (January 1949).

New York City Department of Planning Bulletin, *Puerto Rican Migration to New York City,* February 1957.

"Old Age Insurance for Household Workers," *Bulletin of the Women's Bureau* 220 (Washington, D.C.: U.S.G.P.O., 1947).

"Part-Time Jobs for Women: A Study in 10 Cities," *Bulletin of the Women's Bureau* 238 (Washington, D.C.: U.S.G.P.O., 1951).

Pidgeon, Mary Elizabeth, "A Preview as to Women Workers in Transition from War to Peace," *Special Bulletin of the Women's Bureau* 18 (Washington, D.C.: U.S.G.P.O., 1944).

———, "Changes in Women's Employment During the War," *Special Bulletin of the Women's Bureau* 20 (June 1944).

———, "The Employed Woman Homemaker in the United States: Her Responsibility for Family Support," *Bulletin of the Women's Bureau* 148 (Washington, D.C.: U.S.G.P.O., 1936).

———, "Trends in the Employment of Women, 1928–1936," *Bulletin of the Women's Bureau* 159 (Washington, D.C.: U.S.G.P.O., 1938).

———, "Variations in Wage Rates Under Corresponding Conditions," *Bulletin of the Women's Bureau* 122 (Washington, D.C.: U.S.G.P.O., 1935).

———, "Wages of Women in 13 States," *Bulletin of the Women's Bureau* 85 (Washington, D.C.: U.S.G.P.O., 1931).

———, *Women in the Economy of the United States of America: A Summary Report* (Washington, D.C.: U.S.G.P.O., 1937).

Programs and Services of the Women's Bureau: How to Use Them (Washington, D.C.: U.S.G.P.O., 1955).

Report on Women's Bureau Conference, "The American Woman: Her Changing Role" (Washington, D.C.: U.S. Department of Labor, February 17–19, 1948).

"Recent Unemployment Trends," *Monthly Labor Review* (May 1950).

"Regular Jobs for Household Help," *Monthly Labor Review* (October 1965).

"Report of the Committee on Protective Labor Legislation to the President's Commission on the Status of Women, October 1963" (Washington, D.C.: U.S.G.P.O., 1963).

"Report of the Committee on Social Insurance and Taxes to the President's Commission on the Status of Women, October 1963" (Washington, D.C.: U.S.G.P.O., 1963).

"Report of the Secretary of Labor on Manpower Research and Training Under the Manpower Development and Training Act of 1962" (Washington, D.C.: U.S.G.P.O., 1966).

Report on 1948 Women's Bureau Conference (Washington, D.C.: U.S.G.P.O., 1948).

Robinson, Mary V., "Domestic Workers and Their Employment Relations," *Bulletin of the Women's Bureau* 39 (Washington, D.C.: U.S.G.P.O., 1924).

Runner, Diana, "Changes in Unemployment Insurance Legislation in 1994," *Monthly Labor Review* (January 1995).

Schiltz, Michael E., *Public Attitudes Toward Social Security, 1935–1965*, U.S. Department of Health, Education, and Welfare Research Report No. 33 (Washington, D.C.: U.S.G.P.O., 1970).

"State Laws Affecting Working Women: Hours, Minimum Wage, Home Work," *Bulletin of the Women's Bureau* 40 (Washington, D.C.: U.S.G.P.O., 1924).

"State Minimum-Wage Laws and Orders, July 1, 1942 to July 1, 1958: Part I—Historical Development and Statutory Provisions," *Bulletin of the Women's Bureau* 267 (Washington, D.C.: U.S.G.P.O., 1959).

"The Effects of Labor Legislation on the Employment Opportunities of Women," *Bulletin of the Women's Bureau* 65 (Washington, D.C.: U.S.G.P.O., 1928).

"The Federal Social Security Programs," *Monthly Labor Review* (January 1950).

"The Occupational Progress of Women," *Bulletin of the Women's Bureau* 27 (Washington, D.C.: U.S.G.P.O., 1922).

"The Share of Wage-Earning Women in Family Support," *Bulletin of the Women's Bureau* 30 (Washington, D.C.: U.S.G.P.O., 1923).

"Training Mature Women for Employment: The Story of 23 Local Programs," *Bulletin of the Women's Bureau* 256 (Washington, D.C.: U.S.G.P.O., 1955).

U.S. Department of Labor, Office of the Secretary, Women's Bureau, *Women Private Household Workers: A Statistical and Legislative Profile* (Washington, D.C., 1978).

U.S. Department of Labor, Women's Bureau, *1993 Handbook on Women Workers: Trends and Issues* (Washington, D.C., 1994).

———, *Milestones: The Women's Bureau Celebrates 65 Years of Women's Labor History* (Washington, D.C.: 1985).

———, "The Outlook for Women in Dietetics," *Home Economics Occupations Series Bulletin 234–1* (Washington, D.C.: U.S.G.P.O., 1949).

———, "The Outlook for Women as Food-Service Managers and Supervisors," *Home Economics Occupations Series Bulletin 234–2* (Washington, D.C.: U.S.G.P.O., 1952).

———, *Toward Better Working Conditions for Women: Methods and Policies of the National Women's Trade Union League of America* (Washington, D.C.: U.S.G.P.O., 1953).

U.S. Bureau of the Census, "1985 Service Annual Survey," *Current Business Reports* BS-85-01 (August 1986).

———, "1986 Service Annual Survey," *Current Business Reports* BS-86-01 (September 1987).

———, "1987 Service Annual Survey," *Current Business Reports* BS-87-01 (September 1988).

———, *Census of the Population,* 1900–1990.

"Variations in Employment Trends of Women and Men," *Bulletin of the Women's Bureau* 73 (Washington, D.C.: U.S.G.P.O., 1930).

Visa Applications 1963, "Immigration," "Hearings Before Subcommittee No. 1 of the Committee on the Judiciary, House of Representatives, Eighty-Eighth Congress, Second Session, on H.R. 7700 and 55 Identical Bills, to Amend the Immigration and Nationality Act," (Washington, D.C.: U.S.G.P.O., 1964).

"Wages and Hours of Labor," *Monthly Labor Review* (May 1931).

Waggaman, Mary T., "Efforts to Standardize the Working Day for Domestic Service," *Monthly Labor Review* (August 1919).

Watson, Amey E., "Household Employment in Philadelphia," *Bulletin of the Women's Bureau* 93 (Washington, D.C.: U.S.G.P.O., 1932).

Wistrowski, William J., "Family-Related Benefits in the Workplace," *Monthly Labor Review* (March 1990).

"Women in the Federal Service, 1923–1947: Part I, Trends in Employment," *Bulletin of the Women's Bureau* 230-I (Washington, D.C.: U.S.G.P.O., 1949).

"Women Workers—Employment Trends, 1900–1950," *Monthly Labor Review* (January 1951).

"Women Workers in the Third Year of the Depression," *Bulletin of the Women's Bureau* 103 (Washington, D.C.: U.S.G.P.O., 1933).

"Women Workers in Ten War Production Areas and Their Postwar Employment Plans," *Bulletin of the Women's Bureau* 209 (Washington, D.C.: U.S.G.P.O., 1946).

"Women's Jobs: Advance and Growth," *Bulletin of the Women's Bureau* 232 (Washington, D.C.: U.S.G.P.O., 1949).

"Working Women's Budgets in Twelve States," *Bulletin of the Women's Bureau* 226 (Washington, D.C.: U.S.G.P.O., 1948).

Wool, Harol and Lester M. Pearlman, "Recent Occupational Trends," *Monthly Labor Review* (December 1947).

INTERVIEWS

Alphonse, Minette (pseudonym), interview with author, Maplewood, NJ, August 2005.

Banas, Kinga, interviews with author, New York City, June 1992.

Cooke, Marvel, interview with Kathleen Currie, Women in Journalism oral history project of the Washington Press Club Foundation, Harlem, NY, November 1, 1989, in the Oral History Collection of Columbia University and other repositories.

Cooke, Marvel, interview with author, Harlem, NY, January 25, 1996.

Cox, Debbie, Debbie's Cleaning Service, interview with author, New York City, May 16, 1993.

de Grazia, Victoria, interview, New York City, April 6, 1995.

Frye, Gleason, President of Lindquist Group, parent of the A.E. Johnson Agency, interview with author, Greenwich, CT, June 2, 1995.

German women #1, #2, #3, interview with author, New York City, March 19 & 26, 1995.

Irish Echo advertising manager, telephone interview with author, February 1996.

Johnson, Virginia, interview with author, New York City, May 29, 1992.

Lederman, Sarah Henry, interview with author, New York City, October 1993.

McDonald, Beverly, interviews with author, Maplewood, NJ and East Orange, NJ, summer 2001.

Mensch, Jean Ulitz, interview with author, New York City, July 13, 1992.

Moore, Ana Maria Valverde, interview with author, New York City, September 20–22, 1996.

Opdyke, Leo, interview with author, Brooklyn, New York, June 2, 1992.

Peterson, Helen Hoff, interview with Jon A. Peterson and notes to the author, July 6, 1992.

Ricci, Dana, interview with author, Montclair, New Jersey, August 24, 2005.

Romano, Nick, interviews with author, Maplewood, New Jersey, February, 2005.

Silvestri, Norma, interview with author, Leonia, New Jersey, September 13, 1992.

Williams, Patricia, talk at Columbia University, May 5, 1995.

Wu, Charlotte, interview, New York City, May 20, 1992.

ARCHIVAL COLLECTIONS

Library of Congress, MSS Division, WPA Federal Writers' Project Collection, Beliefs and Customs—Folk Stuff, Folklore New York.

Mrs. A. E. Johnson Agency records, c/o The Lundquist Group, Greenwich, CT.

Municipal Archives of the City of New York, Office of the Mayor, Impelliteri, Vincent R., 1950–53.

———, Office of the Mayor, Lindsay, John V., 1966–73.

———, Office of the Mayor, Wagner, Robert F., Subject Files 1954–1965.

National Archives. Record Group 47. Social Security Administration.

———. Record Group 86. U.S. Department of Labor, Women's Bureau.

Young Women's Christian Association of the U.S.A., National Board Archives, New York. Records File Collection.

LAWS AND COURT DECISIONS

Matter of Tucker, In Deportation Proceedings, A-17455405, July 25, 1967, in Benjamin Gim, "Seminar in Immigration and Naturalization Law," Fall, 1977, Installment II (Columbia University School of Law, privately printed).

McKinney's Consolidated Laws of New York—Annotated—Book 30, Labor Law (2 vol., §§ 1–449 & §§ 500 to End): § 160, § 220, § 560, § 562.

NEWSPAPERS, PERIODICALS AND FILMS

Abbott, Shirley and Bonnie Slotnick, "The Gas Range," *American Heritage* (May/ June 1991).

Alice Adams (film, RKO, 1935).

Barry, Joseph A., "An Open Letter to Husbands," *House Beautiful* (September 1953).

——, "Housekeeping by Contract," *House Beautiful* (September 1953).

Bloodworth, Bess, "Summary of February 17 Afternoon Session, 'American Women on the Job,'" *The American Woman* 104.

Bonner, Raymond, "A Woman's Place: Report from Kuwait," *The New Yorker* (November 16, 1992).

Bromley, Dorothy Dunbar, "Are Servants People?," *Scribner's Magazine* 94 (December 1933).

"Center Opened to End Bronx 'Slave Markets,'" *New York Herald Tribune*, May 2, 1941.

Cheever, Susan, "The Nanny Track," *The New Yorker* (March 6, 1995).

Cooke, Marvel, "Bronx Slave Market: Where Men Prowl and Women Prey on Needy Job-Seekers," *Daily Compass*, January 9, 1950.

——, "Bronx Slave Market: A Personal Experience," *Daily Compass*, January 10, 1950.

——, "Bronx Slave Market: $3.40 a Day," *Daily Compass*, January 11, 1950.

——, "Dixie Girl Exposes Racket of Employment Agencies," *New York Amsterdam News*, April 24, 1937.

——, "I Was a Part of The Bronx Slave Market," *The Sunday Compass Magazine*, January 8, 1950.

——, "Modern Slaves," *New York Amsterdam News*, October 16, 1937.

——, "'Paper Bag Brigade' Learns How to Deal with Gypping Employers," *Daily Compass*, January 10, 1950.

——, "'Mrs. Legree' Hires Only on the Street, Always 'Nice Girls,'" *Daily Compass*, January 11, 1950.

——, "Some Ways to Kill the Slave Market," *The Daily Compass*, January 12, 1950.

——, "Times Bad? Employment Heads Insist Things Are Picking Up," *New York Amsterdam News*, July 17, 1937.

——and Ella Baker, "The Bronx Slave Market," *The Crisis*, November 1935.

CORE magazine (Summer 1973).

Cowan, Ruth Schwartz, "Less Work for Mother?" *American Heritage* (September/ October 1987).

Dixon, Hume, "Maid in U.S.A.," *House & Garden* (February 1946).

Downs, Hugh, "Must We Age?," *Parade Magazine*, August 21, 1994.

Ehrenreich, Barbara, "Maid to Order: The Politics of Other Women's Work," *Harper's Magazine* 300, no. 1799 (April 2000).

Encore (Summer 1972).

"Expose Brings Move to Rid New York of 'Slave Market,'" *Daily Compass*, January 18, 1950.

Ferguson, Mrs. Walter, "One Woman's Opinion: The Cruel Housewife," *News* (April 7, 1933).

Glastris, Paul, "The Alien Payoff," *U.S. News & World Report* (May 26, 1997).

"How Recessions Happen," *Newsweek* (November 10, 1997).

Hubbard, Mary Coates, "Two Worlds: Observations of a Sentinel Set Between Them," *The New York Times Magazine*, June 22, 1924.

"I Want a Job," *The Brown American* III (August 1939).

"Is That So!" *Good Housekeeping* (January 1955).

Jackson, Jay, "Tisha Mingo [comic strip]," *New York Amsterdam News,* August 21–November 27, 1937.

Lee, Audrey, "Moma," *Negro Digest* (February 1969).

MacKenzie, Catherine, "Katie is Leaving—Again," *The New York Times Magazine*, August 31, 1941.

Made for Each Other, film (David Selznick Productions, 1939).

Martha and Ethel, film (Jyll Johnstone, 1995).

"Minimum Wage Coverage For Household Workers Urged," *The Crisis* (September 1971).

Minus, Marian, "Girl, Colored," *The Crisis* (September 1940).

New York Newsday, 1990–1995.

Powell, Michael, "The Working Poor: Just Hanging On," *New York Newsday* (May 17, 1992).

Pressman, Sonia, "Job Discrimination and the Black Woman," *The Crisis* (March 1970).

Rafkin, Louise, "Dirty Laundry," *The New York Times Magazine,* January 28, 1996.

Real Estate Record and Builders Guide, 1920–1930.

Ripley, Josephine, "To Change the Subject: Too Many Cooks . . . No, Indeed," *Christian Science Monitor,* September 11, 1941.

Roche, Mary, "The New 'Servants': Machines and Husbands," *The New York Times,* June 5, 1955.

Santiago, Chiori, "It All Comes Out in the Wash," *Smithsonian* (September 1997).

Seely, Evelyn, "Our Feudal Housewives," *The Nation* (May 28, 1938).

Seipel, Cindy, "Payroll Tax and Immigration Laws for Domestic Service Employ," *The CPA Journal* (April 1995).

Thackrey, Ted O., "Modern Slave Market," *Daily Compass,* July 9, 1950.

The Architectural Forum, 1930–1935.

The Best Years of Our Lives (film, Samuel Goldwyn, 1946).

The Crisis, 1930–1975.

The Irish Echo, 1991–1995.

"The Last of Frankfurt-on-the-Hudson," *The New York Times, film,* August 27, 1992.

"The Negro Woman Goes to Market," *The Brown American* I (April 1936).

The New York Times, 1920–2005.

The New-York Amsterdam News, 1920–1976.

"Turning Tide in the Domestic Servant Market," *The New York Times Book Review and Magazine,* December 5, 1920.

"What One Home-maker Thinks," *Women's Press* 22 (February 1928).

"You and Your Maid in a Changing World," *House & Garden* (April 1947).

Index